Societal Development & Minority Rights

Y. N. Kly

Clarity Press, Inc.

ISBN: 0-932863-23-X

In-house Editor: Diana G. Collier

LCCCN: 96-072543

Cataloguing in Publication Data:

Kly, Y. N. (Yussuf Naim), 1935-

Societal development & minority rights

Includes bibliographical references and index.
ISBN 0-932863-23-X

1. Minorities - Civil rights. 2. Pluralism (Social sciences).
3. Equality. I. Title.

JC575.K59 1997 323.1 C97-920000-8

CLARITY PRESS, INC.
Ste. 469, 3277 Roswell Rd. N.E.
Atlanta, GA. 30305
Tel.: 404-231-0649
Fax: 404-231-3899
Toll free order: 1-800-533-0301
Internet: http://www.bookmasters.com/clarity
E-mail: clarity@islandnet.com

Table of Contents

Preface

For the past century, scholars have focused on the ideal of the nation-state as the fundamental unit of global socio-political organization. However, as it became clear that political, cultural and economic exigencies would prevent a full realization of this ideal, there emerged, along with increased acceptance of cultural diversity, the conceptualization of the multinational state, and along with this bow to empirical reality, the dialogue on the international legal protection of minorities or the minority rights approach.[1]

At the beginning of this exploratory research[2] it was our intention to limit our analysis to a small area of this emerging dialogue so as to demonstrate that a composite minority rights model[3] is serviceable to the promotion of sustainable human centered societal development (hereinafter referred to as SHCSD).[4] Originally, we intended to present and describe the various existing models of constitutional-legal arrangements for minority rights in most multinational states, and correlate the historical presence or absence of unmanageable minority / majority socio-economic or political conflicts associated with each model. Then, by comparing the attributes and liabilities of all models in relation to conflict management, we intended to construct an ideal model composed of the attributes rated highest from all models examined.[5] We would then compare the ideal model with the models evolving in Canada through the First Nations' land settlements and self-determination negotiations, and the Quebeçois search for constitutional-legal recognition of special rights for the province of Quebec, whether conceived of as sovereignty-association, special status or internal political independence.[6] However, after an extensive examination of minority rights and minority conflict resolution literature in international law, political science, social anthropology, and international relations, the communications of the OSCE[7] High Commissioner on National Minorities, the output from the numerous meetings of the Project on Ethnic Relations (PER), as

Table 1:
Trends in selected indicators of the quality of life

Indicators	Low-income countries	Middle-income countries	High-income countries
	1989 U.S. Dollars		
Per capita gross national product (GNP)	80-500	581-5 999	6 000-29 880
Life expectancy at birth			
1965	49	58	71
1989	62	66	76
Daily per capita calorie intake			
1965	1 988	2 482	3 082
1988	2 331	2 834	3 398
Average number of years of complete schooling per worker around 1980	1.8	4.8	9.6
	Percentage		
Adult literacy			
1960	26	49	98
1985	56	75	99
Average annual GNP growth rate, in real terms 1965-89	2.9	2.3	2.4

"Quality of life" is a pluralistic conception of well-being that is closely linked to the notion of development and human progress. While at the common-sense level the term seems clear enough, it can mean different things to people with different standards of living and cultural viewpoints. Since there is no common mould to fit the term, quality of life is best measured by a combination of social and economic indicators and by subjective measures of a person's relative satisfaction with his or her conditions of life and well-being. As discussed in the present chapter, there exists in most countries an ambiguous relationship between physical and economic betterment, on the one hand, and social progress and satisfaction with the quality of life on the other.

Those elements of the quality of life that are readily measurable by economic and social indicators reflect some of the most important dimensions of human existence. Per capita gross national product (GNP) in particular is a proxy measure of human well-being and social progress at the national level: the higher the income, the higher society's potential capacity to provide improved health care, education and other services. However, per capita income measures have serious flaws when it is a question of assessing the quality of life. To capture social reality more comprehensively, those measures must be complemented by other indicators. Table1 accordingly presents additional indicators — of life expectancy at birth, caloric intake, adult literacy and educational attainment.

Life expectancy at birth is important as an indicator of human welfare, as it sums up the combined effects of nutritional status, public health, the general physical environment, and the circumstances in which people are born, live and die. Literacy and educational attainments have a favourable impact on the quality of life by enlarging human choice and participation in material and social progress. Nutritional status data are also included in the table, in view of the importance to general well-being of adequate food and a proper diet.

The social indicators utilized in Table1 also reflect the distribution of social progress among population groups. An improvement in longevity, caloric consumption and literacy means that at least the proportion of people sharing such benefits has risen, even if the improvement does not explicitly identify how the benefits it reflects are distributed among specific segments of the population. With regard, for instance, to improvement in life expectancy and caloric consumption, it can be assumed — in view of the natural biophysical ceiling already (nearly) attained by their indicators among the well-to-do — that the greater benefit accrues to the poor.

As may be seen in Table1, improvements in social conditions and living standards are strongly and positively correlated with economic growth. These improvements have proceeded at rates that, historically speaking, are high compared with those of the industrialized countries at comparable stages in their development.

As literacy becomes more nearly universal in the developed countries, other social betterment objectives, including improved universal education, have assumed a higher priority in recent years. That is one reason why average number of years of completed schooling was included in Table 1; the other reason was that each year of education beyond the literacy level could be presumed to have a favourable impact on the enlargement of people's capabilities, choices, participation and life opportunities in modern society.

Individual indicators provide useful measures of improvements that have occurred for various dimensions of well-being; however, the design of composite indicators that provide an overall measure of the quality of life involves greater difficulty. All efforts to this end have met with thorny conceptual and theoretical problems of coherence and causality. In all cases, arbitrary assumptions have had to be made in selecting the weights for combining and aggregating the respective indicators within one quality-of-life index. The underlying arbitrariness of quality-of-life indices reduces their credibility as objective measures for classifying and ranking countries according to welfare criteria.

Additional conceptual problems (besides the methodological ones of integrating, calibrating and summing composite indicators) have hindered efforts at developing indices of political freedom and civil rights. That human freedom has an ultimate worth of profound importance to one's personal life and positive self-identity has long been noted in history. The concept of human freedom, however, is too culture-specific to be captured in any general measure. There are complex questions of participation and control in many societies that are not necessarily exhausted by an approach to addressing those questions based on the presence or absence of a particular set of political arrangements. Moreover, while there may be a positive correlation between increased freedom, as conventionally defined, and economic growth, the direction of movement from cause to effect is not clear.

Social indicators also have limitations: they fail to shed light on the less readily measurable elements connected with social well-being, such as people's fears, sufferings, conditioned wants, and satisfaction with life.

Thus, social as well as economic indicators can provide no more than partial and incomplete glimpses of the complex and sometimes contradictory realities that determine and shape the quality of life of both individuals and societies.

Sources: Department of Economic and Social Development of the United Nations Secretariat, based on World Bank Development Report, various years; World Bank, *Social Indicators of Development 1990* (Baltimore, Maryland, Johns Hopkins University Press, 1991); World Health Organization (WHO), *World Health Statistics Annual*, various years; and United Nations Educational, Scientific and Cultural Organization (UNESCO), *Compendium of Statistics on Illiteracy*, 1988.

well as the numerous presentations by scholars at international conferences,[8] we noted:

1. In most cases, the efforts of states to provide special legal and political status to minorities occurred not so much because of governments' foreknowledge and acceptance that certain types of minorities require special rights or special measures,[9] nor because they had international obligations to provide for appropriate minority rights, but rather took place only after significant harm and often irreparable damage to state/minority relations had been allowed to occur, in the course of what was a costly but unnecessary destructive conflict with losses to both parties.[10]

2. That minority demands for special rights or special measures usually were resented by those considering themselves a part of the majority, hence paralyzing the normal function that public opinion plays in providing for peaceful change in modern democratic information societies.[11]

3. In general the very existence of the international legal minority rights dialogue was, like international human rights in general, either unfamiliar, unknown or profoundly confused in popular conceptions with civil rights, natural rights, etc..[12]

We therefore felt that a serviceable analysis should evidence the existence and importance of an international legal dialogue on minority rights, and illustrate how the concept of minority rights serves not only to benefit minorities but to establish a firm foundation for national unity, security, and SHCSD. Thus, we concluded that if there is no interest in or little awareness of the existence of the dialogue on the international legal minority rights approach, then there would be less appreciation of models derived from the tenets of that approach. Therefore, the first requirement will be to expose our readers to the nature, attributes and problematics[13] of that dialogue and its association with SHCSD. Also we felt that for this approach to an analysis of minority rights to be specifically serviceable to justice and human service studies, it should at least provide conjectural bridges connecting minority rights as associated with SHCSD, with its philosophical implications for social policy. In order to accomplish these objectives, we have attempted to occasion a legal justice approach[14] which uses international legal methodology in such a manner as not to ignore political and socio-economic reality and particularly the minority rights issues in the search for societal justice. While we reviewed numerous scholars in justice studies who saw minority rights as essential for a just societal development, there were none who viewed rights as irrelevant to societal development. This means that we attempt to situate our approach in understanding, exploring and highlighting human service implications of the minority rights approach beyond the conceptual tools of rights, although in order to focus on exploring the significance and validity of issues involved in state-minority conflicts, we assume that the concept of justice may (uniquely for this purpose) be viewed as compatible with the subjectivities involved in the search for democracy, quality of life, and ecological sustainability.[15]

John Ralston Saul, a well-known Canadian philosopher and novelist, alludes to the fallacy in not using a human justice approach when speaking about human rights:

> When those from the center onwards to the left talk about rights, it is as if these were free-standing and unrelated to the existence of society, which means unrelated to the existence of the public good. And from the center on to the right, obligations are invoked as if they referred either to a requirement to look after yourself in isolation from society, which usually relates to law and order, defense and moral order. Again, there is no suggestion of the shared role of the citizen in the maintenance of the public good.[16]

In relation to our original desire to focus on the Canadian models, we felt that focusing on them alone would tend to obscure the full potential and yield of the minority rights SHCSD dialogue. Thus we concluded that the developed, articulated and time-tested international models which emerge and are highlighted in our exposé of the minority rights SHCSD dialogue may better serve to interest and inform Canadian public opinion and decision makers. Therefore, in keeping with the requirements and spirit of normative international legal methodologies as it relates to the search for a justice attuned to the societal values of democracy, peace and equality, etc., we shall use as a criteria and highlight aspects and recommendations from those models of multinational SHCSD which have, over time, become widely used international standards of international law and are viewed as having proved themselves as relatively successful in real world situations or empirical application.

We will not, as in most of the social science literature, concentrate on the socio- economic condition of minorities, their consequent political demands, and the resultant need for systemic adjustment; nor, in contrast to most of the international legal literature, will we represent the minority rights dialogue as essentially limited to a search for an international legal consensus as derived by deduction from international legal sources in order to determine whether a legal right exists or not — an approach which is correctly viewed by scholars, particularly those in political science, as irrelevant to empirical evidence and thus real world usefulness. We have, as earlier implied, viewed the minority rights dialogue as it is articulated in international law as a search for justice in the utilitarian sense of providing a basis for peace, human rights, quality of life, etc., as not only concerned with the requirements for meeting states' legal responsibilities, but also amenable to empirical scrutiny and enabling multinational states to achieve democracy and SHCSD. The multi-disciplinary international legal methodology[17] recommends itself for the task of guiding a comprehensive utilitarian human justice approach in the area of minority rights and societal development because the impetus of the modern minority rights dialogue comes from international conventional law which has its origin in international customary law, which itself is the consequence of those policies which statesmen have historically found viable or necessary for managing or resolving minority-majority conflicts. Thus, the utility of minority rights norms recognized by this approach can be empirically corroborated by historical events resulting from their socio-economic and political application.[18]

Further, we shall seek to avoid the numerous terminological confusions which exist in relation to the minority rights problematic even among social science scholars, not to mention national minority spokesmen, the general public, political leaders and government officials. Frequently, terminology that is essential to understanding the dynamics, role and empirical evolution of minority rights in law and societal development is unfamiliar or, when employed in relation to the minority rights problematic, is invested with meanings which are inconsistent with and often irrelevant to the real world minority rights dialogue. The meaning of key terminology varies depending on the discipline or profession of the user. There is little recognition of the way these terms are conceptualized in the real world dialogue, and thus little effort to connect their meaning with its original conceptualization in international law. Key terms such as special rights, special measures, nation, multinational, minority, self-determination, multicultural, affirmative action, nondiscrimination, equality, equal status, social minority, integration, assimilation, segregation, separation, immigrant minority, national minorities, consociated democracy, pluralistic democracy, etc., are often insufficiently specified.

These observations convinced us of the need for key terminology used in this research to be consistently defined within the disciplinary framework of international law, which itself is multidisplinary and historically associated with the development, discernment and codification of the historical output of minority rights politico-legal conflicts, while at the same time correlated with prevailing social science terminology and human justice conceptualizations. This does not necessitate claiming international legal definitions as the only correct definitions, but instead proposing and using them as fixed points that can guide the reader in following and evaluating the utility, salience and validity of the minority rights approach. We therefore recommend that the reader consult an international law dictionary when a definition of terminology used in this research is required.

Also noted in preparing for this research was the political and emotion-laden climate surrounding the study of minority problems, which may have led many scholars to avoid meaningful contributions to this area of research out of fear of being labeled unpatriotic, nationalistic, subversive, irresponsible, anti-statist, racist, anti-religious, xenophobic etc.. We feel that this derives largely from the aforementioned "terminological definitional confusion" and the politicization of the problematic, leading to a deficiency of public information about the crucial association of minority rights with desirable societal development. This emotionally charged climate restricts the extensive undertaking of much-needed research.

Our search of the literature also left us with the impression that there are areas of particular importance to the scientific elaboration of the minority rights / societal development dynamic that still require empirical investigation:

1. The legal, political, cultural, historical and geographic determinants of successful non-hegemonic, non-imperialistic and peaceful assimilation of two or more distinct ethnic or racial groups into one of the existing groups or all into a new group different from any of the original. Both historians and anthropologists tells us that this occurs.[19] What is missing is modern empirical data evidencing the legal, political, cultural, demographic, etc. factors responsible. The concept of "fusion" used by Asbjorn Eide, Chairman of the UN Sub-Comission, and which is a part of the minority rights dialogue in relation to how or why different ethnies can become one nationality hints in this direction, but remains unelucidated. Our chapter on Social Proclivity to Conflict provides a limited example of what is needed.

2. Empirical data on how and why groups form culturally negative images of other ethnic or racial groups. Empirical and psychological data from the recent works by scholars such as Floyd Webster Rudmin and Ervin Staub,[20] etc., reveal the role of societal conventions and institutions, particu-larly the mass media, in encouraging negative imagery of minorities which supports prejudices that may or may not lead to observable discrimination effects (depending on their assonance with economic, political and other conditions and circumstances). However, such studies do not provide empirical evidence on how and why negative images of others serve the interest of existing societal institutions in certain states. What is required is a nonjudgmental empirical investigation of these culturally conditioned images of others, particularly those which may be viewed in the culture concerned as providing reasonable or guiltless reasons for prejudice or discrimination. An investigation of the culturally-based reasons given for the stereotyping of others (common to all cultures) and the consequent tendency to accept the rectitude of discrimination is required in order to discern the cognitive, systemic and institutional nature of, and reasons for, discrimination against minorities. This would also provide information required to discern and compare the phenomena that are so often placed under the catch-all umbrellas of "racism," "chauvinism," "nationalism," and "cultural xenophobia," etc.. Is the impetus to such phenomena the same as their manifestations suggest? An empirical response to this question would facilitate a more utilitarian grasp by government

and the public of the substantive reasons for and functional meanings of such terms as racism and discrimination, and what may be required for their management or elimination. The minority rights dialogue suggests minority rights might assist in deter-mining what type of institutions are needed in the society concerned, and might further assist in the development of parameters for professional education of human service personnel working in multinational environments. Perhaps it is on the foundation of institutionalized negative images and resultant guiltless reasons for discrimination, that fanatics, demagogues, racists and other anti-social destructive individuals are able to build their edifice for ethnic hostility leading to devastating societal conflicts.[21]

3. Finally, and of equal importance to service justice as it relates to minorities, is the need for empirical field studies to ascertain precisely what administrative and functional difficulties are faced by human service workers in multinational milieus attempting to practice normative service delivery methods while under the constraint of social policy which is viewed by one or more ethnic groups in that milieu as not necessarily normative or neutral. Such situations may call for a restructuring of the social service policy making/policy delivery system so as to permit adequate feedback to policy makers about the nature of service delivery difficulties, failures and successes related to policy content. Research such as the above mentioned could be facilitated through cooperation between the universities and UN human service agencies, as well as those of the government.[22]

Working Assumptions

Our presentation of the dialogue evidencing a nexus between minority rights and SHCSD as well as the selection of materials was influenced by several fundamental assumptions derived from an extensive scrutiny of the literature, participation in several international conferences and face to face consultation with a wide range of international legal, international relations, social work, and political science scholars:[23]

1. States do not exist in nature; they are mental and legal constructs which reason and our search for justice compel us to conclude were created for the purpose of better providing for human needs through the creation of political communities,

which were thus able to acquire legal rights and responsibilities. Thus, policies and institutions of states which function to prevent the realization of citizens' needs should, by this logic and the search for justice, be amenable to change. To conclude otherwise would mean that states should exist on the basis of the monopoly of force alone, and for the prime purpose of social control.[24]

2. The nation state is viewed as an ideal concept of the 19th century which was largely never realized beyond the scope of political rhetoric and constitutional-legalism. Thus when scholars speak of the decline of the nation state, essentially they are referring to the decline of the nation state ideology, an ideology which, due to its inadequacies, is today being challenged as the prime model of social organization, particularly by national minorities, religious and political groups facing the problem of meeting human needs, whether they be material, spiritual or social.

3. The international system is viewed as a mental, political and legal construct which provides a collective psychic space where peoples acting through states and sub-national units can view themselves as meeting on an equal status basis with equal rights, thus providing the psychic terrain facilitating good will negotiations and conflict resolution.

4. The technological revolution which occurred over the past few decades has, for perhaps the first time in human history, created a situation wherein modern civilization has the production potential to provide for the basic human needs (food, shelter, primary health care) of the earth's population. Neverthe-less, an estimated 550 million people went hungry in 1990 and today, millions more still go hungry, despite the fact that the global supply of food is sufficient to feed them adequately. [25] Thus as suggested in Francis Moore Lappé's classic research, *Food First*,[26] famine and hunger are caused primarily by a lack of purchasing power on the part either of individuals and families wanting to buy food or of entire countries wanting to import what they do not produce. As Helen Hodge notes:

> When one-third of the world's population consumes two thirds of the world's resources, and then in effect turns around and tells the others to do as they do, it is little short of a hoax. Development is all too often a euphemism for exploitation, a new colonialism. The forces of development and modernisation

> have pulled most people away from a sure subsistence and got them to chase after an illusion, only to fall flat on their faces, materially impoverished and psychologically disoriented. A majority are turned into slum dwellers...
>
> Development planners can pretend that everyone will be able to live like a New Yorker as long as they ignore the fact that natural resources are limited... Economists and technical optimists assume that we will be able to invent our way out of any resource shortage...*ad infinitum.* Such a view is a denial of the fact that the natural world has limits...and conveniently circumvents the need for a redistribution of wealth...[27]

5. The tele-video and transport communication component of the technological revolution has been equally spectacular. It has for the first time in human history made possible a transport and communications infrastructure encouraging a true world civilization adhering to a general but relativistic culture clued to the developing common standards of human rights and international law, and intensifying the multiplicity of cultural, and other exchanges between the center and periphery, periphery and periphery, etc. of the world. While most scholars would agree that one of the most visible consequences of such advances has been the knitting together of all parts of the world in an information technological revolution, which has effectively broken national boundaries with regard to the flow of information and the exchange of values, etc.,[28] the cost is still out.

6. The convergence of global, national, and local values and ideals[29] has created a dilemma for the continuing notion of the absolute authority of the state in local, national and international affairs. States' social policy seems unable to adequately respond to the social consequences of the technological revolution, leaving them and their sub-national units in the position of seeking answers through international organization, thus strengthening the authority of international organization *à propos* the states. Paul Kennedy, Director of the International Security Program at Yale University, writes :

> Everyone with an interest in international affairs must be aware that broad, global forces for change are bearing down upon humankind — new technologies are challenging the way we make trade, and even grow things — these various trends from global warming to twenty-four hour a day trading, are transnational —

> crossing borders — affecting local communities and distant societies at the same time, and reminding us that the earth, for all its divisions, is a single unit.[30]

In *Decolonizing History,* Claude Alvares suggests the impact of these technologically produced changes on socio-economic and political theory:

> The available doctrines of social change have become dated. Indeed it is not clear any more that any one compelling, all encompassing intellectual structure of thought and action can alter the human condition. Nor is it clear that what appear as historically necessary tendencies can in fact prove inevitable.[31]

The demise of the pre-eminence of any one all-embracing theory of social change as well as of the nation-state as the prime political construct for societal organization goes uncontested in today's literature and is expressed in most radical forms by scholars such as Alain Minc :

> Entre ces villes-états, ces regions-états, se mettront en place des réseaux de solidarity, à l'instar des universités du Moyen Age, afin d'exercer une influence plus fort *vis-à-vis* des états-nations qu'elles essaient subrepticement de dépouiller—des Empires mous; des villes-états; des minorités autonomes: étrange carte qui n'a plus rien de commun avec les modèles que les Temps Modernes ont inventés. Elle ne correspond ni a la juxtaposition d'états-nations arc-boutes sur leur frontières, au point de se faire regulierement la guerre comme au dix-neuvième siècle, ni à une communauté d'états en vois de se constituter par abandons de souverainété successif et suivant un calendrier affiché, rêve de l'après-guerre, ni a un monde tellement dominé par le libre échange et les flux économiques, fantasme anglo-saxon, que toutes les autres formes d'identité finissent par se dissoudre.[32]

Our studies lead us to suggest that in relation to multinational states such as Canada, the minority rights challenge is as decisive to the state's future security, unity and societal developmental direction as those of maintaining democracy, social rights, environmental protection, women's rights, etc. Not only are minority rights important but, like other human rights sanc-tioned in international law (social, economic, civil and political rights, etc.), they are also interconnected in such a manner that no one of them can be adequately achieved without sufficient attention to the others.[33]

7. As predicted by the 1960s Club de Rome UN report, *The Limits to Growth,* our research supports the assumption that the accelerating rate of technological change has caused a debilitating gap to emerge between societal economic and technological potential and societal socio-economic or political developmental theories. As earlier suggested,[34] much of the literature speaks of the existing socio-economic or political theoretical vacuum. In relation to political theory, Robert Jackson, editor *of Global Issues 94/95,* writes at the beginning of the annual edition: "Perhaps the most striking feature of the study of contemporary global issues is the absence of any single, widely held theory that explains what is taking place."[35] In attempting to consolidate micro level theory to suggest the possible emergence of general theory from the micro level, Eduardo Canel instead exposes the perplexity also existing at the micro level:

> The older theories assumed the passage from a condition of exploitation or frustration to collective action aimed at reversing the condition was a simple, direct, and unmediated process. The new paradigms, in contrast, propose that this passage from condition to action is a contingent and open process mediated by a number of conjectural and structural factors.[36]

For example, the editors of the journal, *Society and Nature,* credit the inability of the ecological movement to propose an alternative social vision for the movement's gradual withering away. The ecological movement is declining, they suggest, "despite the growing ecological crisis," and highlight the directionless ideological confusion by telling us that the movement in Europe has been integrated into existing social systems, and accepts the liberal democratic state as a vehicle to institute environmental reforms. "The result is its progressive absorption by traditional political parties (social democracy, the Euro-left, idealists or irrational and metaphysical, etc.)..." This seems to reflect the lack of a unified direction, and a high level of ideological fragmentation.[37]

8. The search for solutions to the minority problematic reflects a major world structural and organizational crisis expressed in terms of the need to define, legalize and implement minority

rights and responsibilities in the context of achieving democratic SHCSD. Civil wars and internal conflicts have become the principle cause of violence, destruction and the displacement of people.[38] In 1989-1990, there were 33 armed conflicts in the world, only one of which was between nation states. More than 2 million people fled Yugoslavia as refugees or displaced persons. Internal conflicts have destroyed opportunities for economic and social improvements in several countries such as Afghanistan, Angola, Ethiopia, Liberia, Somalia and Sudan. The human losses in these conflicts were high. During the period 1989-1990, 6000 people were killed in Yugoslavia, and in India, 12,261 between 1989-1991. Millions more lost their livelihoods and homes. These conflicts destroy conditions necessary for economic and social development and redirect scarce resources and human energy from the urgent task of meeting basic human needs, and makes the task of human service workers and human service delivery (note the present case of Rwanda) extremely complex or impossible. [39]

Contemplation of the role played by both the state and minorities in precipitating the service delivery dilemma in these societal developmental tragedies mentioned above, and evidence that states continue to fear the implementation of minority rights due to their belief that minorities seek political independence regardless of the cost to the state's socio-economic and political well-being,[409] suggests that minority responsibilities to the state and to the global village in which they live should be given equal emphasis with that of the state to provide minority rights. There are both legal and political justifications for this conclusion. For example, Article 29 of the Universal Declaration alludes to duties when it affirms that "everyone has duties to the community in which alone the free and full development of his personality is possible." The *African Charter of Human and Peoples' Rights* set forth the duties of the individual towards his family, the state, and the international community. The limitations placed on all rights, to the extent legitimate or legal, are no less than an expression of a duty. As Erica-Irene Daes, Special Rapporteur on Indigenous Populations, stated in our conversation during a UN apprenticeship at the Secretariate of the UN Human Rights Centre in Geneva in 1992: "International human rights are linked to international legal social, moral, economic and political responsibilities." The political implications of this linkage are clear. The ability of all parties concerned to accept the necessary changes in their socio-political reality is needed in order that each give due consideration to the rights and well-being of the others. In short, the minority as well as the state has the legal and moral responsibility to be politically mature.[41]

Conclusion

We assume the existence of integral human societal unity underlying human societal diversity, similar to the ordered pattern that emerges from chaos.[42] While the literature rejects all assertions of universality for any one particular model of societal organization, it does not dispute that there is unity underlying diversity. Human ethnies and communities are interrelated and the causes underlying the problems they face are at least in part to be found in these interrelationships. Thus, to ask for minority rights without agreeing to commensurate responsibilities to the larger community would be similar to asking for a different alternative for each society without reference to the basic unity provided by both the interrelations in which different units stand and the determinants of the historical process. It would be to invite infinite fragmentation which has no reason to stop at the national level but could extend to regional, intra-ethnic and even professional identities. Any search for solutions to the minority problematic that does not seek to foster a new, better or more acceptable political arrangement for living together is liable to lead to disintegration in the sense of developmental devolution.[43] The minority rights approach rejects developmental devolution as a preferred alternative to democratic SHCSD. Likewise it rejects the notion of minority rights for the sake of minority rights, giving privileges or unfair superiority to the minority, or encouraging the expression of minority discrimination against others. In so doing, it affirms both the principle of autonomy, of the right of each collective or social entity to seek its own way to self-realization, as well as the integration of all such entities in a common framework of interrelationships based on agreed values.

Today, most multinational states which do not implement minority rights reject both autonomy and integration as a principle informing human arrangements with the citizen nations (minorities) under their imperium. Their institutional structures, on the whole, are based on a framework of dominance that works through endless fragmentation and tensions. They therefore rely heavily on instruments of violence for social control.[44]

The minority rights and other equally important dialogues (environmental protection, women's rights, etc.) are challenges to modern civilization which have arrived at all levels (local, provincial, national and international) and cannot be ignored without dire consequences because they stem not from theory but from socio-political, economic and environmental realities that mark the present stage of humankind's survival dilemma. It is no longer possible, due to new communications technology and the consequent revolutionary accessibility of public education, for increasing numbers of peoples to believe in or accept the divine, inherited, natural, political or military right of any ruler or ruling elite to hold arbitrary or undemocratic power over the resources, human rights and human needs of others. In relation to this public educational revolution, Zhelyn Zhelev, President of Bulgaria, observes:

> The polity has been shattered; political mediation, the foundation for the very idea of representative democracy, fulfills its function of transforming individual interests into collective interests only partially, if at all. Public opinion polls show that political mediation with the state is increasingly being shunted aside and discredited. It is natural for the public to judge governments according to Max Weber's "ethics of ultimate ends" or results, in line with people's increasing demands in terms of economic justice and security, environmental protection, and human rights.[45]

Today, social policy in multinational states finds itself under increasing socio-political pressure to respond to individual and collective human needs as set forth in the *Universal Declaration of Human Rights*. This occurs at the same time that the older socio-political theories of economics and development (which were theorized at a time when output incentives were major problematics of production) have become obsolete. Nonetheless, outmoded theories which did not countenance changes to the production problematic brought on by the technological revolution over the past few decades remain in vogue with many socio-political policy decision makers. Thus socio-political theorists still dependent on outmoded theories find themselves temporarily unable to convincingly encompass or respond to today's problems.

Indeed, the challenges to political organization in the modern multinational democratic state in this post-industrial information age, are immense. However, if decision makers continue to countenance these challenges with only the tools of yesterday's reality, we run the risk of experiencing Thomas Hobbes' "Leviathan" in reverse -- a situation where the socio-economic policies issued under the authority of centralized but outdated political institutions engender human rights abuse, ecological destruction, socio-economic and political disorder and a loss of democracy,[46]and consequently give rise to a search for the philosophical foundation to define and support the institutionalization of a new search for human justice.

---

1 Hereinafter referred to as the minority rights dialogue. Also see *Nationalism & Ethnic Politics*,Volume 1, Number 1 (Spring, 1995)

2 Jarol B. Manheim and Richard C. Rich, *Empirical Political Analysis, supra.*, pp. 22, 85-86, 96, 132, 201 and 374-375.

3 A model constructed on the basis of characteristics from various real world instances that have over time demonstrated their success in managing conflict and permitting democratic sustainable human centered development.

4 Sustainable human centered societal development refers to a development that provides for all the human rights and in which development is measured by the UN Quality of Life indicators (see Table 1).

5 We found that these cross-national datasets would permit the construction of an empirical composite model:
Ted Robert Gurr, *Causal Model of Civil Strife, 1961-65.* Variables cover magnitudes of conspiracy, internal war, turmoil, and total strife for 114 countries. Also included are measures of deprivation such as economic and political, and long and short term deprivation. Mediating variables such as legitimacy, coercive potential, institutionalization, past strife levels and facilitation of strife are included.
Ted Robert Gurr, *Comparative Studies of Political Conflict and Change: Cross National Datasets.* This combined group of datasets is comprised of three studies: Civil Strife Events, 1955, Conflict Magnitudes, 1955-1970, and Conflict and Society. Civil Strife Events are variously called internal conflict behavior, internal war, insurgency, or political violence. They include any collective, non-governmental attack on people or property that occurs within the boundaries of a political system. Conflict Magnitudes provide a measure of the extent and intensity of a conflict. Data are given in five-year aggregations for ten countries for 1956-1960, in five year annual aggregations for 115 countries for 1961-1965, in five year annual aggregations for 87 countries for 1966-1970, in annual aggregations for 10 countries for 1955-1970, and in annual aggregations for 115 countries for

1961-1970. The Conflict and Society dataset contains indicators of social, economic and political conditions in 86 countries. Data on the conflicts themselves are given for up to 115 countries.

Ivo K. Feierabend, Rosalind Feierabend, Rose Kelly, *Data Bank of Minority Group Conflict, 1955-1965.* This is a preliminary compilation of events denoting conflict between minority groups (ethnic, racial, linguistic, religious) and the predominant group within the society. Data were collected from "Deadline Data on World Affairs" but include only those countries with minority groups. A set of ratings for each country was made regarding the type of policies and objectives pursued by the government toward minority groups and by the minority groups themselves. Data include initiator group, target group, third party to the event, names of the groups involved, and the nature of the issue underlying the dispute. For each type of event, characteristics such as country, date, location, duration, number of persons involved, deaths, injuries, scaling of intensity of event on hostility and amity scales, and outcomes are presented. There are data for 59 types of events in 43 countries.

Inter-University Consortium for Political and Social Research, International Relations Archive, ICPSR. *Domestic Violence, International Behavior and National Attributes of Developing Nations.* A custom data set of International Relations Archive variables for 85 nations. There are 40 variables. Data are drawn from 4 data files: World Military Expenditures, Comparative Foreign Policy Analysis, and World Handbook II (Aggregate file and Event file). Violence data cover 1962-1964 and 1965-1967. Attribute data are for 1965 and behavior data, 1966-1969.

6 The dimensions of the model sought by the Quebeçois remain unspecified.

7 Organization on Security and Cooperation in Europe.

8 See Chapter IV: Social Proclivity to Conflict.

9 Special measures (affirmative action) are viewed as temporary rights designed to compensate for past human rights violations, whereas special rights are associated with the assumption that the rights to be granted will be permanent, and that the state concerned is multinational or pluralistic.

10 Note theUkrainian proactive reaction to the demands for Russian minority rights in the Crimea (internal political independence) as well as the efforts of the OSCE High Commissioner on National Minorities, concerning the institutionalization of democracy in eastern European states, Appendix II. Also see DPI reference paper "The UN and the situation in the Former Yugoslavia, S.C. Res. 25 Sept. 1991 and DPI reference paper "The UN and the Situation in Rwanda," UN, New York, 28 April, 1995.

11 Alain Minc, *Le nouveau moyen age,* Gallimard, 1993, p. 161. Minc provides an elaboration for the theory that information and consequently public opinion provides the modern basis for social change, rather than violence.

12 This was often stated or implied during the PER conferences, 1993-1996, and in the meetings of the UN Sub-Commission and its Working Group on Minorities.

13 Normally the word problematic is used in English as an adjective. However, we have found its French-Canadian usage as adjective and a noun most helpful in facilitating communication of our ideas. When used as a noun, it refers to a situation of complexity wherein there is not one problem but many, so arranged as to make the discovery or solution to one often

dependent on the solution to another, therefore rendering a solution to the central problem problematic or complex.

14 This refers to a multidisciplinary approach which uses the international legal frame of references, but attempts not to ignore any relevant perspectives or contributions to a better or more holistic understanding.

15 We do not attempt to minimize the questions that this approach poses if we think simply in terms of exploring justice for minorities and society. In "Key Concepts in Critical Theory," Milton Fisk writes: The search for a just solution... leads towards the universal — a theory of human nature, of pre-eminant values, or a pattern of relevant factors and away from the particular. The just solution is often not found merely in taking one of the sides to a dispute, for that would... deny the other side the validity of its rights and proclaim a solution by privileging the rights of a particular group." See "Introduction," in Milton Fisk, ed., *Justice*, Humanities Press, 1993, p. 1. Our approach, however, which views justice in terms of societal values such as democracy, quality of life, etc., informed by a pattern of factors (minority rights, multinationalism, etc.) relevant to achieving these values, is similar in principle to John Stuart Mills' attachment of justice to utilitarianism: "Justice transcends disputes over different claims by deciding on the basis of utility to the society what it is right to do, where what is to count as utility is a neutral matter." See *Justice, supra.*, p. 2. However, this only returns us to the question of whether justice must be absolute. Numerous scholars such as David Hume, Alasdair MacIntyre, Michael Sandel, etc. have opposed the utilitarian and absolutist view of justice, and still others allude to the need of justice studies to concern itself with minority rights as a requirement for just societal development (see *Justice, supra.* p. 7).

16 John Ralston Saul, *The Unconscious Civilization*, House of Anansi Press, 1995, pp. 158-59.

17 Georg Schwarzenberger and George W. Keeton, *The Inductive Approach to International Law*, Stevens and Sons, London, 1965.

18 Theo van Boven, "Survey of the Positive International Law of Human Rights," in Karel Vasak, ed., *International Dimensions of Human Rights*, Volume I, pp. 105-110. Also see Luigi Condorelli, "Custom," in Mohammed Bedjaoui, ed., *International Law Achievements and Prospects*, Martinus Nijhoff/ UNESCO, Paris, 1991, pp. 179-197.

19 Andre Julien, *The History of North Africa*, Algiers, Algeria; Ivan van Sertima, *They Came Before Columbus*, Random House, New York, 1977; Janinz Janz, *Muntu*, Seuil, Paris, 1961. The UN Special Rapporteur for the Sub-Commission refers to this occurrence as "fusion." See Chapter on defining a minority for the purpose of international protection.

20 Floyd Webster Rudmin, "Cross Cultural Correlates of War," in *Peace Psychology Review*, Canada, 1995; Ervin Staub, *The Roots of Evil*, Cambridge University Press, 1993.

21 Jan Nederveen Pieterse, *White on Black: Images of Africa and Blacks in Western Popular Culture*, Yale University Press, New Haven and London, 1992.

22 See last chapter, Human Service in the Multinational Village, for an elaboration of the similarity between the UN social service efforts and those of domestic human service agencies.

23 See Bibliography.

[24] This orientation would represent the essence of Hobbesian thought as it relats to the role of the state. However, for justice to be served in this manner, it must be irretreivably attached to theconcept of law and order as a prime good or necessity for human society.

[25] *World Social Situation in the 1990s.* DPI, UN Publication, New York, pp. 122-123.

[26] Francis Moore Lappé, *Food First,* Ballantine Books, 1981.

[27] Helen Hodge, "The Development Hoax," in Chandra Muzaffar, ed., *Dominance of the West Over the Rest, supra.,* pp. 117-118.

[28] Francis Moore Lappé, *supra.,* pp 122-123.

[29] See *Global Issues 94/95,* Annual Editions, The Dushkin Publishing Group, Inc., US.

[30] Paul Kennedy, "Preparing for the 21st Century: Winners & Losers," in *Global Issues 94/95, supra.,* p. 6.

[31] Claude Alvares, *Decolonizing History,* The Apex Press, New York, 1991.

[32] Alain Minc, *supra,* p. 190.

[33] Tadeusz Jasudowica, *Social Rights as Human Rights,* Institute for Human Rights, Abo Akademi University, Finland, 1994, Chapters 2 and 3.

[34] See Claude Alvares, *supra.*

[35] Robert M. Jackson, in *Global Issues 94/95, supra.*

[36] Eduardo Canel, "New Social Movement Theory and Resource Mobilization: The Need for Integration," in William K. Carroll, ed., *Organizing Dissent,* Garamond Press, 1992, p. 23.

[37] M. Bookchin, T. Fotopoulos, A. Frank, M. Fuertss, J.O'Connor, J. Biehl, H. Hawkins, L. Davidoff, D. Foreman, eds., *Society and Nature: The State and Ecological Society,* Society and Nature Press, Athens, Vol. 1, No. 3, p. V.

[38] Ted Roberts Gurr, *supra.* See Dataset up to1970.

[39] *World Social Situation in the 1990s, supra.* pp. 122-123.

[40] See Reports by the Project on Ethnic Relations, 1991-1995. Project on Ethnic Relations, One Palmer Square, Princeton, N.J. 08542-3718.

[41] Here we refer to Bertrand de Jouvenal's concept, in *Le Pouvoir,* that "Political science is the art of the possible."

[42] *Scientific American,* July, 1996.

[43] This is used here to refer to lowering the quality of life as earlier defined, and creating circumstances that make it more difficult for peoples to cooperate and provide for human rights, democracy and SHCSD.

[44] Rajni Kothari, Introduction to *Decolonizing History, supra.*

[45] Zhelyn Zhelev, "Is Communism Returning?" *Journal of Democracy,* Johns Hopkins Unviersity Press, July 1996, p. 10.

[46] John Ralston Saul suggests, "Our reforming elites have rejected the most blatant aspects of Hobbes' fear-mongering to keep us in our place, but accepted almost entirely his view of social organization as a control mechanism. In *The Leviathan,* Hobbes put it that 'during the time men live without a common power to keep them all in awe, they are in that condition which is called war.' The citizen's rights have been buried in law and the citizen states in the hierarchy of professionalism... But it is the law and hierarchy combined which creates the form of a controlled society." See Saul, *supra..*

Introduction

As the dust settles from the recent collapse of the USSR and we strain to see the contours of our present and the parameters of our future, we come to realize that not only has the global political order been dislocated, but more importantly, our vision of the world, of progress, and consequently of order or justice itself has suffered an equal disorientation.

> Avec l'éffondrement du communisme, nous approchons, en revanche, du zero de l'ideologie. Jamais les intellectuals n'ont été aussi nombreux, les socioloques aussi influents, les scientifiques aussi désireux d'échapper aux de carcacs de leur disciplines, les historiens aussi ostensiblement transformes en gourous du futur. Ils ne seront pas de trop pour nous offrir une nouvelle... Toutes nos pensée traditionnelles s'effacent, qui postulaient le progrès, un optimum collectif, et donc le règne d'ordre.[1]

The international systemic disorientation of our conception of progress and socio-economic ideals and ideologies[2] has led to an increase in unmanageable social and political problems on the national and local levels: the exploitation of illegal drug use, a great leap backwards in spending for social programs, an increase in the homeless and other marginal populations, and an intensification of majority/national minority conflicts, with consequent challenges to the authority of the state.

> L état-providence est contesté par des exclues. Ce sont des processus, d'essence certes differente, mais qui tous deux témoignent de l'affaissement de nos structures d'ordre. Ordre, au sens classique du terme, c'est-à-dire soumission à la règle et à la loi. Mais aussi ordre social qui a culminé dans le rève social-democrate d'une population protegée et prise en charge, du plus pauvre au plus riche, le Welfare State. Ce n'est pas cette fois-ci la fin du communisme qui parait la matrice de toutes choses, mais l'épuisement d'un modèle qui avait besoin de 3 à 4 % de croissance par an pour fonctioner sans a-coups. Les éxclus [often

> predominantly the national minorities] constituent, à leur manière, une immense "zone grise": ils dessinent, en éffet, un monde sur lequel l'état a de moins en moins prise. Le nouveau Moyen Age, c'est aussi la réapparition de l'anomie, de la marginalité et de l'invisible: ainsi de cent mille jeunes qui quittent le système scolaire sans diplome et disparaissent dans la société, comme on se perdait autrefois dans des territoires inconnus.[3]

The potential for disorder or loss of freedom heightened by the panic of suddenly not being able to see the contours of our present, and our consequent disorientation in the transitional darkness no doubt holds the possibilities of danger. Perhaps by first discerning what is objectively unique to our present situation, we will be better able to recapture our socio-political and philosophical composure. First we see, as earlier mentioned, that a modern technological revolution interfaces with humankind's millennium of socialization and education experiences, thus animating:

1. The beginning of functional common global values, as exemplified in the recent acceleration in the development and codification of international law, particularly the law of human rights.[4] This does not mean that humankind is becoming less divided. Indeed, it seems more so. But in its dividedness, there is emerging a common understanding and basis for better, more durable and just arrangements for reuniting.

2. Changes in the relationship between the factors of production coupled with the accelerating capacity to produce, introducing the first civilization not only technically capable of providing for global human needs but also capable of doing so without the pharaonic enslavement of human labor.[5]

These two factors alone have opened the door for the eventual possibility of world peace.[6] Indeed, modern civilization is unique in its potential of introducing a world civilization wherein human conflicts become manageable through legal or political structures and processes, wherein common values and mutual agreement informs the nature of the arrangements by which individuals, peoples and nations live together, the way they co-exist and cooperate in resolving environmental and other global problematics. But this is not for tomorrow, perhaps a day or so thereafter. Modern civilization is not unique in its latent tribal heritage nor its resistance to rapid social change (updating socio-economic and political philosophy and social polices so as to keep pace with scientific/technological, educational, and environmental potential and demands). Nor is it unique in being confronted by the age-old challenge, when faced with the need for change, of having to summon from collective and individual spirituality, the political will to do so. Goran Ohlin, participant in the 1995 World Summit for Social Development, notes:

> The philosophical issues involved have been at the heart of theological and political debates in all parts of the world throughout recorded history. Historians cannot agree on whether moral and philosophical values played an independent role in social change in the past, or whether new ideas and ambitions grew out of tensions generated by new social situations. Yet new ideas about the meaning of life and the organization of society have left an indelible mark on all civilizations ... Ideas and visions of change have inspired untold political leaders, and... have penetrated societies where the power holders resisted them... It seems to be taken as a premise that ... a moral, intellectual, spiritual crisis underlies many of the conflicts in the world...[7]

We feel that as the waves caused by the coming future shock settle and humankind has had the chance to assess the new terrain, updated socio-economic and political theory will emerge, guiding humankind to its next social reconstitution — if not from the West then from the East, for the intellectual apparatus and global inheritance of modern civilization is well extended into all parts of the world, despite objections to its materialistic and dominant identification. We should not be surprised if it comes from a resurrected eastern Europe, riding on lessons from developmental successes and failures of China and the former Soviet Union, and serves as the empirical reference for new socio-economic and political theory which recognizes the logical limitations of the global free market system as well as the human and spiritual needs of SHCSD: a multinational, pluralistic, new form of democratic socialist order committed to SHCSD.

Thus, what we witness is not the end of history (Fukayama)[8] nor the beginning of a new Middle Age (Alain Minc, John Saul, etc.),[9] but most complex, the transformation of existing institutions (including the state-centered international system as we know it) under the impact of socio-economic and political globalization, the demand for human rights, and the decolonization of history (Claude Alvares). Has this decolonization caused the former colonizers to bring the devastations of colonization to their own societies? As noted by Jeremy Seabrook:

> What the West practised abroad to such effect faltered in the mid-twentieth century, as the subjugated lands fought for and won their [political] freedom. The experience acquired from this upheaval was, however, repatriated and reapplied at home with great care and skill..In the West, we have seen a colonising of the supposed beneficiaries of empire, the people of the West itself; those who once formed a dangerous and threatening working class, those whose destiny formerly appeared to be a continuous impoverishment that could be terminated only by their own seizure of the agency of their dispossession..."[10]

This is reflected in the downsizing and domestic structural adjustment programs put into effect under the guise of deficit reduction and balanced budgets. To further facilitate western competitiveness within the context of an increasingly non-western European centered international system, international organization is increasingly being used. Its use guarantees that our understanding of history, like capital, globalizes.

While the ultimate reaction of groups and individuals in the global village (aided by the communications and education revolution) to the consequences of the present state of the NAHTAIVEL[11] is yet unclear, the orientation of our present day social movements gives a clear indication that present institutions, including the state as we know it, are becoming increasingly unacceptable. Within the context of a Marxist perspective, Howard Watkins advises:

> We are witnessing the decomposition of class structure of industrial society. Millions of people are in transition, with no stable position in the system of social stratification. Millions are becoming expendable, their labor no longer needed, with growing criminality and social unrest from below and brutality and repression from above...A popular struggle for grassroots democracy, not a class struggle around material interests, is the weak link of this emerging structure of militarized state capitalism. The victims of this restructuring are becoming as deaf to traditional worker-oriented class appeals of the old left as they would be to the old agrarian appeals of the nineteenth century populist movement of farmers and sharecroppers.[12]

M. Fuentes and Andre Gunder Frank go further to suggest a new mobilization away from traditional institutions:

> Whether new or old, the 'new social movements' of today are by far what most mobilizes most people in pursuit of common concerns. Far more than 'classical' class movements, social movements motivate and mobilize hundreds of millions of people in all parts of the world — mostly outside established political and social institutions that people find inadequate to serve their needs — which is why they have recourse to 'new', largely noninstitutionalized social movements. This popular movement to social movements is manifest even in identity seeking and/or responsive social mobilization or social movement with little or no membership ties...[13]

This new movement away from traditional instituitions in the context of the globalization of history imposes inescapable constraints on dominance of the flow of history by the West or East,[14] and instead increasingly transforms it into the input and output of international organization.[15] This process is spurred on by the technological revolution which enables the masses of the global village a greater exposure to education, communication and interaction of values. This acts to intercept the regional orientated dispositions of history, and through the use of international organization to synthesize and redirect it into global history.[16]

For minorities, this globalization of history and its accompanying emphasis on human rights and democratic ideals has animated the demand for decolonzation within states as well as the international level, causing demands for the renegotiation of social contracts in such a manner as to necessitate the further democratization of the state and to concrete the conceptualization of the multinational state. The social contracts of the old world order based on the recognition of conquest and politico-economic and military duress and their resulting structures, institutions and ideologies are finally fading before the pressures of demands for human rights and democratic participation. Its crumbling structures were those which animated gross inequalities and the selfishness that was necessary to sustain global colonialization. The fading of the old order under the impact of the technological revolution disorientates us; while it is the world in which we all must live, its wealth and resources remain controlled by and available to only a few. The new technology has assisted the questioning of traditional institutions by calling into contention the core religious and philosophical assumptions of human society, not excluding those of how wealth and power should be distributed for the attainment of SHCSD.

---

1 Minc , *supra.*, p. 205.

2 Apart from Minc, the disorientation to which we allude is also highlighted in the search for new theoretical frameworks alluded to in the work of William K. Carroll , ed., *Organizing Dissent: Contemporary Social Movements In Theory and Practice, supra.*

3 Minc, *supra*, p. 85.

4 See Wolfgang Friedmann, *The Changing Structure of International Law,* Columbia University Press, New York 1964 .

6 Alvin and Heidi Toffler, *War and Anti War,* Warner Books, Inc. New York, pp. 62-72.

6 "To meet these challenges, and while recognizing that action to secure global peace, security, and stability will be futile unless the economic and social needs of people are addressed..." Declaration on the Occasion of the Fiftieth Anniversary of the United Nations, 24 October 1995, p. 2. SHCSD essentially refers to the political institutionalizon of democracy, human rights, and ecological balance into a dynamic leading towards a human-centered as opposed to rule-centered societal growth. For the purposes of this research, it can be quantitatively measured or observed through the use of the UN Quality of Life Indexes, see pp. 6-7.

7 Goran Ohlin, participant, "Ethical and Spiritual Dimensions of Social Progress" World Summit for Social Development, 6-12 March, 1995 Copenhagen, UN Publication Sales no. E. 95.IV.2 p..46.

8 If we accept Fukayama's reasoning, then we are confined to viewing history within the context of only one philosophical concept. This would mean that each time a philosophical context reaches its logical result, history ends. However, as Hans Koechler noted in "Democracy and the New World Order," (in Hans Koechler, *Democracy and an Alternative World Order,* Jamahir Society for Culture and Philosophy, Vienna, 1996):

"Every epoch has a propensity to eschatologically transfigure its own achievements. In over-generalizing the spirit of the times, one readily invokes the 'world historical spirit' when, in fact, the protection of power interests is at stake. Hegel — like Heidegger later — demonstrated this with his embarrassing spirit-of-the-times opportunism, which was justified by the conception of an irrational idealistic philosophy of history and which found its continuation in the various forms of totalitarianism of our century. Francis Fukuyama, a protagonist of the American way of life, who is overrated as a philosopher of culture, succumbed to the temptation of prematurely transfiguring and immunizing the achievements of the Western system by declaring that the collapse of communism was virtually the end of 'history as such.' [Francis Fukuyama, "The End of History," in *The National*

Interest, vol. 16, Summer, 1989, p. 4] In light of the fact that in the course of this development the 'liberal democracy' of the West proved to be the more successful economic system, Fukuyama argues that it may constitute 'the end point of mankind's ideological evolution.' [*supra.*, p. 5] The factual success of this model of political organization in terms of power politics allows apologists like Fukuyama to almost completely dispense with a critical analysis of the concept of democracy and to speak of a 'remarkable consensus concerning the legitimacy of liberal democracy as a system of government,' [Francis Fukuyama, *The End of History and the Last Man*, New York, 1992, p. xi] even if a completely different system of values is propagated in a great number of states. Statements to the effect that this system is 'arguably free from ... fundamental internal contradictions' [*supra.*] effectively preempt an intellectually unprejudiced encounter with the basic structures of this model of democracy. These interpretations are further reinforced by the fallacious conclusion of power politics that the failure of the opposing model already has proved the correctness — i.e. the democratic adequacy — of the Western system.

"Therefore, after the end of the Cold War, apotheosis has replaced self-criticism. This attitude is embodied in talk about a *new* world order formulated along the basic lines of 'liberal' democracy. All further questions about the specific kind of democracy and about its realization in the model practiced by the West are repressed because this model — which has been postulated as exemplary since the end of the Cold War — represents perfectly the basis of the Western world's universal claim to hegemony and the United States' position as its leading power. [This orientation allows for the consolidation and] revival of the presumably defunct doctrine of [neo-colonialism through] 'just war' in the service of democracy and peace. The extreme, uncritical Eurocentrism of the colonial era was revived with all of its political presumption and arbitrariness when, for example, a representative of so-called 'critical' rationalism, Sir Karl Popper, spoke about the 'states of the civilized world' and implicitly assumed that they could responsibly handle weapons of mass destruction and have the right to discipline 'immature' countries of the Third World. The sublimated racism which allows thinkers like Popper to compare the Third World with a 'kindergarten' corresponds to many editorial commentaries which have frequently justified [past brutal colonial interventions.]... It is the task of a philosophy to critically question claims to legitimacy and not to simply adopt official explanations without testing them...

"For Noam Chomsky, the most determined critic of the Western ideology of democracy, the concept of 'democracy' means nothing more in the prevailing 'political theology' than the 'unhampered rule of the privileged elites' [*Deterring Democracy*, p. 365] in the name of the people. In the final analysis, Chomsky sees democracy as nothing more than a form of 'population control' [*supra.*, p. 369.]...Popper presented [his] ideology in discussions in Alpbach and now — as a philosophically unreflected concoction of Hegelian historical teleology — it is propagated by Francis Fukuyama. Chomsky's fundamental critique of democracy, which is far more philosophically consistent, identifies the liberal model as a form of advanced oligarchy that has resulted in a 'subordination of the political and ideological system to business interests,' [*supra.* p. 375] whereas for

Fukuyama 'the ideal of liberal democracy could not be improved on.' [*The End of History*, p. xi] In this context, Fukuyama relies on a typical immunization strategy, which has been described in various ways by Critical Rationalism and which can be observed with all prophets of salvation, including the ideologists of the 'real socialism' which has failed in the interim: shortcomings are attributed to an 'insufficient realization' of the ideal (i.e. the fundamental principles of freedom and equality) which itself, however, cannot be improved. It is obvious that, if any given order is treated to this degree as an absolute, one is forced to construct a teleology according to which the development of political systems peaks with liberal democracy. In this context, Fukuyama proposes the thesis of a 'coherent and directional History of mankind.'[*supra.*, p. xii.] As so many before him, Fukuyama in fact commits the philosophically inexcusable mistake of eschatologically overestimating the spirit of the times, an error which forces him to make a number of ideological contortions and contrived constructions, such as when he maintains that 'the world's most developed countries are also its most successful democracies' [*supra.*, p. xv] or 'that liberal democracies do not behave imperialistically toward one another' [*supra.* p. xx]. The achievement of these kinds of theses is support — in some respects philosophical, although with a bad ideology — for the claims to power made by the USA and all countries which understand themselves to be liberal democracies.

"With his uncritical glorification of the liberal system, whose primarily oligarchic traits he does not even appear to recognize, Fukuyama operates at a level far below the one which European discussions about democracy have reached. Decades ago, a theorist of culture such as Arnold Toynbee already pointed out that the effective functioning of a genuine democracy had been practically made impossible by 'the increasing complication of affairs under the impulsion of technology' [*The Present-Day Experiment in Western Civilization*, London, 1962, p. 66]. It is clear for Toynbee that the parliamentary system as we know it has more to do with oligarchy than with democracy [*supra.* p. 62]. Fukuyama and the other apologists of the liberal doctrine analyze the political system superficially, merely investigating the formal game rules and abstractly treating the concrete social, economic and cultural conditions under which electoral decisions are made. They cannot see — or do not want to see? — that specific electoral behavior is meaningless in terms of democracy if such behavior is the result of material dependency or the manipulation of public opinion... Furthermore, the thesis of the amorphous structure of the masses and of the political incompetence of citizens — in the domestic and above all in the international sphere — is employed to imply the need for structuring by a responsible elite in the form of representatives (within states) or 'civilized countries' (internationally)."

9 This view is Eurocentric in that, as earlier mentioned by Alvin Toffler, most parts of the world are still at the "stage of the hoe." In relation to their societal development, what does the European Middle Ages represent?

10 Jeremy Seabrook, "The Metamorphosis of Colonialism," in Chandra Muzaffar, ed., *Dominance of the West Over the Rest, supra.*, pp. 117-118.

11 Thomas Hobbes' "Leviathan" in reverse.

12 *Society and Nature, supra.*, p. 71.

[13] M. Fuentes and Andre Gunder Frank, p. 134.

[14] T. Rajamoorthy, "Double Standards, Selectivity and Western Domination," *Third World Resurgence*, No. 31, March, 1993.

[15] Wolfgang Friedmann, *supra*. Also, we have noted over the last decade, more than a three-fold increase in NGOs associated with the UN, along with a phenomenal increase in their variety and scope as well as participation in the international decision making processes. (See Director of NGOs Associated with the Department of Public Information, 1995, UN DPI/1996-July 1995-4M.)

[16] International organization is used in this research in its generic sense and doesn't necessarily refer to the UN alone. The UN is an organization whose international usefulness depends on it not being controlled by any one state or combination of regional states. If this happens to the UN, then it is likely to be replaced by one or more other international organizations.

CHAPTER 1

Critique of the Minority Rights Approach

Introduction

In both the developed and developing countries, the literature by scholars whose formation is not in international relations or international law concerning the changing role of the state as it relates to SHCSD and minority rights seems to have converged under four broad themes which, at the risk of over simplification, may be designated as: free-market globalism, environmentalism, peace research, and participatory democracy theories. Each overlaps and cross-references the others in such a manner as to suggest an increasing propensity towards justice-oriented 'multi-disciplinary' approaches. They have englobed the older Cold War socio-economic theories in a process of deconstruction wherein elements of the older theories re-emerge as postulates of broader conceptual frameworks, which always include such factors as quality of life, spiritual and ecological well being.

Similar to older theories that cater to corporate numerical minorities by promoting social and political policy designed to maximize production incentives for the purpose of maximizing profits without adequate attention to SHCSD, the minority rights approach is often seen as being too narrowly focused around the exclusive needs of minorities without sufficient concern for SHCSD, and therefore is often suspect of being out of step with the present trend towards socio-economic and cultural global interdependence. We feel, however, that such scholars have failed to tune in on the minority rights dialogue, or to cognitize the minority rights approach as it is perceived and communicated through international law: as a tool for achieving stable, ecological and economically viable democratic political re-organization of the state -- a prerequisite for participatory democracy and ethnic conflict management,[1] and therefore for SHCSD.

Those responsible for the development of the international legal approach to minority rights as well as human rights in general do not promote any of these rights as separate from what are viewed as the modern requirements for SHCSD. However, at the beginning of this decade, more emphasis was placed on individual rights than on societal responsibilities. Given the power relation between the citizen and the state, and the fact that many states had abandoned the minority rights concept after World War II, it is not difficult to understand why this occurred. Today, however, the minority rights dialogue promotes a much more balanced approach. For example, Mr. Asbjorn Eide, Special Rapporteur for the UN Sub-Comission, writes:

> The role of the state is declining, and this is likely to increase the possibility for minorities to find solutions to their claim for diversity...Nevertheless, the paramount role of the state will continue well into the foreseeable future as the organizing framework for law and order, to a lesser extent also for the co-ordination of significant aspects of economic and social activity, and less (but still significant) for cultural evolution. Since the state will be the common home for several cultural groups, it has to become functionally adapted to that requirement...Human rights, to be realized, require a functioning legal order. States will for the foreseeable future remain the main frameworks for legal order... and they will be held accountable [for human rights] ...Experiences within many states demonstrate that such accommodations strengthen the stability of the state and weaken the appeal for secessionism.... Article 1 of the International Bill of Rights states that: "all human being are born free and equal in dignity and rights." To be free does not mean a right to do anything one wants, harm others or to deny others' freedom... Order by necessity imposes constraints and obligations on individuals to respect the rights of others, to create the conditions of common welfare, and contribute to the solution of common tasks. Otherwise, there cannot be equity in the enjoyment of human rights.[2]

Mr. Eide also felt that to facilitate states' implementation of protective measures with regard to minority and other human rights, it will be necessary for international law to provide norms that would preserve the territorial integrity of existing states against violent change and promote inclusive democracy at the national level, thereby deepening, expanding and refining the

Table 2:

The Added Value of Minority Rights

Content	CCPR	Dec. on Minorities	Framework Convention	Copenhagen Document
Protection against horizontal discrimination	Art. 27	Art 2(1 Art 4(1)	Art. 5(2) Art. 5(1)	Para. 31
Encourage or promote conditions for identity	Art. 27	Art. 1(1)	Art. 5(1)	
Creation of conditions for identity	Art. 27	Art. 4(2)	Art. 4(2)	Para. 33
Effective participation, including in public affairs		Art. 2(2) Art. 2(3)	Art. 15	Para. 33 Para. 15
Adequate opportunities to learn one's language		Art. 4(3)	Art. 14(2)	Para. 34
Knowledge about minorities in curricula		Art. 4(4)	Art. 12(1)	Para. 34
Teacher raining, textbooks, educational contacts			Art. 12(2)	
Minority interests in national politicies		Art. 5		
Use of language before public authorities			Art. 10(2)	Para. 34
Use of their own radio and television media			Art. 9(3)	
Official recognition of surnames			Art. 11(1)	
Use of traditional local names, street names and topographical indicators			Art. 11(3)	
Protection against altering population proportions			Art. 16	
Non-interference in non-governmental activities			Art. 17(2)	
Conclusion of treaties			Art. 18(1)	
Transfrontier co-operation			Art. 18(2)	

Source: John Packer, "On the Content of Minority Rights," in J. Rakka, ed., *Do We Need Minority Rights?* Kluwer Law International, 1996, p. 165. See Appendix I for international instruments.

social contract within every national society. The international legal approach to minority rights clearly ties human rights to societal as well as group and individual needs. From this perspective, minority rights, like human rights, may be viewed as legitimizing the expectation of, or the demand for, SHCSD.

Empirical evidence that the implementation of minority rights tends to strengthen rather than weaken state unity and security[3] contradicts another notion particularly popular among political scientists: that because human rights, particularly minority rights, is in contradiction to state sovereignty, it cannot be implemented through law and must forever remain essentially a political problematic.[4] Similarly, some social scientists as well as legal scholars argue that even in the internal logic of international law itself, there is a contradiction between minority rights and state sovereignty.[5]

In guise of responding, let us examine the notion of sovereignty in international relations. It is reputed to have been first introduced in Europe in 1576 by the French scholar, Bodin, in his seminal book *De La Repùblique*. According to Bodin, there existed in each state a sovereign authority or supreme power (*summa potestas*); the sovereign in Bodin's time (usually the king) was the source of all laws and of all authority, remaining above all domestic laws of which he was the source, and subject only to natural law.[6] Because Bodin was only referring to the intra-state relations, his theory really had nothing directly to do with international law (other than in the manner that state practices may become sources of international law). However, in the course of time, this notion of sovereignty took on meaning not intended by its author. Sovereignty became confused with total unrestrained power existing above all laws and subject to no higher order (not even natural law). Thomas Hobbes' writings seem to have lent credence to this orientation.[7] However, as evidenced by Oppenheim's international law,[8] the state is not a material entity existing in nature that the authority can put in its pocket. The state is only an idea, the product of human thinking and imagination. In legal terms, the state is a juristic person or a corporate entity. As such, the state has no life of its own: its very existence is intermingled with the superior legal order of international law. Thus, for all legal purposes, state sovereignty should be seen as essentially a legal status within but not above international law — a status that is defined by international law.[9]

The minority rights dialogue suggests that while there is probably a contradiction between the political concept of state sovereignty and the political concept of minority rights, there can be no theoretical-legal contradiction between the international law of minority rights and the international law of state sovereignty. For all legal purposes, minority rights must be interpreted within the context of state sovereignty and vice versa. The minority rights approach promotes the political application of this legal perspective.[10] In line with this technical critique is another, more troublesome one: that since there is no agreed-upon legal classification of minorities that conforms to the needs of minorities within the context of the socio-political and economic situation of the states in which they live, it is legally impossible to provide for specific minority rights or a functional definition of a minority.[11] We found this critique theoretically important but pragmatically inconsequential. Thus we chose to comment on its significance in the conclusion to this research, after more can be said about the minority definitional problematic.

Another popular critique of the human rights approach links minority rights to the effectiveness of the UN and international law, and suggests that both are ineffective and thus should not be given serious attention. Suffice it at this point to suggest that international law should not be confused with the UN; the UN owes its legitimacy to international law, which existed in state practice, customary and treaty form long before the advent of the UN. While saying that the UN is ineffective and that its human rights approach serves essentially as a tool used by powerful states for foreign policy purposes may be a popular way of expressing frustration at the UN's many limitations and shortcomings, this does not square with empirical evidence. For example, the most recent statistics on the UN and collective management of international conflicts provided by the UN Institute for Training and Research (UNITAR) indicates that the UN has been relatively successful in the fulfillment of its prime directive: the management of international conflict and the maintenance of peace (see Table 3). The UN Department of Economic and Social Information and Policy Analysis suggests that it is even more successful in its role as a human service provider (see Table 4).

Perhaps one of the most effective popular critiques of the minority and human rights approach can be gleaned from the

Table 3:

World political issues and all United Nations cases of success (N=74), in percent

		World Political Issues						
		Decolonization						
	N	Easy[a]	Hard[b]	Cold War[c]	Arab Israel[d]	India Pak.[e]	Cyprus[f]	Misc.[g]
1945-50	13	15	23	32	15	15	0	0
1951-55	4	0	25	50	0	0	0	25
1956-60	12	8	46	8	8	0	0	31
1961-65	10	30	50	0	0	0	10	10
1966-70	9	33	11	0	22	11	0	22
1971-75	6	33	0	0	17	0	33	17
1976-80	16	12	12	12	19	0	0	44
1981-84	4	0	0	5	25	0	0	50

[a] Cyrenaica, Togoland, British Cameroon, African High Commission Territories, Kuwait, Panama Canal 1, Gjibouti, Bahrain, Equatorial Guinea, Panama Canal 2, Transkei, New Hebrides, Belize

[b] Indonesia, French withdrawal from levant, Namibia, West Irian, Algerian independence, Mauritania/Morocco, Sakiet raid, attack on Bizerta, Congo independence, Suez War, Aden independence, Ifni, Sarawak/Sabah, Rhodesian U.D.I., Falkland Islands (Malvinas), persecution in South Africa, raids into Angola

[c] Greek civil war, Azerbaijan, Korean negotiations, Russian wives, Cofru Channel, China Seas piracy, status of Lagos, Human Rights in El Salvador, Afghanistan, Corinto mining.

[d] Palestine independence, Palestine truce (1948-56), Israeli borders (1957-66), Six-Day War, Israeli borders (1967-73), Yom Kippuer War, Litani River campaign, Israeli raids into Lebanon, Gaza/West Bank occupation, Baghdad Reactor

[e] Kashmir secession, Kashmir negotiations, second Kashmir war.

[f] Cyprus civil war, Turkish invasion of Cyprus, Cyprus negotiations.

[g] KMT troops in Burma, Lebanon-Jordan civil wars, Wadi Haifa, Buraimi Oasis, Thai-Cambodian border, Tutsi restoration attempt, Katanga exiles, Persian Gulf access, Chilean repression, U.S. hostages in Iran, Burmese refugees, coup in Benin, Farraka barrage, Western Sahara, Malta/Libya, Gulf War, Seychelles invasion, Essequibo.

Table 4:
Estimates of inequality in the distribution of world[a] income
1981, 1985 and 1989

	1981	1985	1989
GDP per capita			
Coefficientof variation	1.69	1.73	1.78
GINI	0.7285	0.7288	0.7324
THEIL	0.7906	0.7965	0.7993
GDP per capita			
Coefficient of variation	1.72	1.76	1.81
GINI	0.7321	0.7328	0.7361
THEIL	0.7994	0.8048	0.8081
GDP per capita			
Coefficient of variation	1.71	1.75	1.80
GINI	0.7298	0.7305	0.7357
THEIL	0.7875	0.8007	0.8064

Source: Department of Economic and Social Development, United Nations Secretariat, based on international and national sources.

Notes:

The co-efficient of variation is obtained by dividing the standard deviation of the distribution by the mean.

The Gini co-efficient varies between 0 and 1. The lower the co-efficient, the closer the distribution is to equality.

The Theil (T) index varies from 0, when incomes are distributed equally to the logarithm of the number of income recipients when all incomes accrue to one the logarithm of the number of income recipients when all incomes accrus to one recipient and none to others.

[a] Based on a sample of 97 countries.

lack of reference to it as a distinct socio-political development approach or theory in itself by most green, peace, left and free market economist scholars.[12] They emphasize instead the importance of socio-economic theory from which human rights is viewed as a desirable outcome, a consequence of the politico-economic determinants. But could the reverse also be true? Can the implementation of human rights, including minority rights, determine or engender democratic socio-political and economic processes? If we accept the view of scholars such as John Packer[13] that the implementation of human rights automatically engenders democracy,[14] and his conclusion — that one cannot implement human rights outside of some form of democratic politico-economic system[15] — it follows that the possibility of the political implementation of human rights (which include minority rights as well as social and political rights) as a contending socio-economic and political theory for SHCSD should be investigated. In short, we suggest the possibility that democracy can only be sustained in states wherein the citizen (*à la mode* John R. Saul) is the chief source of authority, and where a human rights approach animates the orientation of the educational, politico-economic and social policy institutions of the society. Thus the implementation of human rights generates democracy.[16]

> It is partly through the work of the UN that human rights, at least in theory, has gone beyond civil and political liberties to encompass such challenging concerns as the right to development and the right to peace... the UN instruments have ... explored new areas which the UDHR as the inheritor of a liberal-democratic tradition revolving around the rights of the individual could not possibly envisage. In the process, not just human rights thought but political philosophy itself has been enriched...
>
> ...for a number of states which became independent after the UDHR...the various UN declarations and conventions have been a huge reservoir of ideas on human rights, the rule of law, the independence of the judiciary, public accountability and so on. Some of these ideas have taken the form of specific rights enshrined in national constitutions...[The constitution around which progressive elements of the Haitian population recently rallied in order to animate the new democracy platform of

> President Jean-Bertrand Aristide borrowed heavily from the *Universal Declaration of Human Rights.*][17]
>
> It is not just states... which find support in UN documents. Dissidents in many parts of the world have often tried to reinforce their struggle for human rights through the moral and intellectual authority of UN declarations and covenants... For dissidents, universal human rights have become criteria for judging the performance of their governments.
>
> What this shows is that UN instruments and UN institutions have succeeded, to some extent, in evolving universally acceptable human rights standards... In other words, there are certain norms of conduct in the arena of human rights applicable to human beings everywhere, irrespective of their ethnic religious, ideological or national backgrounds.[18]

Viewing Human Rights as a Socio-Economic Approach for SHCSD

What is most obvious as well as most troublesome is that in the world today, given the indivisibility of human rights,[19] most states are experiencing difficulties in recognizing both civil/political and economic/social rights, even some states well known for their democratic aspirations.

> It is often argued that there is a fundamental difference between the state obligations, even of developed states, with regard to social, economic and cultural rights. According to this view, group rights [including minority rights] differ from civil and political [individual] rights in that the latter protects the individual's sphere of freedom from state interference, requiring the state to refrain from state interfering with the individual's freedom, whereas social rights require positive interventions from the state.[20]

The implication here is that intervention to provide for social rights should not be the role of government. Although a part of the *InternationalCovenant on Civil and Political Rights,* minority rights, like social rights, call for positive intervention by the state. Thus the distinction between rights which require intervention and rights that do not raises the question (if we believe that the implementa-tion of human rights doesn't demand changes in the socio- economic and political ideology) as to why such a distinction should be sought by countries that pride themselves as being fully developed democracies, when the rule if not the functional logic of the indivisibility of the Covenants are popular among citizens and have been universally accepted.[21] Is it a question, as John R. Saul and numerous other scholars suggest, of these states being confronted with an internal opposition which challenges corporate democracy, or corporatism in favor of citizen democracy? Regarding this opposition, Saul writes:

> I spoke earlier of three parallel oppositions or struggles... humanism versus ideology; balance versus imbalance; equilibrium versus dis-equilibrium. I can now add two more: democratic individualism versus corporatism; the citizen versus the subject ...[22]

Viewing the human rights approach as a socio-political theory for SHCSD, in the context of the above-mentioned internal oppositions, would suggest that the implementation of the indivisibility of the International Covenants on human rights would set policy criteria that favors the victory of citizen democracy.[23] It is difficult for these developed, democratic states to adopt the International Covenants into positive law without disenabling "reservations"[24] or "understandings."[25] Could the deductive logic stemming from the legal obligations of the International Covenants, like an economic theory implemented in positive law, authorize certain permanent priorities on social policy and thus necessitate certain priorities for public spending which favor citizen democracy and SHCSD?

The International Covenants and other human rights instruments could become prescriptive in domestic law, and militate against systems and ideologies unable to provide human beings with lives free from fear and want. (Note that freedom from fear and want can be defined as *having* one's internationally protected human rights.) As stated in the Preamble of the *Universal Declaration on Human Rights* (UDHR):

> ... the ideal of free human beings enjoying freedom from fear and want can only be achieved if conditions are created whereby everyone may enjoy his economic, social and cultural rights, as well as his civil and political rights...

The duty of each State party to the Covenant is *"to take steps*, individually and through international assistance and co-operation, especially economic and technical, *to the maximum of its available resources*, with a view to achieving progressively *the full realization of the rights recognized*,"[26] and to "guarantee that the rights enunciated..will be exercised without discrimination of any kind..."[27] Thus, governments are requested to marshal national and international resources, *and give priority to the expenditure of those resources* in achieving the full realization of human rights. *Socio-economic human rights are violated where a State either neglects their realization while enjoying adequate resources, or implements them in a discriminatory way.*[28] By asserting that these goals require "the creation of conditions" and that states must "take steps," the International Covenants (*International Covenant on Civil and Political Rights* [ICCPR] and *International Covenant on Social, Economic and Cultural Rights* [ICSECR]) indicate that there is a requirement incumbent on states to act on a governmental policy level with regard to social, economic and political policies, insofar as it is only at this level that action can have sufficiently widespread effect as to be said to alter or "create" conditions, "conditions" referring to the total economic and political environment.

That the creation of these conditions should apply to all of the citizenry, including minorities, is established in the non-discrimination concept. Part II, Article 2 of the ICSECR indicates that these rights shall be exercised "without discrimination of any kind as to race, color, sex, language, religion, political or other opinion, national or social origin, property, birth or other status."

Article 7 recognizes the right to "just and favourable conditions of work," and Article 8 enshrines union rights. Part III, Article 11(1) of the Covenant further declares: "

> The States Parties to the present Covenant recognize the right of everyone to an adequate standard of living for himself and his family, including adequate food, clothing and housing, and to the continuous improvement of living conditions..."[29]

The democratic assumptions underlying human rights equally militate against the creation of any conditions that may reduce human beings to a permanent state of low wages[30] or kill their initiative and enterprise, such as collectivization, centralization of decision making, the threat of unemployment, the removal of the social safety net, particularly as it relates to health care and social security; the turning over of vital economic decision making to corporations, etc.. Part III, Article 6(1) of the Covenant recognizes "the right of everyone to the opportunity to gain his living by work which he freely chooses or accepts." Part III, Article 6(2) of the ICSECR indicates that states are required to assure "full and productive employment under conditions safeguarding fundamental political and economic freedoms to the individual."[31]

The human rights approach therefore suggests, as being more in conformity with human dignity,[32] the extension of the citizen's control of all (economic and social) societal decision-making processes, whether publicly or privately owned. Equally, the human rights standards of non-discrimination suggest this extension must be brought about in rural as well as urban areas, in agriculture as well as in industry, commerce and finance, and among minorities (collective entities) as well as among other citizens as individuals.

Thus, if states are to fulfill obligations under the Covenants in accordance with the logic of these articles, the following axioms might be implied:

1. A principal criterion for all expenditure allocations should be the creation of conditions whereby everyone may enjoy their economic, social and cultural rights, as well as their civil and political rights. Since these rights are universally accepted as fundamental to the human dignity needs of all, we may refer to them as representing a criteria for the general well-being of the population, which is what is meant by human centered as opposed to rule or law and order-centered societal development.

2. Thus, the removal of hardships limiting the ability of all citizens, including members of minorities, to exercise these rights must take precedence over the provision of tax breaks, etc.

3. Non-discrimination requires that the larger interest of the needs of the majority should take precedence over the narrower interests or demands of the few.

4. Thus, a private sacrifice or loss may be inflicted to avoid a public sacrifice or loss, and a greater sacrifice or loss may be averted by imposing a smaller sacrifice or loss. This can be logically derived from 3.

5. The human rights approach applies duties, such as: whichever social sector has most benefited from the system in place should also be first called upon to bear the most costs.

6. "Creating conditions" and "taking steps" as called for in the Covenants implies that those things without which an obligation cannot be fulfilled are also obligatory. (This can be logically derived from 2 and is generally accepted as an axiom of positive law.)

Since general well-being has to be an essential objective of all public spending in accordance with axiom 1, then axiom 6 would require that all physical and social infrastructure projects which help realize this objective through accelerated growth, job creation and need fulfillment should be given priority over those that do not make such a contribution. Even among the indispensable infrastructure projects, axiom 2 would demand priority for projects that would help remove the hardship and suffering caused, for example, by the prevalence of malnutrition, illiteracy, homelessness, lack of medical facilities or the lack of minority rights, etc.. Similarly, the development of an efficient public transport system should acquire priority in accordance with axiom 3 because its absence causes hardship to a majority of the urban population, adversely affecting efficiency and development, and leading to an excessive use of environmentally damaging cars, etc.. Similarly the provision of minority rights should take precedence over the private expansion of a golf course if it causes harm to an indigenous people requiring the land for spiritual or material well-being.[32]

If inequalities of income and wealth are to be reduced, it becomes indispensable, in accordance with axiom 6, to raise the ability of the poor, including the minorities, to earn more through greater and more convenient access to better educational and training facilities and to finance. This would demand giving priority in government spending programs to the establishment of educational and vocational training institutions in all areas of the state, including the minority societal sectors, so that everyone who qualifies has an equal access to them. It is also necessary to restructure the financial system to make financing available to a broad spectrum of entrepreneurs in rural, minority, as well as urban areas to raise self-employment opportunities and to increase the supply of need-satisfying goods and services. Thus, the concept of the human rights approach, which includes minority rights, as a viable developmental approach is important because, if implemented, it would have a decisive effect, not only on minority rights, but also on the social and political policy of the state, as a force for SHCSD.

What remains to be asked, in responding to the omission of the human rights approach as a possibly essential component of SHCSD is whether or not such an approach can be incorporated into functional economic theory as presently institutionalized. After investigating theories of social welfare (at the risk of straying beyond disciplinary competence, and with concepts borrowed from various economists), we suggest that it can. For example,N.G. Marmatakis tells us:[33]

> The social welfare function of a society represents the preferences between alternative stages of the real world. In their effort to create a social analogue to individual indifference curves, economists tried to derive contour lines in the space which represent alternative combinations of factors on which welfare depends. [They found that i]n algebraic form, social welfare function could contain all the economic and non economic elements which represent the preferences of the community and on which the welfare of the individuals and of the society depends.
>
> Since 1938, when A. Bergson introduced the concept of welfare function ...[he believed] that among the elements affecting the welfare of the community during any given period of time, are the amounts of each of the factors of production, other than labour, employed in different production units, the amounts of various commodities consumed, the amounts of the different kinds of work done, and the production unit for which the work is performed by each individual in community during that period of time34 and gives the following social welfare function:
>
> $W = W(x_1, y_1, a_1^x, b_1^x, a_1^y, b_1^y, {}^x n, {}^y n, a_n^x, b_n^x, a_n^y, b_n^y, c^x, d^x, c^y, c^y, r, s, t, \ldots)$
>
> where x y denotes the consumers goods
> a b denotes the two kinds of labor and, worth noting
> r, s, t denotes elements other than the amounts of previous variables affecting the welfare of the community.
>
> Paul Samuelson highlights the function of all the economic magnitudes of a system which is supposed to characterize some

ethical belief — that of benevolent despot, or a complete egotist, of all men of good will, a misanthrop, the state, race, or group mind, God, etc., and gives the following social welfare function:[35]

$$W = W(Z_1, Z_2 \ldots)$$

where the Zs represent all possible variables, many of them non-economic in character. Thus Samuelson also introduces the non-economic variables although he does not specify them explicitly.

S.K. Nath considers the social welfare function as describing the aims of social policy with dependent variable the social welfare and the independent variables, the targets or objectives which policies seek to affect, and the system of non-economic variables affecting welfare, giving the following undefined function:[36]

$$W = W(E, G_1, G_2, R, B, G)$$

where E denotes employment level

G_1, G_2, represent the coefficients of equality of distribution of money incomes and wealth

R denotes the rate of growth of National Product

B denotes the Balance of Payments

G represents the non-economic variables affecting welfare.

Therefore, since the formulation of the concept of social welfare function by Bergson, the inclusion of value judgments is an almost generally accepted approach to welfare analysis.[37] Of course, the sets of values are not clearly defined or if this happens it is done in a general and abstract way or they are considered as given by a political party, an ideology, a religious or ethical system, a government, or a group of individuals or an individual...

[Starting from this logic, it appears that] on the basis of the economic, social and political rights which determine the level of welfare of the members of the community, one may construct a social welfare function... this function [can be] included all the economic, social, ethical and political elements which determine the level of living of the population... and not only the pure economic and utilitarian components. For operational purposes and independently of the intermix and mutual interdependence, we can classify the determinants of this function as economic, represented by a vector U, and non-economic represented by a vector V. In the vector U we can include the factors connected with resource ownership and allocation, with the production of goods, with the distribution, with the consumption and growth which finally determine the level of satisfaction and the level of utility the members of the society enjoy. In the vector Y we can include all the systems of religion, philosophical, social and political values [or the universally accepted product of these systems: human rights]. The general algebraic form of this function [would probably look something like] the following:

$W = f(U, V)$ or
$W (U, V) = 0$ or
$W = F(u_1 , u_2, u_3 , \ldots v_1 , v_2 , v_3 ,\ldots)$

where W denotes social welfare and u , v denote [the human rights (including minority rights) or] the sets of innumerable variables which influence the welfare function of the society. If we keep constant the non-economic variables comprising the value systems under which the members of the society live and work, then the social welfare function becomes the economic welfare function which may be written as follows:

$W = f(u_1 , u_2 , u_3 , \ldots v_1 , v_2 , v_3 , \ldots)$[38]

Therefore, a functionally more wholistic concept of social welfare cannot ignore the political structure of a society, the non-economic aspects of social welfare, the system of prevailing values and the way in which individual or minority well-being is related to the well-being of the society and to the continuous transformation of the conditions under which the socio-economic system operates. At this point, economic theory would converge with sociology, political science, psychology and philosophy.

In short, there are two broad categories of "goods"in the general welfare functions: the economic goods U, and the value systems "goods" V. These two composite goods which a society can afford may be competitive, neutral or complementary, as can be seen from the lines of Figure 1, opposite.

Marmatakis concludes:

One may ask whether more freedom [democracy] and increased emphasis on human rights... produce more economic goods and ... increase faster the economic utility of individuals as it is depicted by the graph, or will the increase of "goods" decrease the production and consumption of good... [In our] opinion... the social, economic and non-economic welfare is increasing when the volume of economic goods increases and when the system of values contained in the declarations of human rights finds universal acceptance and applications.[39]

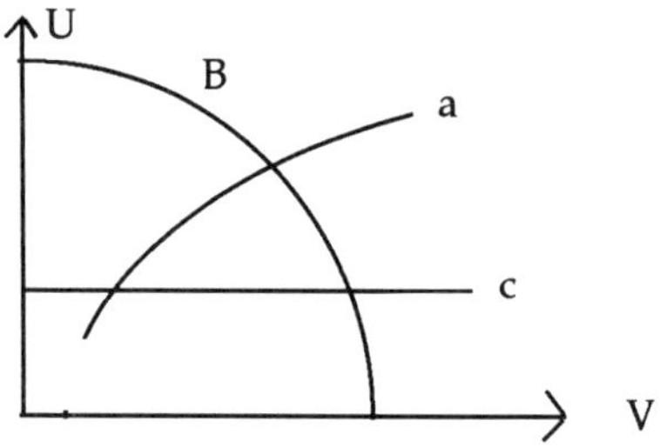

Figure 1:
The Relationship between
Economic and Non-Economic Goods

Finally, to provide for an awareness of a typical Canadian or North American critique surrounding the whole question of SHCSD in relation to minority rights, we have selected five additional short critiques of the human rights/minority rights approach. These particular critiques are empirically based in the sense that they were selected in relation to the frequency in which similar concepts were indirectly expressed by Canadians and reported in *The Globe & Mail* newspaper during the two months preceding and following the Quebec Referendum on independence.[40] Our synthesis of the following critiques is interpreted in relation to the type of critique of international minority rights these propositions implied. Particular attention was given to the opinions expressed by government officials as these, of course, made up the larger proportion of opinions and statements reported. Also, most opinions reported came from outside of Quebec, or from the "No" side inside Quebec. Thus, our critiques are probably not representative of Quebeçois opinion. While there were many opinions that could not be interpreted as critical of the minority rights concept, we only use those that we feel implied a definite criticism, our purpose being solely to discern the contours and essence of popular Canadian criticism.

1. We noted that the word 'minority' was used much more often to describe the First Nations peoples and other non-European minorities in Quebec than it was used in respect to either the French-Canadian minority in relation to Canada or the English minority in relation to Quebec. This suggested discordance with the minority definitional process in international law. (This process will be further discussed in Chapter Two, "Defining a minority for International Legal Protection.") In the English Canadian reaction to the referendum (though not so much in Canadian law or history), the popular approach, as suggested by our quantitative analysis, seems to beinfluenced by the U.S. melting pot theory and experience,[41] which seems to imply that minorities are citizens of non-European origin.

Such a categorization based on physical characteristics makes no distinction between First Nations and recent immigrants widely described as "visible minorities," and further, disregards the minority rights of Canadians of European descent: French Canadians, English Canadians in Quebec or in Nunavut, etc.. Today, there is nothing in the international legal approach that would distinguish between the minority rights of First Nations within the context of their objective and subjective situations and those of other minorities within the context of their situations and needs. The unique situation, circumstances, and consequent needs of First Nations has prompted the relatively recent introduction into international law of the concept of the rights of indigenous peoples. In our reading of international law, indigenous peoples become a category within the classification of minorities, for the purpose of being able to specify rights in relation to situations and needs, and not by race, belief, etc.. Perhaps in the era of the international law which condoned the right of conquest, conditions rendered racial classification less unacceptable; however today, politico-economic conditions which have produced the international law of cooperation and more recently of peace,[42] render such classification increasingly unacceptable.[43] From the perspective of societal human centered sustainable developmental, such approach to classification would only serve to support the shift of societal energy and resources towards the requirements for managing sustained societal conflicts[44] and inhibit the natural processes of ethnic "fusion"[45] and community cooperation in the solution of common problems. Mr. Max van der Stöel, the High Commissioner for National Minorities of the OSCE, states in relation to discrimination against minorities in Europe :

> Conflict prevention is vital to the future of our continent. I do not think that Europe can afford more of the bloody conflicts that devastate some of her regions. If we do not invest enough now and work in advance we will be presented with a much larger bill in the near future...[46]

2. Most statements viewed Quebec to be like all other provinces, as it concerns rights and duties, despite the clear factor that the Quebeçois did not view themselves this way. The relatively smaller number of statements recognizing the minority rights component of the Quebec question suggests that the North American experience may run against the grain of international human rights law in its failure to recognize that subjective as well as objective factors call forth the existence of minorities and necessitate their special rights. For example, the definition of a minority for the purpose of international protection which was accepted by the UN Human Rights Commission in the 1979 report of Francesco Capotorti [UN Doc. E/CN. 4/sub. 2/384/ Rev. 1 at para. 568]), and serves as evidence of the direction that an international-legal decision is likely to take, is:

> a group numerically smaller to the rest of the population of the state, in a non-dominant position, whose members—being nationals of the state—possess ethnic, religious or linguistic characteristics differing from those of the rest of the population and show, if only implicitly, a sense of solidarity, directed towards preserving their culture, traditions, religion or language.

Thus, the international legal approach recognises the subjective criteria for special rights, and thereby differs from what our quantitative analysis of *The Globe & Mail* would suggest is a popular Canadian orientation.

John Packer of the OSCE seems to have expressed the essence of the divergence in the Canadian and probably North American orientation to the definition of a minority, as well as its logical premises:

> Membership (in a minority) is established by free association in relation to a special issue. Hence, humans may associate in order to worship together, they may associate along linguistic lines, they may associate for cultural purposes, they may associate for economic reasons, and so forth. The fact of association, however,

> is a matter of contract..So as not to leave any misunderstanding, it is clearly possible that groupings may be externally established without any consideration of the desire of the members of these groups. However, these associations, which may be characterized as "negative", are simply the result of discrimination for illegitimate purposes...and they may be counter-acted by application of the principle of non-discrimination including, in appropriate cases, compensatory measures of affirmative action or settlement...incidents of negative association include association forced upon the individual against his will and association freely formed by the subjects of discrimination in order to defend themselves and overcome its effects; such association is not for any positive desire of self-fulfillment, but aims only to obtain the enjoyment of the primary human rights...[47]

Thus Mr. Packer's definition would preclude legality of special rights for national ethnic minorities. It would rule out the necessity to recognize the existence of national ethnic minorities when it states that: "To solve the riddle [definition and problem] finally: 'The' or 'a' minority is a group of people who freely associate for an established purpose where their shared desire differs from that expressed by the majority."[48] We will deal specifically in a later chapter with the definitional politico-legal problematic. However, while the orientation towards special rights for national minorities implied by Mr. Packer's definition seems to jell with what our analysis suggests may be the popular orientation of the majority population opinion in Canada and perhaps in North America and with a purely abstract sense of social justice, it runs counter to the international law approach[49] to justice implied in the minority definition approved by the Human Rights Commission, which recognizes the existence of ethnic national minorities as well as their right to special measures, special rights and, under extreme circumstances, to *internal* self-determination, political autonomy and, when all else fails, to political independence and international recognition as a state. Even more telling is the fact that empirical evidence indicates that the official recognition of the existence of ethnic minorities and their special rights is crucial for conflict management in real world situations (particularly where national minorities are concerned).[50]

3. The large number of opinions suggesting that all Canadians should have the right to vote in a Quebec referendum on indepen-

dence and equating majoritarian rule with democracy in a multinational state, indicates unfamiliarity or disagreement with the international minority rights approach to justice and democracy in multinational states, which recommends consociated structures and processes rather than majoritarian ones.[51] Democracy in multinational states will be discussed in Chapter Three of this research. Suffice it here to say that while non-discrimination and equality before the law are perhaps some of the most important tools for the protection of minorities and the assurance of democracy, they have proved insufficient for conflict management in most multinational states.[52]

4. The discussion reported in *The Globe & Mail* was generally in agreement, however, with the right of the English minority in Montreal (where they form a majority) to separate from Quebec, should it separate from Canada. While this concept may conform to a larger concept of social justice, if seriously undertaken, this would be contrary to the international law of peace and cooperation which refuses to recognize the right of minorities who form majorities in a major city or other vital economic area of a state to territorial autonomy, political independence or attachment to another state.[53] Of course, it is not difficult to see why such an attempt would all but guarantee violent resistance and thus find no legality in a law among whose primary purposes and directives is the maintenance of peace,[54] even at the price of limiting justice to the scope of political expediency and law.

5. We observed a large number of statements to the effect that the willingness of the minority rights approach to constitutionally provide for a minority's special status or special rights means that the minority rights approach seeks to create an ethnic ghetto and greater division within the state. While it is possible that any given minority may seek to institute minority rights for an internationally illegal or unjust reason, this misconstrues the purpose of the minority rights approach. As earlier mentioned and which will be elaborated with empirical evidence in later sections of this research, the minority rights approach evolved from the efforts of multinational states to resolve ethnic conflicts and to create mutually acceptable institutions, laws and conditions whereby different ethnic groups are able to live together peacefully in political unity and work towards common goals. We feel that in most but not all real world conflicts, this goal indicates a search for a just solution. To this point, Asbjorn Eide, Special Rapporteur

and Chair of the UN Sub-Commission's Working Group on Minorities, reminds us that most states are multicultural, etc., and that the more constructive way to deal with ethnic tensions and management is:

> to transform the national society, with its existing borders, into a community at a higher level, by making the inhabitants feel that they belong together, that they identify with each other. It must not, however, be done through policies of assimilation... [which] have had particularly negative consequences [for some groups, it breaks down the ethnic identity]. The only acceptable road *in our time*[55] is that of pluralism, with equality and non-discrimination in the common domain but where the different lower-level communities can co-exist and continue to have their primary identity, while co-operating and participating in the common domain with the state. A human rights based approach in plural societies must combine efforts to ensure equality in the common domain with acceptance of diversity in the separate domain.[56]

6. In the guise of concluding this chapter, we call attention to perhaps the most popular Canadian critique of the minority rights approach, centered around the general themes of the vagueness, insufficiency and non-enforceability of international human rights law in general: that in those few areas in which minority rights laws exist (see Appendix I for the international instruments), they tend to be vague and difficult to interpret into domestic positive law; or in areas where laws are required, they do not exist; or even when they do exist and are adequately precise, there seems to exist no adequate means for their enforcement. Indeed, this is a critique that is often made of international human rights law. Perhaps behind these open critiques, as suggested by our survey, is a general disbelief in the justice approach of international law, and consequently in the minority rights approach itself. In the case of minority rights law, the most obvious reason for its vagueness and incompleteness is that the post World War II codification of this law only began in earnest around 1979 with the acceptance by the Human Rights Commission of the Report of Francesco Capotorti on the situation and rights of minorities.[57] True, most minority rights law is "soft" law, reflecting what likely exists in international customary law, yet providing only moral and political commitments rather than strictly legal ones.

From the strictly legal perspective there are valid controversies and many ambiguities as to who the beneficiaries of minority rights are or should be (*ratione personae*), scope of commitment, etc.. There remains a definite need for the classification of minorities as a step towards an actual agreement on a definition [we shall return to this subject in the next chapter], and further codification and specification of the rules of law. However, on the positive side, it appears that in recent years and in conjunction with the increasing salience of the minority problematic to issues of world peace and SHCSD, the evolution of minority rights law continues at a slow but accelerating pace, following the quickening trend towards the maturation and up-dating of societal political policy in relation to minorities, democracy and SHCSD, and the alarming recognition that national minority conflicts have become a serious threat to global peace and consequently to SHCSD, if not always to the search for justice itself.

---

1 William K. Carroll , *supra.*

2 Asbjorn Eide, '"Minorities and Indigenous Peoples: Equality and Pluralism," in *"Nouvelles Formes De Discrimination/ New Forms of Discrimination"* UNESCO/FMDH Conference, Olympia (Greece) 13-14 May,1994, Editions Pedone Paris, 1995, pp. 230-231.

3 Mr. Eide calls attention to the experiences of modern Spain and other states, and their avoidance of civil conflict and perhaps secession by providing for minority rights, *supra.* p. 230. On the other hand, note the caseof Rwanda, Czechoslovakia and Bosnia, etc., where minority rights were not implemented.

4 Wesley L. Gould and Michael Barkun, *International Law and the Social Sciences,* Princeton University Press, New Jersey, 1970; Hans Kelsen, "The Essence of International Law," in Deutsch and Hoffman, eds., *Structures and Processes in International Law* ; Karl W. Deutsch, "The Probability of International Law," *ibid.*; M. Kaplan and Nicholas B. Katzenbach, *The Political Foundation of International Law,* John Wiley & Sons, Inc., New York, 1961.

5 Yoram Dinstein,"State Sovereignty and the Rights of Minorities,"in *New Forms of Discrimination, supra.* p. .217.

6 J Bodin, *De la Republique* 1 Chapitre 8, pp. 122-161 (1583 ed.).

7 T. Hobbes, *Leviathan,* Part 2, Chapter 18 (1651) pp.113-120, Oaksshott ed, 1957)

8 R. Jennings & A. Watts, *Oppenheim's International Law,* 9th edition, 1992.

9 H. Steinberger,"Sovereignty," 10 EPIL 397, 408 (1987).

10 See PER Conference comments and correspondence of the OSCE High Commissioner on National Minorities (Appendix II), etc. on the actual approaches governments are pursuing. Also note the interpretation of

minority rights by the Sub-Commission Rapporteurs, other international legal scholars, and minority rights politico-legal instruments, Appendix I.

11 See UN Doc. E/CN.4/AC/4/1996/WP-1 (definition of minorities) and E/CN.4/AC.5/1996/WP-2 (minority classification).

12 For example, nowhere in William K. Caroll's *Organizing Dissent: Contemporary Social Movements, supra.*, is the human rights approach analysed. Indeed it is almost exclusively in international legal studies and specialized international relations that this approach is discerned and given adequate attention.

13 Mr. Packer is Associate Human Rights Officer with the UN and Advisor to the High Commissioner on National Minorities of the OSCE.

14 Here we need his definition of democracy. However we have interpreted democracy within the context of the definition proposed in this research (see chapter on The Search for Democracy in the Multinational State.)

15 John Packer and Kristian Myntti, eds., *The Protection of Ethnic and Linquistic Minorities in Europe*, Institute For Human Rights, Abo Akademi University, 1993, 1995, Turku/Abo Finland.

16 While we accept the principle implied by Mr. Packer, we suggest that a functional democratic model is required, but not necessarily a western liberal democratic model. Our meaning here will be discussed in the section of this research on The Search for Democracy in the Multinational State. The meaning of human rights is sufficiently clear through a study of UN human rights instruments.

17 Not only is this obvious from a survey of the constitution itself, but also it seems to be popular knowledge among the Haitian population, particularly the dissidents who supported and fought for the Aristide regime.

18 Chandra Muzaffar, *Human Rights and the New World Order*, Just World Trust, Penang, Malaysia, 1993, pp. 144-147.

19 *Ibid.*, pp 43-45. Social, economic, civil and political rights are interdependent, and require the implementation of all types to be guaranteed the benefit of any one type.

20 *Ibid.* p. 44. See also Canadian government negotiations to secure the inherent rights of First Nations.

21 "Universally accepted" means, in the language of international law, have successfully gone through the international legal procedures required to be declared "in force."

22 John R Saul, *supra.*, p. 33. Also see John Kenneth Galbraith, *The Culture of Contentment*, Houghton Mifflin, Boston, 1992. Galbraith's analysis complements that of Saul.

23 Citizen democracy here refers to Saul's concept of individual citizens' satisfactory participation in the decision making processes of the state. In the minority rights approach, this concept is englobed in the concept of SHCSD.

24 Legal techniques used by states to accept a UN convention without accepting all of its content.

25 *Ibid.* These act to assure that the potential of a state's legal interpretation is limited to the law of the its Constitution.

26 General Assembly Resolution 2200 (XXI) of 19 December 1966, entered into force 3 January 1976 (*International Covenant on Social, Economic and Cultural Rights*), article 2(1).

27 *Ibid.*, article 2(2).

28 James C. Hathaway, "'Fear of Persecution' and the Law of Human Rights," *Bulletin of Human Rights*, 91 / 1, p. 108. Note also the international tribunal's response to the Canadian report, submitted under articles 17 and 17 of the ICSECR (UN Doc. E / C.12 / 1993 / 5) which inidcated the tribunal's findings that Canada was not using its resources according to human rights priorities. The influence of NGOs on the tribunal's findings (see"The Right to an Adequate Standard of Living in a Land of Plenty," submitted to it by the Canadian National Anti-Poverty Organization, May 17, 1993) is explicit'y acknowledged in Article 18 of this document.

29 This means that state intervention in socio-economic spheres of the society is required.

30 Many human service scholars express the opinion that workfare would have that effect.

31 While "political and economic freedoms" as cited might be interpreted as favoring private enterprise, this interpretation cannot be promoted as advocating private enterprise at the expense of fulfillment of other Covenant requirements.

32 One of the more severe recent conflicts between Mohawks in Canada and the provincial government of Quebec was generated by that First Nation's protest at the proposed expansion of a private golf course into a First Nations burial site.

33 The 'creation of conditions' providing human beings with lives 'free from fear and want.'

34 N.G. Marmatakis, "The Welfare Function of the Third Universal Theory," in *La Realite Internationale*,Cyprus, 1995. The citations in the quote that follows are those of Mr. Marmatakis.

35 A. Bergson, "A Reformulation of Certain Aspects of Welfare Economics," *Quarterly Journal of Economics*, February, 1938.

36 Paul A. Samuelson, ***Foundations of Economic Analysis,*** Cambridge, Harvard University Press, 1947, ed. 1971, p. 221.

37 S.K. Nath, *A Reappraisal of Welfare Economics*, London and Henley, 1976, p. 146.

38 See, for instance, J.M. Henderson, R.E. Quandt, *Microeconomic Theory: A Mathematical Approach*, McGraw-Hill, London, 1958, ed. 1971, p. 280.

39 See, for instance, Robert Pinker, *The Idea of Welfare*, Heinemann, London, 1979, p. 3, etc.. Also see Phillipe d'Iribans, "La consomation et le bien-être: Approche Psycho-socio-economique," *Revue d'économie politique*, LXXXII, 1972, p. 29; Michael J. Brennon, *Theory of Economic Statistics*, Prentice-Hall, Inc., 1970; Maurice Dobb, *Welfare Economics and the Economics of Socialism*, Cambridge University Press, 1969, ed. 1978, p. 110-114.

40 N.G. Marmatakis, *supra.*.

41 See *The Global & Mail*, 1995. A quantitative analysis of this paper over the dates mentioned was made to ascertain the most salient postions held by Canadians on the question of Quebec's right to secede or to be granted constitutionally recognized special rights or special status. Time and other restraints on this research would not permit a satisfactory review of the attributes and liabilities of all critiques; this is particularly true since it appears from the literature that different regions, civilizations, as well as different states approach the question of minority rights and consequently

critique the minority rights approach in international human rights law from different perspectives corresponding to different subjective and objective ambient factors. Indeed, although we have attempted to empirically discern a North American critical orientation, we limit ourselves to responses designed simply to highlight the conventional international legal premises as applied in international organizations (the Human Rights Committee, The International Court of Justice, etc.) and to help render more visible the complexity of the problematic.

42 Y N Kly, *The Anti-Social Contract*, Clarity Press, Inc., Atlanta, 1989.

43 Wolfgang Friedmann , *The Changing Struture of International Law*, Columbia University Press, 1964.

44 Max van der Stöel, High Commissioner on National Minorities, Keynote Speech to the Seminar on Early Warning and Preventive Diplomacy, Warsaw, 19-21 January 1994, CSCE Office for Democratic Institutions and Human Rights *Bulletin*. Also see Diana Chigas "Building Capacity for Conflict Resolution" in same *Bulletin*, page 1.

45 See the situation in Rwanda, for instance.

46 Max van der Stöel, *supra.*

47 See John Packer and Kristian Myntti, *supra.*

48 *Ibid.*, pp 40-45.

49 Georg Schwarzenberger and George Keeton, *supra.* Also see Wolfgang Friedmann, Oliver J. Lissitzyn and Richard C. Pugh, *International law: Cases and Materials*, West Publishing Co., St. Paul, Minnesota, 1969, pp. 11-33.

50 See Appendix V for a more concrete view of the real world minority problem, keeping in mind that it is the UN, using the international minority rights model (where appropriate), that was first to be called in for conflict management, while NATO was eventually called into the Bosnian-Serb conflict to move the conflict from a military stage to a politico-legal struggle by the use of military power to force the combattants to accept commonality of international norms and standards sufficient to permit the implementation of international law and thus the eventual return of the UN. See Wesley L Gould and Michael Barkun, *supra.* In this chapter, the author speaks about the intermingling of law and bargaining. Many other scholars express the opinion that international law represents, to a significant degree, important aspects of socio-political reality. See Curtis Arthur Amlund, "Toward the Establishment of World Law: From Possibility to Probability," *Southwestern Science Quarterly*, Vol. 46 December 1965, pp. 281-288, etc..

51 Arendt Lijphart, *Democracy in Multinational States: A Comparative Exploration, 1977.* Janusz Symonides, "TheLegal Nature of Commitments related to the Question of Minorities, " in *New Forms of Discrimination, supra..* pp. 197-212. Yoram Dinstein, *State Sovererеignty and the Rights of Minorities, supra.* pp. 218 - 227.

52 See Appendix II, see also reports from the PER, *supra.* This statement represents the predominant opinion expressed in the literature. We came across no opinion of scholars to the contrary, nor did any empirical investigation suggest otherwise.

53 Oscar Schachter, *General Course In Public International Law*, CCHAIL 1982,VOL.178. Once the nation had successfully achieved political independence or exercised its right to self-determination, such an action

would violate its right to control over its economic and natural resources. Ironically, should the same occur before independence, if the province was not viewed as autonomous with special status and the inhabitants wished simply to join it to another province in which their culture was the the majority culture, the problem posed would be quite different, similar to that posed by the French speaking Jura region of a predominantly German speaking Canton in Switzerland. However, being members of the dominant group in the province before Quebec's independence were to occur, means that the claim of the English minority in Montreal to minority status would be in question.

54 Percy E. Corbett, *The Growth of World Law*, Princeton, 1971, pp. 7 -32

55 Italics added.

56 Asbjorn Eide, *supra* . pp. 237-240. The common domain refers to the area where the laws and expectations are the same for all citizens; the private domain refers to those areas left to the control of the minority or which exclusively concern the minority.

57 See UN Doc. E/CN.4/Sub.2/384/Rev.1.

CHAPTER 2

Defining a Minority for International Legal Protection

In accordance with most justice concepts as well as the legal axiom that 'no one should be the judge in his own case,' the problematic of national minorities in multinational states is perceived by international legal scholars as an appropriate subject of international law. The actualization of this perception is due in large part to the evolution of international law over the years from a law of co-existence towards a law of cooperation and peace, to the increasing impact that minority conflicts are having on international peace, and to the difficulty observed in attempting to mediate minority conflicts on the national level and solely within the context of domestic law.

The international laws of cooperation and global peace are seen as interdependent. Both are viewed as necessary for, and contingent on, the implementation of human rights (including minority rights) which in turn depends on the existence of democratic ideals, processes and institutions. Thus, increasing civil conflict and gross violations of minority rights since 1945 due to the failure of multinational states to peacefully and justly[1] process national minority demands at the state level, has reanimated the minority rights dialogue, and engendered a renewed effort, on the international level (as manifested through the UN) to codify new minority rights standards,[2] the purpose being to provide multinational states with international legal guidelines for the treatment of national minorities and management of minority related civil conflicts.

Given the often decisive role that minorities and their struggles for self-determination have played in both ancient and modern history, it seems ironic that two of the most important inquires about minorities today should concern "What is a minority?" and "How are minorities classified?" Nevertheless, this is the case.

In popular every day usage, the terms "French-Canadian," "Indian," "ethnic group," "Roma," "Anglo-Quebeçois," "women," "children," "Black," "homosexual," "immigrant," "the poor," "Native people,""colored peoples," "ideological and political communities," etc., are all thought of as referring to minorities. In most cases, such popular usage reflects the unique social and historical development and politics of the state concerned.[3] However, as earlier suggested, this research approaches the subject not from a popular usage perspective,[4] but a perspective which is informed by popular usage in such a manner as to corroborate and evaluate the degree to which normative international legal evidence accords with empirical reality.[5]

We have observed that most scholars tend to approach the problematic of defining a minority for the purpose of international legal protection from what can be divided into three distinct bearings: 1. *sociological* (sociologists, social work scholars) 2. *strictly political* (political scientists); and 3. *legal* (scholars of international law).

1. The ***sociological orientation*** generally is concerned with designating what are called *social minorities,* such as women, the poor, gays, radicalized Canadians, etc. in relation to societal discrimination and meeting human needs. However, such groups are viewed from the international legal perspective as receiving international protection from human rights instruments other than minority rights.[6] As far as minority rights in international law is concerned, the sociological bearing accords best with international legal advocacyon behalf of what the international law of minority rights should include *(lex ferenda)* based on human needs. Scholars in the sociological orientation do not, as a general rule, concern themselves with the legal sources of human rights (particularly as derived from historical state practice), or the politico-legal problematic of creating legally binding human rights law *(lex lata).* This provides them with the widest latitude for focusing on human needs and rendering indispensable contributions to the minority rights dialogue.

The political impact of sociologists and social workers through their influence on international social policy decision making and its influence on local and national social policy is so recent that it has not yet been cognitized or fully recognized in social services, advocacy or delivery policies.[7] However, it is often the writings by social work scholars (spurred on by social work's advocacy mission) that influences the multinational state's definition of minorities and consequently (through NGOs or state practices) that of international law.[8] The writing by these scholars is focused on individual and group (minority) societal needs, rights and citizenship responsibilities vis-à-vis the state and its socio-economic policy. Thus, their main contribution to the evolving international legal definition of a minority should be in the area of minority classification in relation to societal needs. This contribution may be indispensable to creating political consensus on a minority classification, and consequently an international legal definition.

2. *The* ***strictly political orientation***, most clearly discernible in writings by international relations/political science scholars such as M. Kaplan, A. Schlesinger, S. Huntington, etc., often seems to presume the nation-state to be a given of nature, a naturally occuring phenomenon arising from a developmental need for socio-political control instead of a provisional result of historical processes accepted by individuals and groups with a view to meeting human needs through the establishment of a political community. Consequently, it seldom represents minority demands as demands for just structural changes to achieve a more mutually beneficial and acceptable arrangement (social contract) for equal-status political unity, but instead as a natural tendency of individuals and groups to return to the anarchic state of nature described by Hobbes.[9] Hence, the struggles of minorities for minority rights are usually portrayed as analogous to the anarchic struggles of individual against individual or nation against nation -- a strugglereconcilable only by submission to a monopoly of power, as opposed to a struggle of ideas seeking to fulfill human needs through acceptable legal, socio-political or eocno-mic changes in the local, national or international structures, and which are amenable to good-will equal-status negotiation, mediation, and just conceptualizations, etc.. From this strictly political perspective, minorities (national minorities)[10] are most frequently viewed as submerged nations owing their loyalty to a dominant state culture; concomitantly, minorities fail to demonstrate their loyalty to the state if, by

demanding minority rights, they refuse to acquiesce to the status-quo version of the historically evolved constitution and politico-legal institutions. For example, Samuel P. Huntington writes:

> It is my hypothesis that the fundamental source of conflict in this new world will not be primarily ideological or primarily economic. The great divisions among humankind and the dominating source of conflict will be cultural. Nation-states will remain the most powerful actors in world affairs, but the principal conflicts of global politics will occur between nations and groups of different civilizations.[11]

Similar to M. Kaplan in "The Coming Anarchy,"[12] Huntington goes on to equate the increase in global civil conflicts almost exclusively with the breakdown of the existing order, effectively obscuring the possibility of the disorder he sees being related to systemic transformation towards greater sustainability by animating greater socio-political, economic and ecological justice.

Most importantly, this strictly political orientation ignores or relegates the changes in world standards of the *International Bill of Human Rights*, the enlarged U.N. socio-economic and peace-keeping roles,[13] and the new international law of cooperation and peace, which were manifested after World War II, to the realm of utopian ideals, and formulates its premises exclusively on the older axioms of power politics and the chaotic consequences of challenges to the unfettered sovereignty of the nation-state. Different from scholars of the sociological approach, such scholars focus their attention on what we term *national* minorities, which are seen as emerging within pre-existing nations by political will, due to the technological revolution, socio-economic circumstances, and consequent subtle shifts in political power. While this view tells us little about how to define a minority for the purpose of international legal protection, it contributes to the minority rights dialogue by calling attention to, and providing information on, the political factors that should be given consideration in attempting to achieve political consensus for a legal minority definition.

3. *The* ***strictly legal orientation*** should be divided into two methodologies: the deductive (positive) and inductive (neutral or natural). The deductive method, which is associated with the positive law approach used to formulate domestic law (law which exists inside of states) would offer minority definitions

based on a combination of international legal authority and logical deductions derived from legal axioms and "black letter rules." It sometimes employs such domestic concepts as *steris decisis*, etc. Definitions derived from this method seek to create an international minority rights law that could be set before a court (particularly a domestic court) with the rules of law so well elaborated that the judge would be able to determine which groups are or are not minorities regardless of such factors as how the group thinks of itself (self-definition), the majority popular consensus in relation to the group, or a functional consideration of a group's historic and socio-economic circumstances in relation to other groups in the same state (restorative justice). In international law, this minority rights method runs smack into the old legal principles, *lex non cogit ad impossibilia* (law will not force one to do the impossible). Also, its tendency to separate or ignore political and extra-legal law creating factors, opposite to the sociological orientation which is not essentially concerned with creating or determining legality, creates another legal problem insofar as the prime directives of peace, cooperation and justice are central in any given case to the interpretative processes of modern international law. Often the requirements for the maintenance of peace, justice and cooperation defy deductive legal reasoning (see Figure2). In its attempt to substitute deductive logic for accepted practices, it is thus misleading in that it encourages a confusion of *lex lata* with *lex ferenda.*[14]

This understanding of the interplay of international law with socio-economic and political factors to achieve *lex lata* can be seen in the recommendation to states by the Sub-Commission of the UN Human Rights Commission that 'in dealing with minority problematics, they [should] rely less on force [including legal enforcement] and more on democratic principles, procedures and institutions."[15] We view this Sub-Commission advice as reflecting the majority approach to an understanding of the multi-faceted nature of the law-creating processes in international law. Our research suggests that the legal guidelines*lex lata),* in relation to the definition of minorities, are inimical to the use of the deductive methodology. This approach, in seeking to create a positive international law, becomes inapplicable in real world conflict situations and is largely responsible for the view that international law is ineffective.

Figure 2:
The content of the right to peace

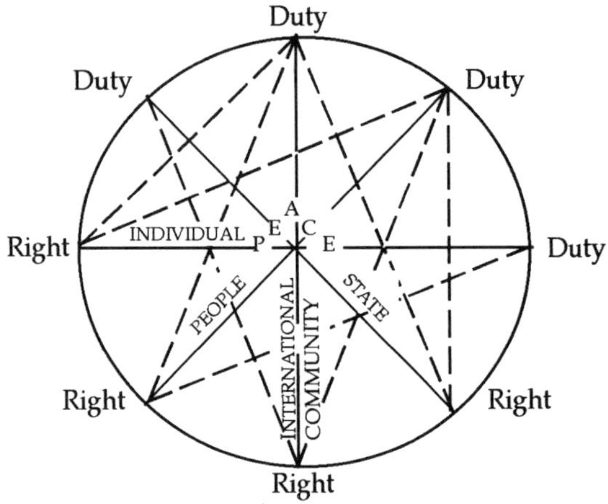

Source: Adrian Nastase, "The Right to Peace," in Mohammed Bedjaoui, *International law: Achievements and Prospects*, Martinus Nijhoff Publishers, UNESCO Paris 1991, p. 1224. The right to peace is inalienable, it is not *a faculty which may or may not be exercised*, according to the will of the subject. For this reason it can not be viewed *ut singuli*, but in its logical *summation* and, as a result, none of its subjects can renounce its right to peace, because thus the right of other subjects to peace would be affected.[16]

In attempting to ignore or specify the independent political and socio-economic variables underpinning the international process of law creation and enforcement, it also seems oblivious to the fact that the success of positivism in domestic law is heavily dependent on the monopoly of authority and of force enjoyed by the government of the state concerned. Even in domestic law, if this were not true, the government must resort to negotiations and mediation, etc., processes which permit the interplay between law creation and socio-economic and political forces, or enter into civil war (which is exactly what modern international law seeks to avoid).

The lack of this monopoly of authority and force is a starting point for understanding the nature, structure and processes of international law. Two of its earliest and perhaps most fundamental principles — *sovereign-equality*, and *no state can be subject to a treaty to which it is not a party* — not only reflect this lack of monopoly, but also appear to contradict the (mistaken) notion that international law *seeks* to base law creation and enforcement on obtaining a monopoly of authority based on a monopoly of physical force by the UN or some yet to be imagined world government. Instead, by necessity as well as by its professed ideals, international law seeks a more democratic socio-economic, political and moral basis for law creation, acceptance and adherence.

In consideration of the above, the circumstances and prime objectives of international law suggest that the majority methodology for determining what is international law is most appropriate. This method is often referred to as ***the inductive method***.[17] The inductive method, which illuminates our dialogue on the minority rights approach, can be seen as resulting from a cross between positive and natural law. It is a method which one may say recognizes international law as an evolutionary process of providing what was essentially natural law and customary practices with some of the attributes of positive law which had evolved domestically: a legitimate body of laws and rules, legitimacy of sources, a system for legal interpretation, etc.[18] It also provides for attributes not common to domestic law: heavy dependency on moral, political and economic sanctions for enforcement; non-punitive, restorative justice; an ecologically sustainable human rights centered legal orientation, etc..

Regardless of its indeterminacy, this method holds international law to an interpretation of what, in any given case, was actually accepted by state parties to an agreement, thus allowing the political, socio-economic or ecological issues which led to the agreement in the first place to continue to interact with the legal law-creating processes. This approach is often referred to as conservative, but conservatism in relation to international law creation has little meaning because it is the enforcement and conflict solving effectiveness of international law that deserves prime consideration.

In relation to the minority definition problematic, this method leads to the conclusion that at present, due to the lack of sufficient international agreement on legal sources, there is no legal definition for what is a minority for the purpose of international legal protection, and it is unlikely that one will soon be forthcoming.[19] *However, there are legal guidelines and recognition of groups as minorities according to these guidelines as well as an international legal concept of self-definition in relation to minorities.* These guidelines plus this concept conforms to the fundamental human rights paradigm that the human dignity and rights of the individual or group exist outside of any positive or state law (although state law must be given appropriate consideration) and are acquired simply by being born a human being. "The basic principles of international human rights law are thus derived from a universal notion of the inherent dignity of the human being. They existed independently of, and before, the state."[20] In relation to the 'minority definitional problematic', these guidelines formulated through the inductive method provide legally accessible and internationally recognized frameworks which groups use both to gain recognition, and to recognize and define themselves for the purpose of international minority rights protection. Because the guidelines do not block the operation of the principles of *self-definition* and other democratic political processes, they can be theorized to permit the appropriate influence of political, socio-economic and environmental factors on the evolution of international law toward the eventual achievement of the conditions prerequisite for a legal definition of a minority for the purpose of international protection, as well as for an appropriate classification of minorities according to socio-political needs and circumstances.

The inductive method as used in the U.N. Sub-Commission produced the following 1950, 1979, and 1985 proposed definitions of a minority for the purpose of international protection :

> 1. "The term Minority includes only those non-dominant groups in a population which possess and wish to preserve stable ethnic, religious or linguistic traditions or characteristics markedly different from those of the rest of the population... Such minorities should properly include a number of persons sufficient by themselves to develop such characteristics... The members of such minorities must be loyal to the state of which they are nationals."[21]
>
> 2. "A group numerically smaller to the rest of the population of the state, in a non-dominant position, whose members — being nationals of the state — possess ethnic, religious or linguistic characteristics differing from those of the rest of the population

and show, if only implicitly, a sense of solidarity, directed towards preserving their culture, traditions, religion, or language."[22]

3. "A group of citizens of a state, constituting a numerical minority and in a non-dominant position in that state, endowed with ethnic, religious or linguistic characteristics which differ from those of the majority of the population, having a sense of solidarity with one another, motivated, if only implicitly, by collective will to survive and whose aim is to achieve equality with the majority in fact and in law"[23]

Although on all three occasions, UN efforts to achieve a political consensus sufficient to support an international legal definition of the term minority (as used in Article 27 of the *International Covenant on Civil and Political Rights* [ICCPR]) have not yet succeeded, the amount of international support thus far received recommends them as legal evidence of what a definition might be like. Thus, they serve as international legal guidelines. In relation to the legal classification of minorities which is viewed as the first step to enable the achievement of a political agreement on an international legal definition, minority rights specialists meeting at the UN in April, 1996 for the second sitting of the newly created Working Group on Minorities (to which this researcher was invited) did raise the classification question for the first time as an item for the agenda of the forthcoming UN Sub-Commission. They suggested that minority rights, like solutions to a minority problem, should be tailored to correspond to the situation and circumstances of the particular minority and state concerned, and that the situation of some minorities, i.e. the Roma, the indigenous peoples, the involuntary immigrants to the Americas, etc. requires special attention and classification, and that such classification would make agreement on a minority defintion more feasible.[24] In an earlier document, the Chairman of the Working Group and Special Rapporteur to the Sub-Commission, Asbjorn Eide, contributed to the classifi-cation effort by suggesting that:

Groups are therefore best understood when examined in the context of the conflicts in which they might be involved:

1. The conflicts between a dominant center and a peripheral group... *The most typical, but not the only one, is the situation of*

indigenous peoples: groups whose traditional way of life and resource base is challenged by a dominant center which exploits the resource base of the group and in the process also destroys the capacity of the peripheral group to reproduce and to develop its own culture, including language and religion. In defence, such groups have in recent decades mobilized in resistance and sought international support for their right to be separate, to have a degree of self-government within which they can reproduce their culture, preserve and consolidate their resource base.

2. The second category of situations are efforts of discriminated groups to obtain equality. Most visible are efforts by groups discriminated because of their colour or race, but many experience discrimination based on their ethnic or religious origin. *Their identification as a group arises primarily because of the negative attitudes towards them by the dominant or host society. Their primary struggle is for equal enjoyment of civil, economic and social rights.* In some cases their struggle is for citizenship and full political rights. This applies mainly to recent immigrants, but in some cases even long-standing residents have experienced difficulties in obtaining effective citizenship. [This category seems to concern groups such as Afro-Canadians, Chinese Canadians, etc.]

3. A third situation consists of conflict between communals ... they are "culturally distinct peoples, tribes, or clans, in heterogeneous societies who hold or seek a share in state power". They are different from ethno-nationalists in the sense that the group or its leaders do not seek to dominate culturally or linguistically the national society as a whole, nor do they try to secede from the national society, but they seek to enhance their own position or to maintain their position when challenged by other communal contenders. [This situation concerns what this research refers to as national minorities. In relation to Canada, French Canadians seem to fit this category.]

4. Ethno-nationalists are persons using a relatively large and compactly living ethnic group as a basis, who either seek to dominate a heterogenous national society or to secede from it (dominate or separate). Dominating the national society would at best consist in assimilating the non-dominant parts of the population into the culture and language of the dominant ethno-national group; at worst exclude members of other ethnic groups from the national society, either by denial or deprivation of

> citizenship, or by outright ethnic cleansing. [Segregation in the U.S. South before 1970, apartheid in South Africa before 1990, and the Serbian minority in Bosnia seem to represent this type of situation.][25]

The April 30, 1992 Stupava conference of the PER in Czechoslovkia provided some empirical indication of how the minority classification and definitional problematic affect the treatment and situation of a minority. In summarizing the problem of the Roma minority, Milena Hubschmanova[26] described what she called the Czechoslovakian policy of forced assimilation after World War II:

> The Roma were labeled a social group with a dying ethnic identity; they were not allowed to have Romani teachers for their children, nor could their language be used in classrooms... *as a social group, the Roma themselves could be blamed for their lot, but if they were an ethnic group, the host societies would have to take some responsibility for their disadvantaged status...* another aspect of the redefinition of Roma identity was the transformation of ethnic and cultural differences into social deviance ... *Young Roma thus became increasingly alienated and isolated from the host society, experiencing an enforced social retardation which led to withdrawal, aggression, and other forms of antisocial behavior.* While policies of forced assimilation did not achieve their stated goals, they were successful in a purely negative sense: they destroyed traditional social structures, occupational skills, and values without providing replacements.[27]

During the 1991 PER Bucharest Conference, the definitional problematic is explored within the context of seeking a balance between the civic individual orientated society and the collective or ethnic-orientated society. The discussions that follow seem to revisit the individual vs. collective rights debate, which was legally resolved in the international law of human rights by concluding that both the *International Covenant on Civil and Political Rights* (individual rights oriented) and the *International Covenant on Social, Economic and Cultural Rights* (group rights oriented) were equally important, and that one could not be fully implemented without the other.[29]

> In the West, there is a generalized understanding of the privileged position of the majority concerning political and economic access

relative to the minorities. In the United States, it has even become standard practice to consider discrimination as possible only against minorities by the majority. *In consequence, the general proposition that redressing ethnic discrimination policies requires a change or compromise largely on the part of the majority is fairly non-controversial. However, this proved not to be the case among the Romanians, who perceived themselves as one ethnic group in the midst of a struggle for basic rights with other ethnic groups, indicating a level of national insecurity reminiscent of that which existed in 1918* [when the concept of individual rights was subordinated to group or ethnic rights].

Three other definitional debates resurfaced throughout the symposium. The first concerned the issue of violence against the Rom or Gypsy population. Romanian government and academic participants consistently characterized this as a social conflict, as did Attila Pok,[29] the participant from Hungary, when discussing the same problem in his country. Rom participants, particularly Nicolae Gheorghe,[30] pointed out that the ethnic nature of the violence alone required that it be treated at least as a problem of both social and ethnic relations...

Perhaps the most problematic issue discussed by participants was that of collective or group rights vs. individual rights. A basic division appeared in the debate between the American specialists and Romanian specialists... and other Romanians, including the great majority of non-Romanian ethnic participants...

It emerged that the standard American approach to the management of ethnic tensions is to sublimate ethnic identity within a larger state identity and to emphasize individual rights rather than group rights. The general approach of the ethnic minority participants at the conference appeared to be just the opposite: to foster/create an ethnic identity where only a weak identity existed before, and to gain a recognition of group rights by the Romanian State.

The goals of the ethnic minority participants ranged from the minimum quest for group protection to a maximum of establishing special community rights. For example, as Nicolae Gheorghe explained, for the Rom minority the primary problem has been managing ethnic conflict so that it does not become violent... On the other hand, for the Tatar-Turk and Armenian minorities, the crucial problem was one of gaining access to resources enabling them to print journals and books in their native tongues and so aid them in fostering ethnic group identification.

Participants from the German and Hungarian minorities stressed the need for a guarantee of group rights. According to Paul Phillipi,[31] the Germans were originally called by the state to be part of the power structure with specifically defined rights and duties. The model then, the "universitatus Saxonus," was the prevalent one before the French Revolution. Now [after World War II], however, group rights have been replaced with public and private rights, leaving the individual to confront the state directly — an uneven match at best.

Geza Domokos[32] also stressed the importance of minority group rights. While noting that the predominant Romanian fear is that minority rights will lead to autonomy and then to territorial loss *a la* the Vienna Diktat of World War II... *without group rights, Domokos argued, the majority can dominate the minority in the name of democracy*. Attila Pok added that real equality sometimes demands positive discrimination which is only possible if certain collective rights are guaranteed.

According to Kenneth Jowitt,[33] the conflict over collective and individual rights was an artifact of the antagonism existing between the civic, state, and ethnic orientations of the modern nation-state. *Ideally, an impersonal secular state provides for the equal treatment of all.* However, this conflicts with the gemeinschaft identification of ethnic orientations. Moreover, civic and ethnic antagonisms arise because: *1) The civic orientation is individualistic while its ethnic counterpart emphasizes the importance of the collective or group. 2) The civic orientation is inherently democratic and critical towards authority while the ethnic orientation, by stressing solidarity within the group rather than the rights of the individual, is inherently more authoritarian. 3) The civic orientation is universalistic and inclusive since it implies a relationship between democratic citizens world-wide, while the ethnic orientation is inherently exclusionist and* parochial. *The point, Jowitt emphasized, is not that ethnic is bad but that civic and ethnic orientations are not only different, but are conflictual as well...The central dilemma is whether the state in new conditions would continue to be defined in old ways — whether state and ethnic definitions would be dominant or, rather, whether they would remain important but secondary. The desired aim is not the elimination of ethnic identity, but*

> *the victory of the civic identity*. A citizen-based Romanian state is a primary condition for political and economic democratization.
>
> ...Donald Horowitz[34] suggested that the degree to which a supra-ethnic identification has been created is one way of placing Romania on a spectrum from the Third World to the developed West. While Italian-Americans, Japanese-Americans, etc., all consider themselves Americans, and German-Swiss and French-Swiss perceive themselves as Swiss,[35] there are no Burmese or Ghanaians.

Given the intensity of the political and social controversies surrounding minority classification, identification and other related problematics (civil rights model vs. collective ethnic rights model, the meaning of democracy in multinational states, etc.), it should not be difficult to imagine why international law remains vague on these subjects. Even the question of what is a "nation", with which the term minority is often associated, may be so dependent on other subjective factors, including socio-political and economic philosophy, that it remains beyond international legal definition. The eminent British commentator on nationalism, Hugh Seton-Watson, has written that after a lifetime of study, he was driven to the conclusion that it was not possible to devise a scientific definition of a nation. "All I can find to say is that a nation exists when a significant number of people in a community consider themselves to form a nation, or behave as if they formed one." Perhaps the same can be said of a minority. Thus, we may conclude that, due to the continuing minority classificational and definitional incompleteness, the law that defines who is a minority remains in an abstract state (*ex facto jus oritur*) until a minority successfully proclaims itself and effectively seeks recognition by the state in which it lives.

In calling for the subjective factor in all three of the international legal guidelines and accepting as minorities falling within the perimeter of that guideline, those ethnic, linguistic and religious groups which have successfully recognized themselves as minorities, international human rights law has provisionally endorsed the concept of *self-definition* particularly when achieved through a democratic process.

Types Of Minorities

In its present stage of development, international law designates three types of minorities[36]according to the characteristics that make them different from the rest of the society: ethnic,[37] religious and linguistic minorities. However, international law up to the present has avoided the classification of these three types into socio-political categories for the purpose of specification of rights according to real world needs and circumstances.[38]As earlier suggested, state practice and many international legal scholars have historically divided or placed ethnic, religious and linguistic minorities into three comprehensive categories: ethnic, religious and linguistic *social minorities, immigrant minorities and national minorities.*[39] While admitting in its *travaux preparatoires* that social and immigrant minorities do exist and receive protection, the UN and international legal scholars usually interpret both historical state practices as well as Article 27 (largely a codification of custom and state practices) to exclude all but *ethnic, linguistic and religious,* often called *national* minorities, from international protection under Article 27 of the ICCPR.[40] This conclusion is evidenced by a casual analysis of the *travaux preparatoires* of the special rapporteur on minority rights:[41] immigrant minorities are said to desire, and have freely chosen and contracted for, assimilation into the dominant civic culture,while social minorities are viewed as not seeing themselves as significantly different or wanting to remain significantly different from the majority ethny.[42] However, all three proposed minoritydefinitions required the group to show a desire to remain different and not to seek assimilation into the culture of the dominant group. Similarly in the *travaux preparatoires,* immigrant and social minorities are said to be expected to achieve adequate international legal protection under other provisions and instruments of general international human rights law. This does not mean that what one state might refer to as a national minority cannot be referred to as a social minority in another state.

While we have our doubts about the possibility of this interpretation creating unjust exclusions, we agree that much of the legal basis for the special rapporteurs' interpretation which seems to justify the omission (under Article 27 of the ICCPR) of social and immigrant minorities can be found in international customary law. As earlier suggested, we feel that historic state practice indicates that all types of minorities have usually been classified under the three comprehensive categories: social, immigrant and national minorities, and only national minorities have usually qualified for protection under Article 27. Thus minority rights as envisioned in Article 27 would extend to the categories of *national,* ethnic, linguistic and religious minorities, and their sub-categories. However, modern international conventional law has just begun to cognitize and elaborate the problematic of classification of minorities in relation to the problem of finding a universally applicable legal definition of a minority.[43]

John Packer's "associational" definition would resolve this problem by providing a definitional framework which permits the three types (ethnic, religious and linguistic minorities) and three comprehensive categories *(social, immigrant,* and *national minorities)* to be combined in such a manner as to extend the scope of groups protected under minority rights law (inasmuch as 'association' can be based on socio-economic, political, immigrant or ethnic, religious, or linguistic determinants). The democratic logic of Mr. Packer's proposed definition would certainly provide for minority rights within the context of non-discrimination, and would be one which governments of multinational states as they now exist would no doubt find theoretically easier to implement if for no other reason than that the "associational definition" would, from a politico-legal perspective, effectively disassociate the term "minority" from its historical association with "nation" or "nation-state," disassociating the concept of minority rights, including self-determination, from the rights of secession and political independence, and by moderating the ethnic identification associated with collective rights, insofar as a democratic state's population can be seen as endlessly combining and re-combining arrays of associations, whose contending claims mitigate the claims of any one ethnic type in particular.

However, under the present real world political situation, it is doubtful that the 'associational model' would be acceptable to national minorities. Thus in keeping with our proposed comprehensive classification within the context of the international legal guidelines, *associational* minority falls within the purview of *the social minority category(ies),* and is unprotected under Article 27. Consideration of the Packer definition would also raise the legal question of whether, and under what conditions, international conventional law can delete rules of international customary law. However, non-acceptance by national minorities would be the most important consideration, since minority rights, as a part of international law, must give priority to democratic conflict resolution and the maintenance of global peace. It seems that this may be true, even if the maintenance of peace could not include the maintenance of the state or the protection of the minority. However, international law in its present phase does not provide clear responses to such questions.[44]

Another difficult political problematics in seeking a politically acceptable minority definition is the existence of ethno-nationalist minorities or groups who for various reasons seek not equal status but dominance. The alternative strategy for ethno-nationalists who are unable to dominate the national society is to secede from it, by establishing an independent state which their ethnie can dominate, or by redrawing borders to become part of another state dominated by their own ethny. The South's secession leading to the U.S. Civil War seems to represent this type of situation in North American history; other instances seem to be the attempted secession of the Ibo in Nigeria or the Serbs in Bosnia. In these types of situations, the classification of such groups as minorities and the promotion of minority rights would not contribute either to promoting peace, human rights or SHCSD. Thus, as earlier noted, it is only through the designation of a minority and minority rights in relation to socio-political and international legal criteria that this misuse of the minority rights approach can be discouraged or avoided.

However, most multinational states are not torn by ethno-nationalist efforts to dominate. Most are better characterized as in a process of (imperfect) fusion. Whether subjected to an assimilationist ethno-national domination or to a process of fusion, some groups seek to defend their own cultural identity, to maintain their own language and traditions. This is usually done without any intent to dominate others and without objecting to equal treatment in the common domain. This seems to apply to Quebec's search for sovereignty-association. "States have emerged and their borders are set by a multitude of factors, including conquest, colonialism, and feudal struggles. Even in the few cases where states have emerged as a consequence of joint, free action by human beings, the present borders nearly everywhere contain some groups who had no choice but who were forced to submission and who now live within these borders."[45]

This comment of the Special Rapporteur should be viewed in light of our earlier assumption concerning the reason for the existence of the state. It raises a crucial question: if all nations should not be given states as this might lead to chaos and international stability, *does the effort to maintain state unity at the expense of a minority's oppression equally lead to chaos and international instability*? Note the present situation unfolding in the Indian state of Kashmir.

The following is a review of the type of groups states prefer to designate as their ethnic groups or minorities for public demographic purposes. This representative sample is taken from our research covering 152 states. We have chosen to present them in the text of this chapter rather than in an appendix, so as to highlight the culturally subjective and political nature of the definitional problematic.[46]

States' submissions for demographic purposes often do not concur with the configuration of ethnic groups reported to the UN in UN Doc E/CN.4/Sub.2/384/Add 6, entitled "Brief Survey on the Existence, Size and Proportion of Ethnic, Religious and Linguistic Minorities Within the Population of Some Selected Countries." Also note that the same type of minority, called a linguistic social minority in one state, may be considered a linguistic, ethnic or national minority in another state; or a type of minority considered an ethnic national minority in one state may be called a religious or social minority in another, etc.

States in the Americas, including the U.S. but not Canada, often list ethnic groups according to biological race, particularly as it relates to "black-white" people. Only the United Kingdom does this in Europe (and this despite the fact that their most serious ethnic conflict involves the Irish Catholic ethnic community. India also uses biological race unrelated to ethnic identity as an ethnic classification, which is unique for Asia. This also does not concur with the Special Rapporteur's finding in the before-mentioned documents, which notes the existence of a confusion between race and ethnic groups, but goes on to analyse ethnic group as referring to all the common characteristics, including biological race, history, lifestyle, philosophy, religion, comportment, language, etc..

CANADA

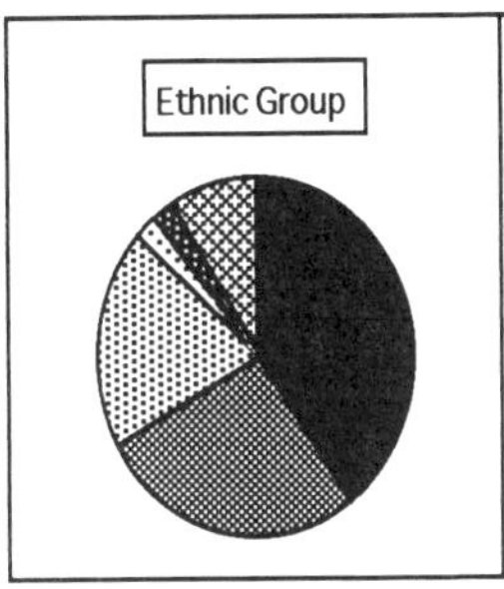

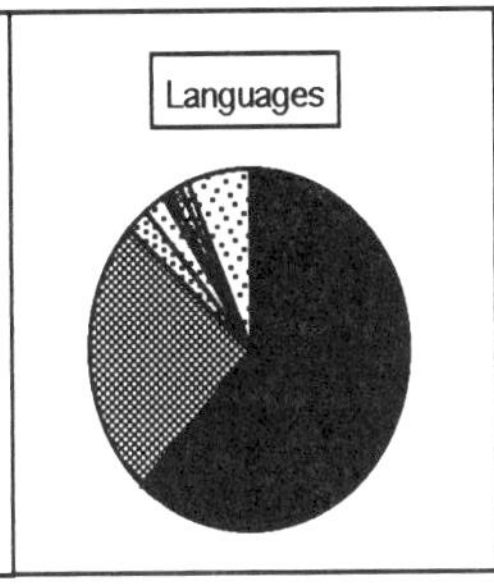

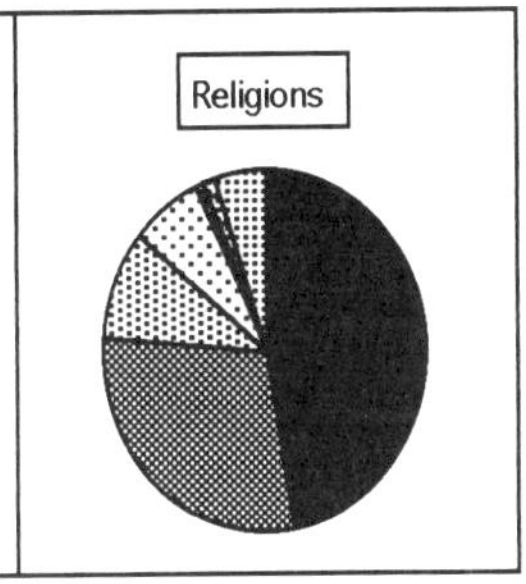

40% British
27% French
20% European/Other
2% Asian
2% Amerind & Innuit
0% Other

62% English*
25% French*
2% German
2% Italian
1% Chinese
1% Portuguese
1% Amerindian
6% Other

47% Roman Catholic
29% Protestant
10% Anglican
7% Nonreligious
1% Orthodox
1% Jewish
5% Other

UNITED STATES

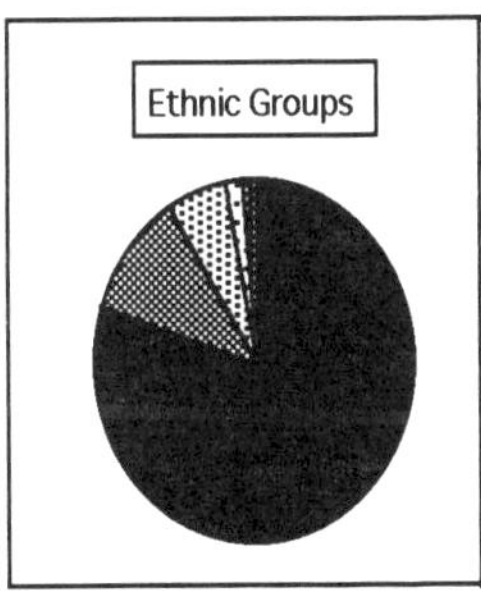

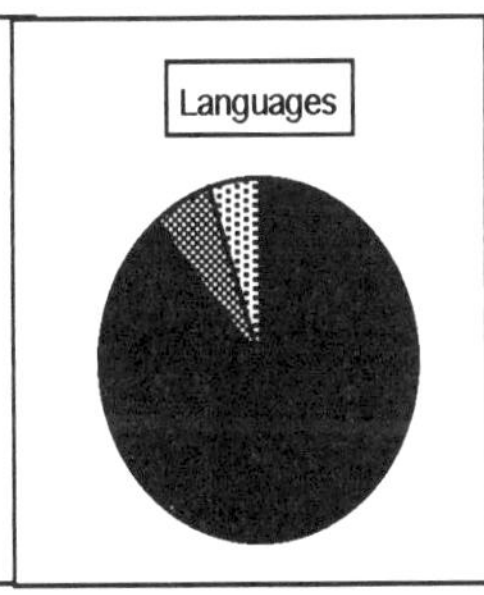

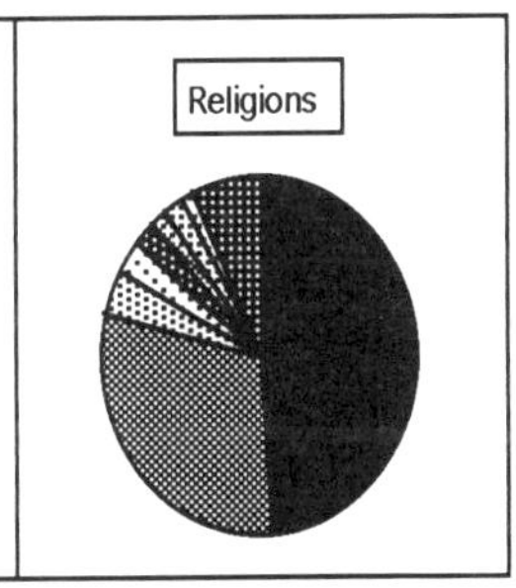

80% White
11% Black
6% Hispanic
2% Asian
1% Amerind & Other

89% English*
6% Spanish
5% Other

49% Protestant
30% Roman Catholic
4% Christian, other
3% Jewish
2% Anglican
2% Orthodox
2% Muslim
1% Mormon
7% Atheist & other

* Official languages

SWITZERLAND

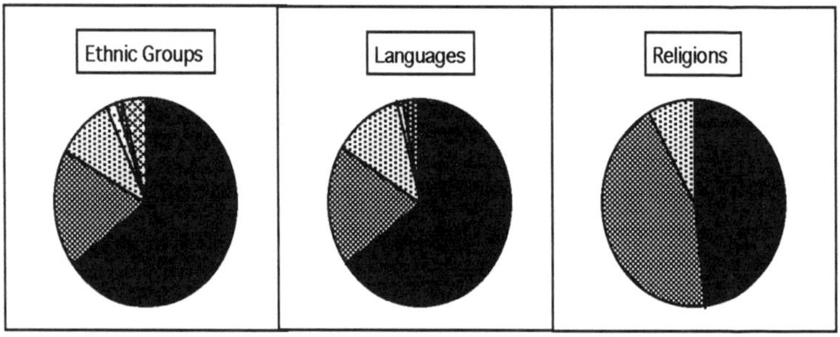

Ethnic Groups	Languages	Religions
65% German	65% German*	48% Roman Catholic
18% French	19% French*	44% Protestant
10% Italian	12% Italian*	8% Other
2% Spanish	1% Romansch*	
1% Romansch	4% Other	
4% Other		

UNITED KINGDOM

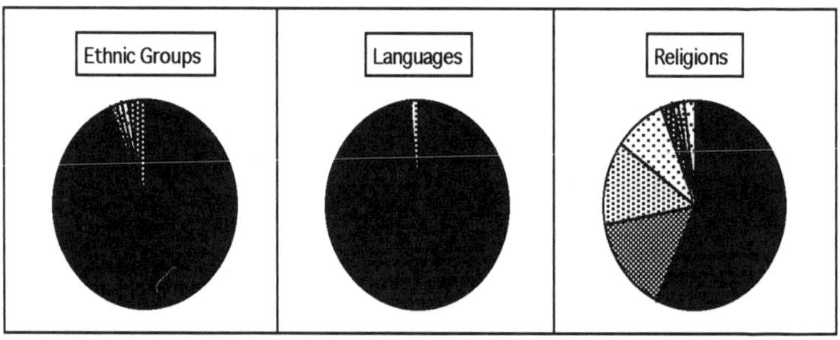

Ethnic Groups	Languages	Religions
94% White	98% English*	57% Anglican
1% Indian	1% Welsh	15% Protestant
1% West Indian	-- Gaelic	13% Roman Catholic
1% Pakistani	1% Other	9% Nonreligious
3% Other		2% Christian, other
		1% Muslim
		1% Jewish
		2% Other

* Official languages

CAMBODIA

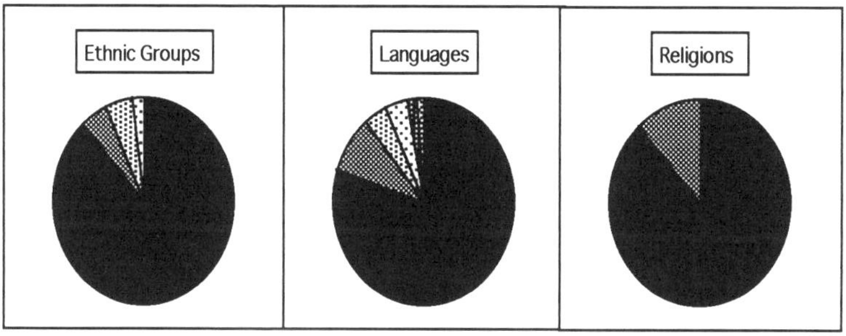

88% Khmer
5% Chinese
5% Vietnamese
2% Other

80% Khmer*
9% Kuy
4% Chinese, Mandarin
4% Cham
1% Other

88% Buddhist
12% Other

COLOMBIA

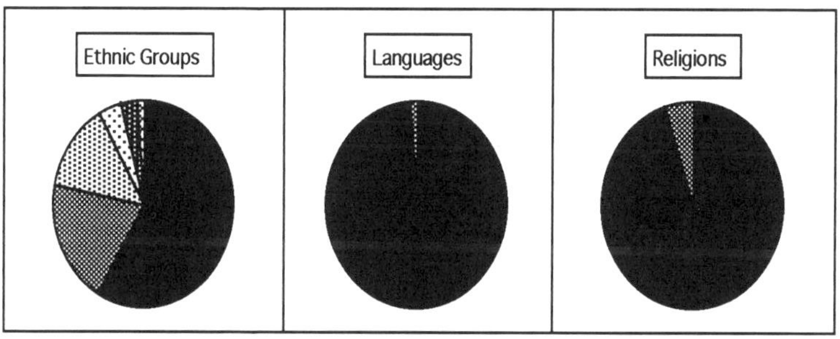

58% Mestizo
20% White
14% Mulatto
4% Black
3% Black-Amerind
1% Amerind

99% Spanish*
-- Amerindian
1% Other

95% Roman Catholic
5%

* Official languages

ALBANIA

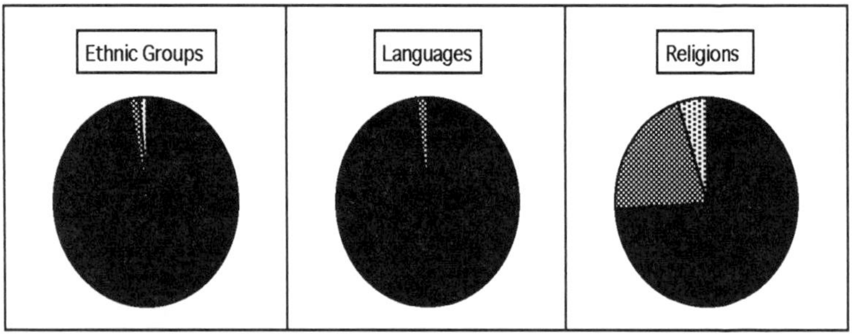

97% Albanian
2% Greek
1% Other

98% Albanian*
2% Greek

74% Nonreligious
21% Muslim
5% Christian

BOSNIA - HERZEGOVINA

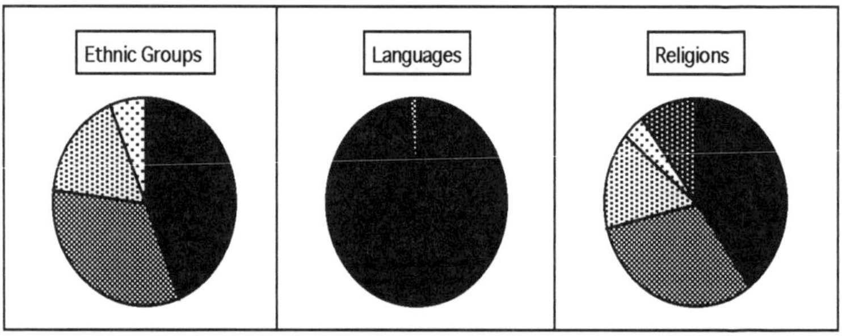

44% Muslim
33% Serbian
17% Croatian
6% Other

99% Serbo-Croatian*
1% Other

40% Muslim
31% Orthodox
15% Catholic
4% Protestant
10% Other

* Official languages

GUATEMALA

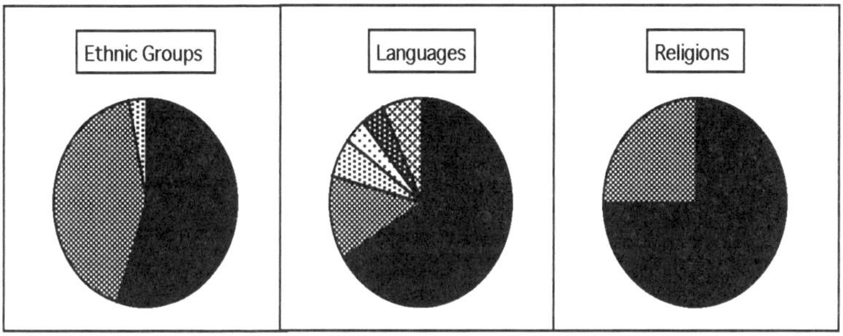

55% Amerind
42% Ladino
3% White & Black

66% Spanish*
13% Quiche
6% Calchiquel
4% Mam
4% Kekchi
7% Mayan, other

75% Roman Catholic
25% Protestant

INDIA

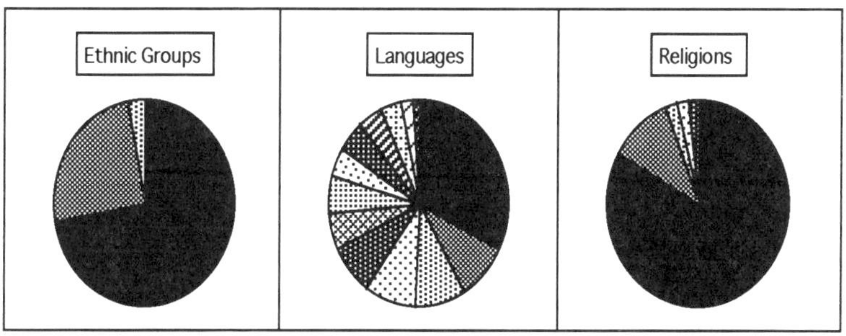

72% Indo-Aryan
25% Dravidian
3% Mongoloid & other

28% Hindi*
8% Telugu*
8% Bengali*
8% Marathi*
7% Tamil*
5% Urdu*
5% Gujarati*
4% Kannada*
4% Malayalam*
4% Oriya*
3% Punjabi*
2% Assamese*
1% Kashmiri*
--- Sanskrit*
--- English*
13% Other*

83% Hindu
11% Muslim
2% Christian
2% Sikh
2% Buddhist & other

* Official languages

ISRAEL

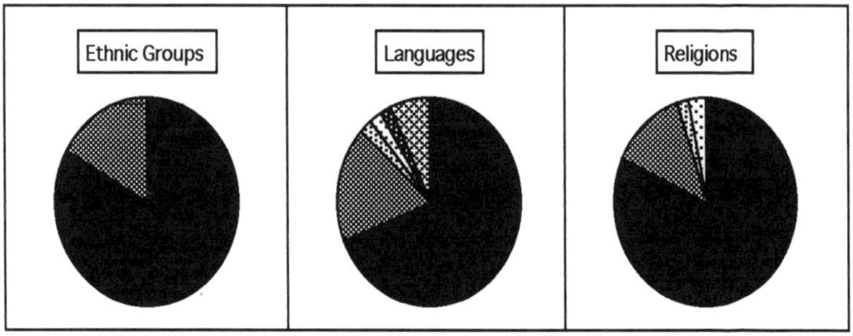

83% Jewish
17% Arab & other

69% Hebrew*
18% Arabic*
2% Yiddish
2% Russian
2% Romanian
7% Other

82% Christian
13% Muslim
2% Christian
3% Druse & other

LAOS

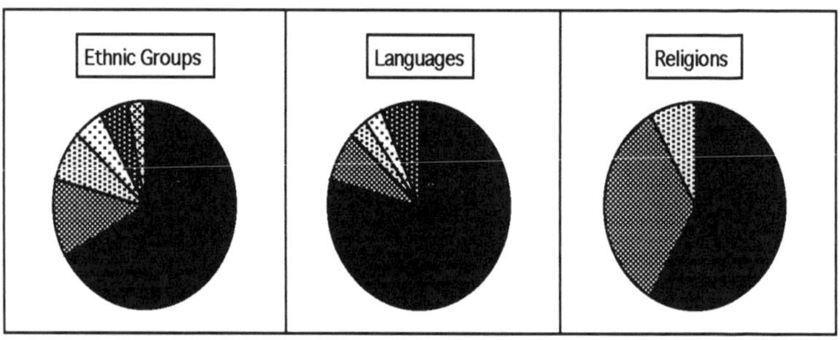

67% Lao
12% Palaung-Wa
8% Tai
5% Miao (Hmong), Man
5% Mon-Khmer
3% Other

79% Lao*
8% Khmu
3% Hmong
3% Phy Thai
7% Other

58% Buddhist
34% Trad. beliefs
8% Other

* Official languages

MYANMAR

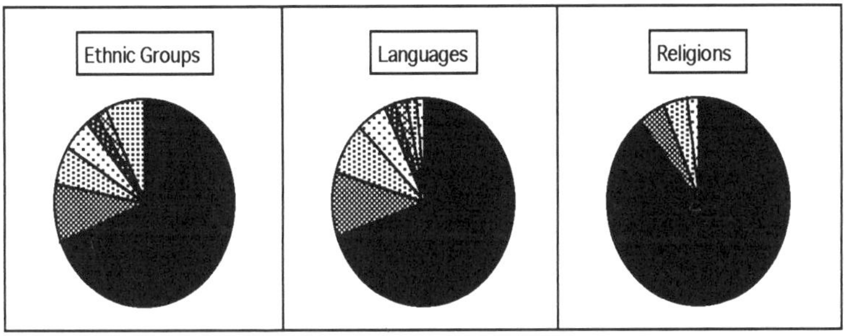

69% Burman
9% Shan
6% Karen
5% Rakhine
2% Mon
2% Chin
7% Other

69% Burmese*
10% Karen
8% Shan
5% Tibeto-Burman
2% Mon
2% Jingpo
2% Mon-Khmer
1% Parauk
1% Other

89% Buddhist
5% Christian
4% Muslim
2% Other

NICARAGUA

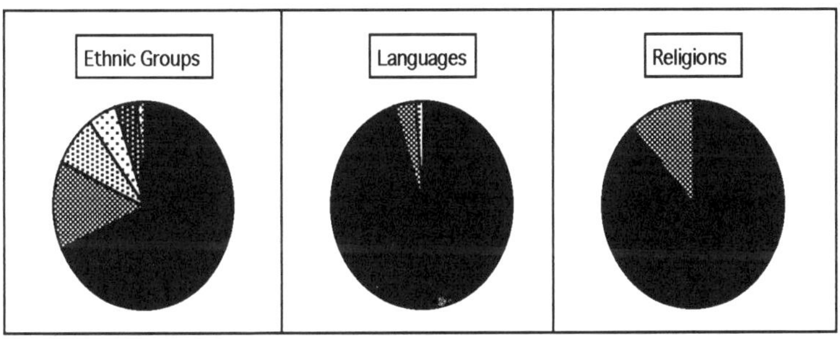

68% Mestizo
14% White
8% Black
5% Zambo
4% Amerind
1% Other

95% Spanish*
4% Miskito
1% Creole English

88% Roman Catholic
12% Other

* Official languages

PERU

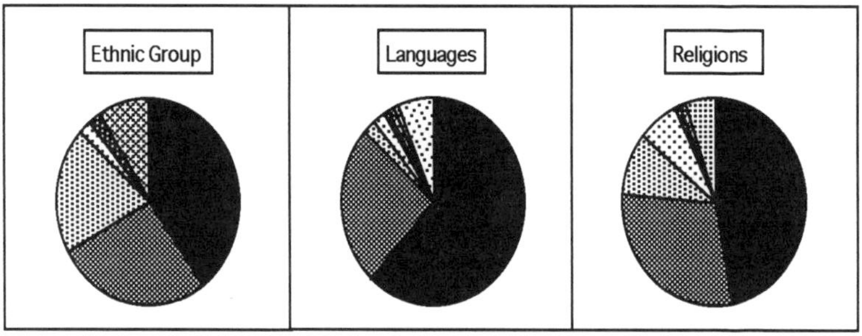

47% Quechua
32% Mestizo
12% White
5% Aymara
4% Other

68% Spanish*
27% Quechua*
3% Aymara
2% Other

92% Roman Catholic
8% Other

PHILIPPINES

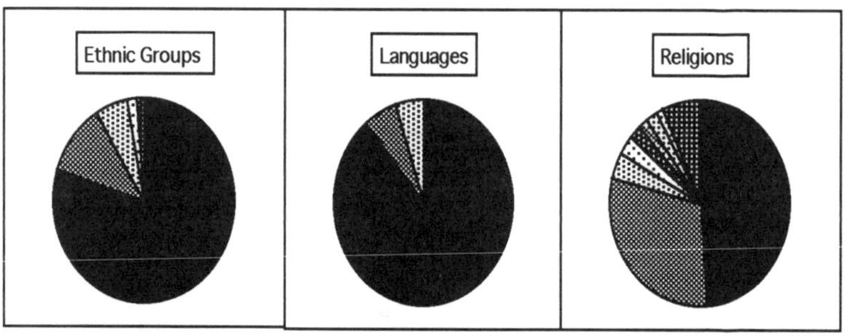

92% Malay, Christian
4% Malay, Muslim
2% Chinese
2% Other

24% Cebuano
24% Tagalog*
11% Ilocano
10% Hiligaynon
7% Bikol
5% Waray-waray
3% Pampangan
2% Pangasinan
-- English*
14% Other

84% Roman Catholic
6% Aglipayan
4% Protestant
4% Muslim
2% Other

* Official languages

SOMALIA

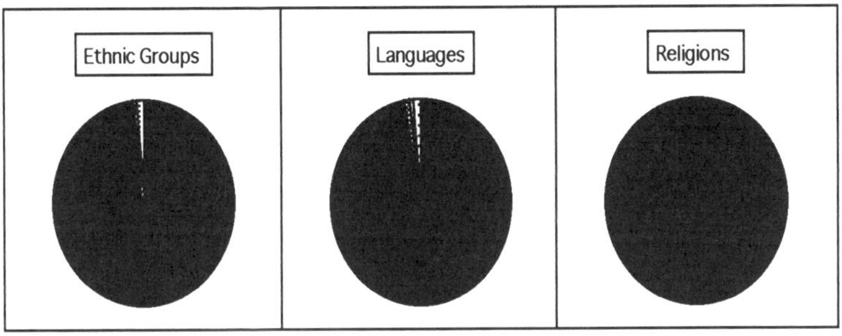

98% Somali
1% Arab
1% Other

97% Somali*
1% Arabic*
1% Swahili
1% Other

100% Muslim

SOUTH AFRICA

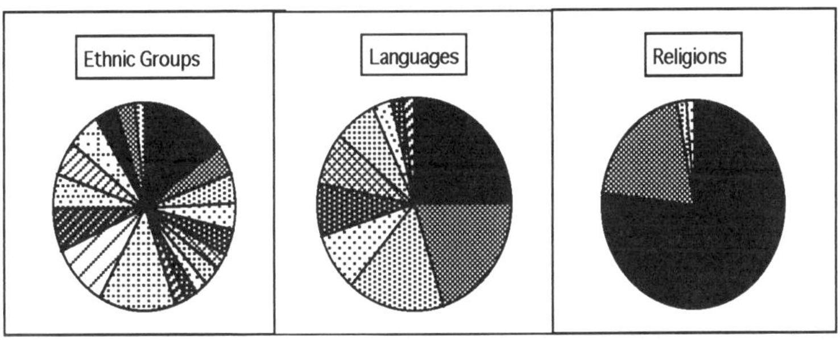

24% Zulu
18% White
12% Black, other
10% Sotho, North
10% Xhosa
10% Coloured
7% Sotho, South
6% Tswana
3% Asian

25% Xhosa
20% Zulu
16% Afrikaans*
9% English*
8% Sotho, North
8% Tswana
7% Sotho, Sotuh
3% Tsonga
2% Swati
2% Venda

77% Christian
20% Trad. beliefs
2% Hindu
1% Muslim

* Official languages

TURKEY

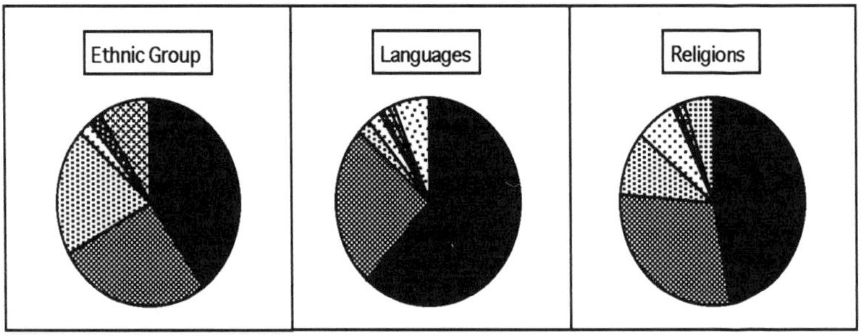

86% Turkish
11% Kurd
1% Arab
2% Other

90% Turkish*
9% Kurdish
1% Other

99% Muslim
1% Other

UGANDA

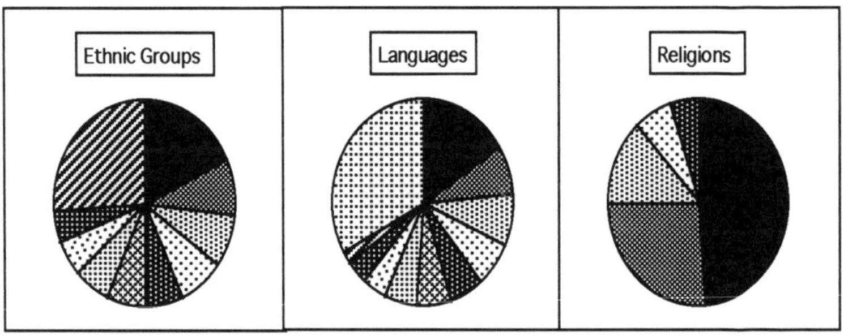

16% Ganda
9% Teso
8% Nkole
8% Soga
7% Giau
7% Chiga
6% Lango
5% Rwanda
5% Acholi
26% Other

16% Ganda
8% Teso
8% Nyankole
7% Chiga
6% Nyoro
6% Rwanda
6% Lango
4% Acholi
4% Lugbara
2% Karamogon
__ Swahili
--- English*
33% Other

49% Roman Catholic
26% Anglican
13% Trad. beliefs
7% Muslim (Sunni)
5% Other

* Official languages

Linguistic and religious minorities are often listed as ethnic groups as well as social and immigrant groups, thus suggesting, as we have proposed, governmental recognition of the existence of linguistic, religious and ethnic social minorities, immigrant minorities, as well as national minorities. However, this recognition we find through state practices is accompanied by different expectations and rights for each category.

In Table 3 concerning states suffering from armed civil conflict, our research revealed that none of the states mentioned had implemented a policy recognizing minority rights before the outbreak of civil conflict, etc. and that most had official governmental policies which could be described as forced assimilation or forced invisibility.[47] This is true although their constitutions may have indicated the existence of minority recognition. Thus, the minority rights definitional problematic seems but a reflection of the confusion existing in the real world situation.

Conclusion

Peoples have always sought the right to express their unique differences and to establish institutions supportive of such expression. Indeed for most nations or peoples, the right to establish such institutions was viewed as an integral part of their right to life and development. However, history also records that, when two culturally different peoples inhabited the same political territory, the establishment of the institutions unique to one (usually the strongest) over the territory common to both often meant stifling the expression and thus the societal development of the other. A consequence of this is seen in the unending histori-cal drama of human energy and resources being wastefully channeled into what in modern times have come to be known as liberation politics against hegemonic political elites, pro and anti-hegemonic terror, violence and wars, thus stifling the SHCSD of all. The minority rights concept (a revisit to, and update of, social contract theory) evolved in international law as a tool to enable societies to bypass the repetition of this age old drama as it relates to the recognition of group identity, needs, and the problematic of appropriately sharing resources and political power. We feel this problem poses one of the chief dilemmas for giving appropriate priority to sustainable ecological, balanced human-centered development.

Observations made at the Moscow, New York and Stupava conferences of the PER highlight the extent of this age old drama:

> As several participants noted, the appearance of ethnonationalism since the dismantling of Communism should not have been unexpected. Ethnic feelings and tensions had been long present in this part of the world, although the Communist regimes swept them under the rug. But surprising or not, ethnonationalism is nevertheless troublesome because it threatens the stability that could be achieved in a post cold-war world...[48]
>
> The violence directed against the Roma in all the former socialist states is pervasive. Since the beginning of 1990, Roma have suffered more than 45 attacks, resulting in the deaths of twenty Roma and the destruction of over four hundred Roma dwellings. The violence has been especially well-documented in the former Czech and Slovak lands and in Romania and Hungary, but it has also taken place in Poland, Bulgaria, and former Yugoslavia... Although from the perspective of the Roma, the important aspect of anti-Roma violence is grounded in deep-rooted prejudice and racism, it became clear during the course of the conference that there are demographic variations in the specific nature of the violence and the rationalizations and justifications behind it... in the Czech Republic on September 12, 1991, fascist skinheads, claiming a desire to "protect racial purity" attacked a Romani club, beating its members and killing a Rom. In Romania, however, as Nicolae Gheorghe pointed out, violence against the Roma was generally a rural phenomenon, usually consisting of assaults on local Roma inhabitants after some real or imagined precipitating event. In Bolentina, on April 6-7, 1991, after a Rom allegedly raped a village woman, the villagers drove 137 Roma families from their homes — the entire Roma population of the village — and burned the homes of 26 Roma to the ground as "retaliation"... There has been a marked reticence on the part of state and municipal authorities to recognize the ethnic nature of the violence and a corresponding tendency to underplay any fascistic and facist incidents. For instance, a member of the law faculty at Comenius University in Bratislava asserted that it took him six months to have an article on such attacks published... Likewise, according to Aldar Horvath,[49]the skinheads have had the help of the police on the streets of Hungary, and the justice system there has made no public comment on demonstrations against the Roma. Manouch Romanov[50] described how, in

> Bulgaria, Roma were "chased like dogs in the street," and Djuric[51] asserted that, after he had received several death threats, his home was ransacked by state authorities and he was forced to leave Belgrade and Yugoslavia...[52]
>
> ...One of the Serbian participants noted that the principal struggle the "moderates" have to wage is for the "modernization of ethnicity"; i.e. for making manifestations of ethnic loyalties compatible with twentieth century ethical and social norms of behavior. *Alongside the entirely "internal" norms referred to above, such behavior should provide for a broadly interpreted structure of regional security and for an international "umbrella," or international intervention by political means to guarantee the rights of minorities.*[53]

As noted by UN Special Rapporteur Asbjorn Eide. the international concern with the protection of minorities has historically gone through several stages with different approaches:

> From the time of the Westphalen treaty (1648) onwards the focus was on religious freedoms included in peace treaties. Then came the period of the League of Nations which was characterized by the concern with what was then called racial or national minorities in Central and Eastern Europe as an outcome of the settlements after World War I; the focus during the League of Nations period was on equal treatment for the groups as such as well as for the individual member of the group. During this last period of the United Nations from 1945 onwards the overarching concern has been with universal human rights for the individual, including non-discrimination and equal treatment for individuals irrespective of racial, national or ethnic background. There was during this period also an emphasis on the right to self-determination for the populations of non-self-governing territories (colonial territories or territories occupied after the illegality of annexation by the use of force had been established in international law, particularly with the adoption of the United Nations Charter Art. 2, para. 4).[54]

It is suggested that now there is a fourth period which started with the end of the Cold War, where a greater concern for a balance between individual and collective rights is proclaimed. There is an accelerating return to a focus on minorities, together with the question of the rights of indigenous peoples (a special minority classification). What is of particular interest is the shift from the first post-World War II period where a tension between individual and collective approaches existed and many scholars indicated that the balance between the emphasis of international law on collective and individual rights had been more positive during the period of the League of Nations than during the period of the United Nations. However, in the latter part of the 1990's, even while the ideal and authority of the state itself dominates, there is another shift in focus towards a greater balance between rights and responsibilities, and the promotion of human and minority rights within the context of the requirements for democracy and sustainable human-centered societal development.

---

1 Here 'justly' refers to being able, through democratic processes and institutions, to implement a mutually acceptable arrangement with national minorities for living together within one state.

2 See Appendix I.

3 For example, in states where biological race plays or has played a significant role in their historical evolution (Latin America, the U.S., India), or where biological race served politico-ideological purposes (the United Kingdom, India), popular notions of minorities or ethnic groups reflect this orientation.

4 The sociological perspective seems less correctly disposed to provide for minority definitons in relation to national minorities and international legal exigency.

5 As elaborated in Wesley L. Gould and Michael Barkun, *International Law and the Social Sciences, supra.*. In short, we seek an international legal, not a popular, definition and we assume that an international legal definition will provide for the appropriate influence of socio-political reality.

6 The development of minority rights in modern international law (since 1945) grew largely out of the interpretation and elaboration of article 27 of the *International Covenant on Civil and Political Rights* by various special rapporteurs of the UN Sub-Commission, and the consequent work done by the Sub-Commission of the UN Human Rights Commission. This seems to be the case although each of the special rapporteurs used international customary law to specify and corroborate their findings. The rights of social minorities are viewed as being protected by treaties such as: *The Convention on the Elimination of All Forms of Discrimination Against Women, The Convention on the Rights of the Child,* the *International Covenant on Civil and Political Rights,* the *International Covenant on Social, Economic and Cultural Rights,* etc.

7 See *Proceedings of the Joint Meeting on Human Rights and Social Workers,* Strasbourg, 8-10 April, 1987, Council of Europe publication DH-ED(X7)13.

8 For example, in writing about the rights of the poor and the legitimacy of the state, Frederic Lesemann, in the *International Review of Community Development,* (1986 p.4,) notes: "que peut faire l'état pour combattre la

pauvrété? ... C'est l'état lui-même qui est à la source des maux qu'il entend combattre... l'état est-il même illegitime si elle dépasse les strictes limites des garanties formelles de protection?" Mr Lesemann obviously does not raise this question to provoke a response from international law but rather as suggestions. However, today such suggestions often find their way through human service NGOs into forums where international conventions are being prepared. The crucial role of human service NGOs in drafting the *Convention on the Rights of the Child* testifies to this new potential.

[9] Hobbes viewed nature as a state of all against all, and life under such conditions as necessarily crude, brutish and short.

[10] This term refers to a minority classification category to be discussed later in this chapter. It is the most problematic category for multinational states.

[11] Samuel P. Huntington, "The Clash of Civilizations," in *World Politics: Annual Editions 95/96*, p. 8.

[12] Kaplan, M., "The Coming Anarchy," *Global Issues, supra.*

[13] See Appendix V.

[14] It confuses what states and other subjects of international law actually have accepted as legal obligation with what one logically should accept as legal obligation.

[15] Asbjorn Eide in *New Forms of Discrimination, supra.*, p.233, notes; "states should increasingly replace coercive power by responsibility and accountability, which is the essense of democracy." He goes on to say that this should be done by accommodating all groups, extending to each an equal respect for their identity...allowing for effective participation and ensuring consultation whenever their interest is involved.

[16] Adrian Nastase, "The Right to Peace," *Supra..*

[17] Georg Schwarzenberger and George W Keeton, *The Inductive Approach To International Law, supra.* Also see Wolfgang Friedmann, Oliver J. Lissitzn and Richard C. Pugh, *International Law: Cases and Materials, supra.*, pp. 11-33.

[18] This evaluation is conditioned by such legal axioms as: promises must be kept; a state can only be bound by a treaty to which it is a party; sovereign equality, the right of self-defence, and collective security.

[19] Browse the graphs in this chapter, which show the confusion in the way states prefer to define minorities or ethnic groups at the national level. Note that biological race and ethnicity are occasionally confused.

[20] Tunguru Huaraka, "The International Protection of Human and Peoples Rights," in Mohammed Bedjaoui, *supra.*, pp. 1061-1132.

[21] See UN Doc. 4/ CN.4 / 358 of January 30, 1950.

[22] See UN Doc. E/CN.4/Sub. 2 / 384/Rev. 1 at para. 568.

[23] See UN Doc. E / CN. 4 / Sub. 4 / 1985 / 31 of 14 May 1985 at para. 181.

[24] See UN Documents from the Working Group, Appendix I.

[25] Asbjorn Eide, *New Forms of Discrimination, supra.*, p. 231-2.

[26] A spokesperson on behalf of the Roma.

[27] *PER Conference Report*, Stupava , 1992, pp. 13-14.

[28] Krzysztof Krzewicki, Catarina Krause & Allan Rosas, *Social Rights as Human Rights, supra..*

[29] Attila Pok, the Institute of History, Hungarian Academy of Sciences, and the Europa Institute.

[30] Nicolae Gheorghe, Romani CRISS, Institute of Sociology of the Romanian Academy.

[31] Paul Philippi, Institute of Theology, Romanian Academy.

[32] PER listing not available.

[33] Kenneth Jowitt, University of California, Berkeley.

[34] David Horowitz, Duke University School of Law.

[35] While Horowitz' comments imply a preference for the civic model with a lessening of emphasis on ethnic identity/minority rights, it should be observed that the Swiss model he cites is *not* a strictly civic model, but rather one which has so successfully integrated minority rights and needs to share political, social and economic power within the national and sub-national political and legal structure, that the Swiss have no need to view their system as one of minority rights. Indeed, the Swiss political system assures that national ethnic groups that wish to preserve their distinct ethnic identity can do so by using the political and legal institutions available to each. By referring to their system as not a minority system, the Swiss imply that no national ethny is placed in a dominant or a non-dominant position.

[36] See Article 27 of the *International Covenat on Civil and Political Rights.*

[37] Ethnic is often viewed in international law as interchangeable with racial. This international legal definition of race, which combines the life-style,biological and ethnic characteristics, is the only universally functional definition. Thus it is worth noting because it permits us to view racism as a destructive by-product of collective efforts towards dealing with historic socio-political and economic priorities and problems, as well as a fear of others provoked by and institutionalized attitudes.

[38] See Appendix I. The classification of indigenous people as a category of minority seems to be the only exception.

[39] Article 27 provides us with a classification of three fundamental types of minority. However, we have noted in practices by states and their institutions, as wells in the writings of scholars, that these fundamental types of minorities are often subsumed within the categories of social, immigrant and national minorities. In light of state practices and popular practice, there are linguistic, ethnic and religious social minorities. Likewise, there are linguistic, ethnic and religious immigrant minorities. Also, national minorities can be ethnic, religious or linguistic. In short, the three categories in popular usage all include the three fundamental types of minorities designated by Article 27. However, as to be mentioned, Article 27 rules out minority rights for what in popular usage are social and immigrant minorities, and accepts minority rights only for what in popular usage are national minorities. Also, it appears that an immigrant minority, using the minority definitional legal guidelines, cannot be a national minority.

[40] This conclusion is warranted by he materials and sources (state practices, minority treaties, etc.) that the Special Rapporteurs for the Sub-Commission choose to use in the search for an international legal definition of the term 'minority' used in Article 27. Content analysis confirms that these materials and sources dealt essentially with national minorities.

[41] See U.N. Doc. E/CN.4/Sub.2/384/Addenda.

[42] Christos Theodoropoulos, "The International Protection of Immigrant Populations," in *New Forms of Discrimination, supra.*, p. 47.

[43] See Yussuf Kly, section entitled "Notes on the Current State of Law and Balancing Sources of Law," in the Proceedings of the Hamline Conference on Self-Determination, *Hamline Law Journal*, Vol. 17, No. 1, Fall, 1993.

[44] See John Packer, *supra.*

[45] See Benjamin B. Ferencz, "The International Law of Peace," in *Global Survival*, Oceana Publications, Inc.,1994 pp. 1 - 37

[46] Asbjorn Eide in *New Forms of Discrimination, supra*, p. 231-2.

[47] See Muzaffar, *Dominance of the West Over the Rest, supra.*, p. 37. "To be invisible, we have learned, is to have no voice, to gain no recognition. To be forced into invisibility is to be dominated, to be oppressed and marginalised. And to be made invisible is the routine experience of power-less persons and powerless groups."

[48] Project on Ethnic Relations, *Ethnonationalism: Fears, Dangers, and Policies in the Post-Communist World*, Moscow, Russia, January 20-21, 1995.

[49] Aldar Horvath, listing not available.

[50] Manouch Romanov, the Roma Union.

[51] Djuric not available.

[52] Project on Ethnic Relations, *The Romanies in Central and Eastern Europe: Illusions and Reality*, Stupava, Czechoslovakia, April 30-May 2, 1992.

[53] Project on Ethnic Relations, *Interethnic Relations in Serbia/Yugoslavia: Alternatives for the Future*, New York, September 27-28, 1993.

[54] Asbjorn Eide, *supra.* Eide cites A. Bredimas as the source of the latter notion.

CHAPTER 3

The Search for Democracy in the Multinational State

In this chapter, we do not intend to describe what democracy in a multinational state is, but rather to describe the chief contexts, problematics and frameworks in which the search for it is being pursued within the context of the minority rights dialogue. Concepts of democracy are most often elaborated and analyzed within the conceptual framework of the nation-state, where there is said to exist one nation composed of citizens who have consented under the terms of a social contract to be interpreted as a single indivisible political unit governed through a procedural and structural instrument called a state or a nation-state.[1] Only in relatively recent history has this same problematic been revisited in relation to the concept of the multinational state. Scholars such as Arendt Lijphart with his notion of consociated democracy and others such as Asbjorn Eide, Gudmundur Alfredsson, etc. seem to have led the way in this exploration. They raised the question as to whether today's modern multinational states should rightly refer to themselves or functionally conceive of themselves as nation-states (states founded by and consisting of only one nation or people). They suggest that by so insisting, such states sow the seeds for distorted rule centered development, civil conflict and international disorder. This in turn damages the moral substructure for the rule of law and the protection, promotion and respect for human rights, thereby stifling the development of these prerequisites for the expansion and continuance of democracy.[2]

The issues raised by these scholars are important to international law and relations because the majority of states in the world today are viewed as multinational (states containing one or more founding nations or peoples).[3] A review of the major atlas and other research tools[4] reveals that the groups mentioned as ethnic minorities invariably share the following common characteristics:

1. They are groups established in the state over a long period of time.

2. They are usually identified with the founding of the state and\or, for specific historical reasons, viewed as possessing special rights,[5] and are often referred to by scholars and state governments as *national minorities*.[6]

3. They have often been politically integrated into the state under conditions of outright conquest or economic/military duress at a time when international law recognized the right of conquest, imperialism and colonialism.[7]

4. They were preponderantly those minorities involved in violent or unmanageable civil conflict which often threatened the survival of the state.[8]

It is important to remind ourselves for the purpose of better appreciating the roots of many present day minority conflicts, that often the political integration of national minorities into states had little to do with the processes of mutual consent associated since World War II with democracy and SHCSD, but instead was determined by the prevailing economic and military power configurations of the past. Thus, socio-legal institutions and structures for the cohabitation of ethnic nations in multinational states are often remnants of an earlier undemocratic international system that recognized the right of conquest, imperialism and colonialism. Although the standards of this system were most visibly transformed after World War II with the advent of the*Universal Declaration of Human Rights*, decolonialization, and the emerging international law of peace and cooperation,[9] many structures of that past were preserved at the intra-state level. Emerging recently from the human rights corpus, minority rights is viewed as a tool enabling multinational states to effectively deal with the remnant of past standards based on conquest, economic duress and gross violations of human dignity by recognizing past injustices and creating, where necessary, new social contracts based on democratic principles of mutual consent and equal status participation in democratic decision-making processes.

Given this contradiction between modern international standards and the remnant of the old at the national level, it is only logical to expect national minority/state conflicts to get worse before they can get better. In multinational states, it is probable that the implementation of minority rights is a necessary component for achieving peaceful conditions required for effective establishment of equal status democratic processes and institutions.

As a casual survey of any atlas and the charts on state ethnic composition included in Chapter Two indicate, the homogeneous nation-state is an exception in this world. Of the 132 major states with more than one million inhabitants, only 12 can be described as ethnically homogeneous. Another 25 states have a single ethnic group constituting 90% of the population. In 31 states, the dominant ethnic group accounts for between 50% and 74% of all people. There are 39 major states where no single ethnic group accounts for half of the population.[10] Therefore, it seems logical to infer that any attempt to view the multinational state as the instrument reflecting the will and interest of only the nation(s) that control the state apparatus often leads towards unmanageable civil conflict, if not national disintegration or anarchy. We feel it was the cognizance of the potential of this contradiction between the ideals of the present as represented by international standards and remnants of past standards as inculcated in the structures and institutions of some multinational states that led scholars such as Kaplan, Huntington, Minc, Toffler, etc.,[11] to predict a future of anarchy and chaos, insofar as, if we were obliged to give each ethnic group a nation-state, we would have several thousand states. Though not conclusive, present evidence suggests that if viewed within the light of the present global economic, social and ecological crises, such mini-states would be extremely unstable economically and politically, creating such international disorder as to disrupt modern international socio-political and technological cooperation, trade, etc., and propel the world towards the new Middle Age predicted by Minc.[12]

The minority rights dialogue, however, suggests that there are other alternatives. What other manner than through statehood can the apparently growing desire for group identity as a democratic right[13] be accommodated, if not through the concept of minority rights as evolved in international law in response to the possibility of just such a challenge? The only other alternatives seem to be ethnic oppression (U.S. and the former USSR), ethnic cleansing (Yugoslavia) or genocide (Rwanda).

Given the multinational / multicultural nature of the international system, as well as that of the states within that system, combined with the demand for individual as well as collective rights, a definition of democracy is required that is cross-culturally applicable, and responds to appropriate individual and collective (minority) rights as well as the need for cross-cultural implementation. While the details of democratic institutionalization must by logic be culturally relative, at the risk of describing rather then defining, we have proposed the following inductively conceived structural-functional and subjectivist definition:[14]

> *the establishment of a series of institutions (structures) and processes in any self-determined political entity in such a manner as to permit the appropriate degree of citizen participation in political and socio-economic decision making required to enable, over time, successful conflict management of contending demands as presented by individuals, collectives and minorities; maintenance of state political unity; and mutual acceptability to most individuals and opinion makers so that collectives and minorities view the authority and decisions of government and its societal institutions as sufficiently just and beneficial.*

This definition stresses the degree of citizen satisfaction with their participation (as individuals and collectives) in political decisions as a key measure of democracy.

We realize this approach to defining democracy differs qualitatively from traditional approaches.[15] Scholars such as Terry Lynn Karl,[16] addressing democratic minimalism, would probably equate it to "the fallacy of electoralism," believing, according to Larry Diamond "that mistakes consist of privileging electoral contestation over other dimensions of democracy and ignoring the degree to which multi-party elections, even if genuinely competitive, may effectively deny significant sections of the population the opportunity to contest for power or advance and defend their interest, or may leave significant arenas of decision-making power beyond the reach or control of elected officials."[17]

On the other hand, scholars denoting the maximalist orientation remind us that:

> ...in addition to regular, free and fair electoral competition and universal suffrage, [democracy] requires the absence of 'reserved

> domains' of power for the military or other social and political forces that are not either directly or indirectly accountable to the electorate... [democracy] requires 'horizontal accountability of officeholders to one another, the resigning of executive power, constitutionalism, the rule of law, the deliberative process, political and civil, individual and collective, pluralism.'[18]

Professor Diamond's latter prerequisite for democracy extends, however, only to recognition of the *nondiscrimination rights* of cultural, ethnic, religious and other group needs, insofar as in a democracy, "Cultural, ethnic, religious and other minorities... are not prohibited legally or in practice from expressing their interests in the political process, and from using their language and culture."

Our definition does not contest the content of either the minimalist or the maximalist contentions. It suggests instead the necessity of encompassing the human subjective factor satisfactorily within the normative formula for discerning democracy, and thus questions whether democracy can be universally defined through the perspective of any one discipline, culture, or temporal historical period. In short, can democracy be universally defined within the context of any set of societal institutions, politico-legal processes, etc. whose form and contents or perimeters are set by a given culture or civilization?

It is puzzling that such an approach should be so widely popular among scholars of international relations and political science, since even the methodological texts in these disciplines, where comparative analysis is an indispensable tool, warn of the necessity (when attempting to investigate the same phenomena in different states [in a different systemic design]), to choose indicators that travel, or be prepared to find different indicators in a different system designed so as to measure the same phenomena. This means that often the same institutions, processes or structures in one state may serve a different purpose in another, and vice-versa—the same phenomena may be represented cross nationally by different institutions, political processes, structures, etc.. In the popular text, *Empirical Political Analysis*, Jarol B. Manheim states: "The important point here is that each country may offer its citizens different modes for expressing preferences or complaints about what the government does."[19] The acceptance of societal pluralism is associated by many traditional American scholars with democracy and perceived in terms of constitutional and civil rights law, individual and public opinions, etc.. However, Ziad Abu Amir suggests that balance of power among the tribal and political factions would, in the instance of Palestinian society, be an appropriate indicator of the existence of pluralism. He writes: "Palestinian pluralism is less a matter of principle than an extension of the variety that marks the world of tribal or familial relations, and is determined by the balance of social power and considerations of mutual interest."[20]

Lahouari Addi of the University of Lyons, France, further reminds us that "[democracy] needs to be analyzed in relation to the history of each country, taking into account specific political, cultural and ideological circumstances. There is assuredly no universal model of democratic transition that one can recommend..."[21]

As Collier and Levitsky denote, these efforts among many traditional minimalist and maximalist scholars to contextualize a universal definition of democracy within the parameters of western philosophical paradigms suffer from 'conceptual disorder.' These scholars seem to automatically bind the concept of democracy, which has become a universal notion, to the institutional and structural expressions as evolved in western states, particularly the U.S.. By so doing, they downplay the importance of culture, socio-economic and political environment, and subjective human factors. Indeed, similar to attempting to institutionalize the One Truth, the effort to institutionalize and operationalize a universal concept of democracy no doubt adds more to the disorder observed by Collier and Levitsky than it contributes to definition. The most obvious problem exists in the tendency to universalize the models of democracy conceptualized in the major western states, which in turn serves the interest of western power politics:

> Obviously there is a peculiar definitional fallacy attending the meaning of the term democracy, i.e. the assumption that democracies are simply those political systems commonly called democracies...Now if the political systems of the USA, UK, etc. which are denoted as democracies, themselves constitute the meaning of "democracy," then, clearly, no future—or postulated —political system could be correctly called a democracy without the meaning of the word being changed. Thus, if the American

> political system is a democracy, then any system that does not correspond with the American system cannot be called a democracy. And America calls itself a democracy—with the result that many other political systems, not only in the West, but in the East, the North and the South, have fallen in step with the American prescription... Professional politicians, party hacks, social "analysts" and other propagandists have successfully conned all of us into believing that the multiplicity of antics engaged by party activists is the essence of democracy. But democracy—the real stuff—is based on a rather simple faith: no one person is really fit to rule; so rule must be exercised in common by all. That is, democracy is government by the self, rather than government by others.[22]

In a recent speech, Mikhail Gorbachev also hinted at the definitional fallacy of democracy.

> Gorbachev ... refused to concede that the West had "beaten" communism in Eastern Europe. He said no country had any right to impose its model on any other. "Every nation is a great nation and capable of choosing. Let us not impose another model on them." Not everything in the West was the best, he said. He also insisted that there was no single model of Western democracy: every country chose its own path.[23]

Our approach only provides a functional definition of democracy. It is limited by how it is indigenized in each state, suggesting that different processes will be used by individuals and groups to achieve human rights and their concept of human dignity. Thus it defines democracy as a process. The minority rights approach seems predicated on the definition of democracy used in this research. It lends support to the increasingly universal search for democracy by accepting the existence of citizen-nation, legalizing and focusing the attention of governments, citizens and citizen-nations on instruments cross culturally found to be essential for minority-majority conflict resolution within the context of providing for democracy. The search for democracy within this logic suggests that on the macro level of international political organization, and as delimited by cultures operating within the context of historical determinancies, we may have liberal free market-based democracies (both European and American), Islamic democracies, socialist (Chinese, eastern European, etc.) democracies, African democracies, and so on. Then, on the national level of political organization, we may have nation-states and consociated states. In short, a universal definition of democracy must, according to democratic principle, avoid an institutional or policy conceptualization (if the global village views democracy as essentially adequate participation in the decision-making processes that determine individuals' lives and human rights) that is circumscribed by the philosophies of Montesquieu, Locke, Rousseau, Hobbes, Bodin, St. Augustine, etc., and accommodate democracy as it might be viewed by the followers of Buddha, the Prophet Muhammad, or in the *Upanishads*, etc.. Likewise, democracy in multinational states would accommodate, on an equal status, all national minorities, insofar as:

> [I]t is perhaps necessary to clarify that, according to human rights philosophy, "democracy" is not an end in itself but a means to an end, i.e. the enjoyment of human dignity through the fulfillment of the self or, in Stoical terms, the "attainment of complete selfhood". Moreover, democracy is not a singular notion, but rather a composite of principles and subsidiary rules as mentioned above. Thus, it should be understood that "democracy" does not exist outside, beside or intertwined with human rights, but, as a term, is really an abbreviation for a certain collection of human rights relating to participation in the polity and facilitating control over one's own destiny. This understanding explains, inter alia, why "democracy" does not have a "generally established meaning" unto itself; it is a composite. It also explains why there is no 'right to democracy per se: there a rights to various other entitlements which , together, would amount in practice to what is generally referred to as democracy.[24]

In writing about corporatism and democracy, J. R. Saul notes the relation between democracy and citizen participation: "The most powerful force possessed by the individual citizen is his government....there are other mechanisms but they reduce the citizen to the status of a subject...people ask : What kind of government? How much government? I think the primary question [for the democratic state] is: Whose government?" Similarly, the primary question raised by national minorities seeking democracy in multinational states that refuse to recognize their collective existence is: Whose police force? Whose social service organization? Whose educational institution? Whose government? Indeed, whose state? That of the dominant ethny? These questions denote the philosophical and political dilemma of multinational states in attempting to decide what structures, institutions and legality to establish in order to achieve democracy in political entities which are composed of two or more nations or national minorities all asking these types of questions. A. Buchanan, Professor at the University of Denver, sees a paradox in such questions for the search for liberal democracy. He writes:

> A historical paradox is that while national determination [ethnonationalism] is viewed as profoundly antidemocratic, self-determination presupposes a democratic worldview although in order for it to be accomplished it must depend on the concept of an existing nation as a natural historical given. This is why the right of secession can never be based solely on the liberal argument of consent and self-determination.[25]

Hannah Arendt[26] suggests that a related paradox is apparent in the potentiality for contradictory consequences ensuing from democratic rights of citizenship and nationality which are complementary. The first imposes on the state a democratic demand to guarantee non-discrimination and equality before the law for all citizens; the second exacts democratic demands which view the state as an instrument of national or group interest. Thus, in a multinational state, we have a situation wherein two or more nations (national minorities) view the democratic state as constrained not only to provide for equality before the law or non-discrimination but also to seek the national interest of each or a national interest common to each. The minority rights approach attempts to bridge this potential contradiction by institutionalizing concepts which serve to encourage a rapprochement between the interests of the dominant ethny and those of its national minorities.

In the Third World, similar democratic problematics exist for newly formed or emerging multinational states but in much more of an anarchical environment and ambiguous politico-economic and social context. These multinational states (usually cognitized as nation-states) often emerged at the impetus of a transcendent nationalism generated within ethnic, linguistic, religious, etc. groups occuping a colonially delimited territory in order to sustain an anti-colonial (actually, colonial territorial) struggle against the center of a traditional or colonial empire. But these new would-be nation-states seem unable to establish the civil model on the national territory, due to the conviction held by the diverse ethnic groups within them (national minorities) that to fully be a citizen in fact requires them to possess certain predetermined national characteristics common to the dominant group or majority. They fear that the cultural majority will reject them in spite of the law and policy declarations of the national government.[27]

Thus, a further, narrower drive for national identity, arising from the struggle of a national minority in the new state against the new state, itself, often results from the success of the first struggle to form a new multinational state, insofar as this struggle has been conducted within the context of the nation-state ideal. It derives from the contradiction between the desire of national minorities, impacted by the success of the establishment of the new state, for institutions geared to expressing and preserving their own particular national identity, and the ill-advised efforts of the new state governments to implement imported western democratic civic models which seek to forceably assimilate national minorities into a state identity which is usually that of the dominant ethny(ies), thereby rendering them socio-politically invisible.[28]

Lacking the implementation of or the ability to implement a mutually acceptable minority rights policy, such governments often find within the territory of their states the gray areas eluded to by Minc and Kaplan[29] — areas in political and socio-economic disorder and, occasionally, military conflict — areas populated by national minorities who, however tied to state governments by their need for human services, also wish to escape control by these majoritarian states with whom they do not identify. As often witnessed by international human service workers in places such as Rwanda, Bosnia-Herzegovina, Cambodia, etc., such states risk no longer representing either the law or the dominant nation within, but rather finding themselves confronted with nationalities (the dominant and non-dominant groups) transformed militarily into political interest groups or ultimately, anti-government guerillas. It is under such conditions that the distinction between the state and the nation becomes clearly visible, and the line between democracy and totalitarianism often becomes indistinct.

Similar to the manner in which the search for democracy in non-western multinational states, conditioned by cultural history, regional philosophies and politico-economic circumstances, differs from one to another, the problematic in Canada and North America differs from that of Europe and other parts of the western world. North American states are influenced by the consequences of their history of voluntary and forced immigration, territorial conquest, and the desire to create new solutions to traditional problems such as minority persecution. In North America, the cultural ideal was to establish a citizen's democracy wherein the notion of individuals living together in equal status, functional harmony and relative economic prosperity is realized through the implementation of non-discrimination and equality before the law. Recognizing the difference between this ideal and what actually occurred, and dealing with the consequences thereof, remains a major North American challenge. Asbjorn Eide, Special Rapporteur of the UN Human Rights Commission's Sub-Commission, notes a significant degree of success of the North American model (with the possible exception of the situation of the African Americans, the indigenous peoples, and certain Hispanic peoples).[30]

Although historically unique, the North American model is, in its philosophical and functional aspects, extremely important as it relates to the search for democracy in multinational states. Insofar as it influences governments and sub-national units throughout the world, it deserves special attention. The following excerpts from "On the Definition of Minorities" are reprinted with permission of the author, John Packer,[31] an associate UN human rights officer, assistant to the High Commissioner of National Minorities of the Organization for Security and Cooperation in Europe (OSCE), and former Professor of Human Rights at Åbo Akademi University. This excellent historical and theoretical critique, recognized by Mr. Packer as a theoretical expansion beyond the present state of international law as it relates to minorities,[32] typifies the North American contribution to the international minority rights dialogue,[33] seeking to extend democratic pluralism beyond the present limitations of the majority rule as it concerns minority positions on a spectrum of policy issues. In the section of his article entitled 'The philosophy of human rights: situating the minority issue and sorting out the democratic puzzle,' John Packer writes:

> While it is asserted that the fundamental values underlying human rights are universal, there may be no doubt that their articulation in international human rights law follows directly from liberal conceptions espoused by Western philosophers.[34] While the pursuit of "justice" may be said to be somehow rooted in all philosophy, St. Augustine advanced the notion of justice as the foundation of the State in The City of God. To obtain justice, St. Augustine borrowed Aristotle's concept of "the rule of law" as being the "constitutional State" in opposition to "rule by might". The Greeks, of course, were not egalitarians, and nor was St. Augustine. However, while recognizing the innate inequality of humans, the Greeks devised the principle of "equality before the law" for all citizens and, later, the principle of "rule by the people" (also meaning citizens). In this last respect, early Christian philosophers such as St. Augustine were hardly supporters of the principle of democracy, but they had through their Christian philosophy enlarged the sphere of "justice" in equality to pertain to all human beings; the rule of law, however, was that of God.
>
> Modern notions of equality and democracy did not evolve until several centuries later with the Protestant reformation opening the way. In "A Defense of Liberty against Tyrants", the French Huguenot "Brutus" (a pseudonym for an anonymous refugee author) reasserted the democratic principle in its enlarged Christian sense through his theory of two covenants: the first between God and King, with the King acting for God as agent and for the people as "subjects", and the second between King and people where the King promises to govern "justly" (according to God) and the people promise to obey so long as governed justly. This innovative contractarian theory allowed the transition of "the people" from "the King's slaves" to his "subjects" and heralded the conversion of European monarchies from absolute to conditional and constitutional. Hence, legitimate government could be discerned by at least a certain measure of consent.
>
> The Protestant reformation was, of course, religious in nature, although many of its influences were commercial and its effects went well beyond the church. The fact of evolving disputes led, for example, to the Peace of Augsburg in 1555 which confirmed

the principle of *cuius regio eius religio* (by which the ruler of a country determined the religion of its inhabitants), but which also allowed religious dissidents to freely choose their faith provided they emigrated: sovereignty (which Bodin had defined as "the absolute and perpetual power of the State, that is, the greatest power to command") still rested with the King. A century later, however, this principle was challenged by Thomas Hobbes in his reinvention of the contractarian theory of "mutual covenants one with another" such that "the sovereign" obtained legitimacy through these covenants which served "the Commonwealth." In only this way, argued Hobbes, could man "escape from the state of war" that was nature.

From Hobbes to revolution was not a large step, and it was manifested in England's Glorious Revolution at the end of the seventeenth century. But the constitutional state was problematic in its complexity, and new concepts were needed both to explain and formulate order. Most significant among the new revolutionary thinkers was John Locke who, *inter alia*, contributed the fundamental notion of "equality" among all "free men" (i.e. property owning male adults) who, by nature, possessed "rights". Of course, what Locke meant was that those men who had, by nature, obtained a certain status should be equally free to participate in the organization of society and equally free to enjoy the benefits of organized society. For Locke, despite the innumerable variations in the distribution by nature of individual talents and capacities, society was homogeneous insofar as the distribution of equality was concerned; each man would achieve his status if free and equally able to exercise his rights. The purpose of the state, therefore, was to guarantee this freedom—which the legitimate state did and the illegitimate state did not. *As for "justice," Locke introduced the notion of "majority rule" since, no man being more equal than another, the basic social compact must be that the majority would 'have a right to act and conclude the rest." In other words, Locke estimated that the tyranny of the majority of property owning male adults was better than the tyranny of a single property owning King.*[35]

Locke's postulates of "equality" and "natural rights" were crucial contributions to the development of modern human rights philosophy, but they soon proved inadequate to the times and required several subsequent adjustments. These came one-half century later in the contributions of Montesquieu and Rousseau. First, informed by the English law and practice of his time, *Montesquieu championed the doctrine of the "separation of powers' which so well accommodated his idea that "in a democracy the people are in some respects the sovereign, and in others the subject;"* as described in *Spirit of the Laws* (1748), the "body politic" is the "united strength of individuals" which is constituted by "a conjuncture of all their wills" both in the formation of the laws and in their application, i.e. consent to make and obey the laws. It was Rousseau, however, who managed to locate the "conjuncture of all their wills" in "the General Will" which he introduced in his "Discourse on Political Economy" (1755) and developed in *The Social Contract* (1762). According to Rousseau, the problem was one of "association" which was inevitably linked to specific issues: the General Good is seen as an object or aim, while the General Will is a subjective matter which originates in all and applies to all. *Accordingly, Rousseau recognized that the state was not the only group with a General Will; there would be particular societies and associations within the state with a General Will in relation to their members.* Rousseau acknowledged, of course, that in a society of many individual wills, there would not always be a common will or interest on every issue, and so he distinguished between the Will of All (common interest) and the General Will which is the composite "sum of particular wills". *To resolve the problem of dissent, Rousseau simply retrieved Locke's "majority rule" in asserting that the vote of the majority binds the minority—which gave rise to Rousseau's perverse and dangerous idea that the minority could be "forced to be free;" consent was found in the minority in the conclusion that "residence constitutes consent" since Rousseau judged that dissenters were free to leave.* Rousseau's ideal state, therefore, is a community of free men living in a small state where democracy is practiced directly (Rousseau rejected representative government) for personal enjoyment and advantage and with shared responsibility for the welfare of the whole.

The ideas of "association" and "the General Will" led inevitably to minority concerns in the large state, especially insofar as philosophers had argued that justice for all was to be found in the "majority rule". Rousseau had already synthesized the notions of "good government" and "self-government" in *The Social Contract*, but there were evident limitations in accommodating discord and dissent especially in larger communities: in the words of one commentator,[35] the classical liberal concept of the individual and the state is "unduly limited" and Rousseau had run aground on these limitations. *Rousseau's insistence that there should be "no partial society within the State" was simply unrealistic and, moreover, implied an unnecessary uniformity of practices within the state, i.e. he did not envisage parallel orders of, e.g., family law applying to different groups within the state.* In seeking to resolve interests of discordant groups, the liberal democratic ideas had to evolve further.

Classical liberalism and the majority rule were, of course, flawed from the outset. Subsequent thinkers quickly observed that status was often not achieved in equality of nature as Locke asserted, but was the result of privileges conferred by a pre-existing socio-political order. As such, Lords did not so much earn their status by the exercise of any talents as they did inherit their status by the pure fortune of birth. *Likewise, the calculation of the majority rule in no sense assured justice for all much less for the minority which was practically obliged to conform; the majority rule was simply a useful and relatively just procedural invention — "a practical necessity" as Rawls[37] has put it — through which, in the absence of anything better, it was hoped that justice would be delivered.* With regard to the first fiction, Rousseau had already distinguished natural inequality (which, in Thomistic fashion, he judged not substantial) and political inequalities (which he sought to eliminate). That all men were nevertheless equal in their dignity, however, was a thought that could be retained from the universalism of both the ancient Stoics and the rational humanists and became an essential component of human rights philosophy from Montesquieu to the present. *But, it was John Stuart Mill who managed to reconcile natural inequality with essential equality in advocating the positive obligations of the state to breathe life into Locke's "equality of right" by realising "equality of opportunity" for all.* Central to this logic was the understanding that natural inequalities (e.g. strength of arm, power of wit, fortune of birth) were, in Thomistic terms, "accidents" and that all human beings irrespective of such accidents were/are the same. Consequently, government must not merely ensure freedom by the maintenance of a minimum order (consisting largely in keeping the peace) and otherwise desisting from interfering in the lives of human beings (as Locke and the later "laissez-fairists", especially Montesquieu, would have it), but, somewhat to the contrary, government has a duty to materially facilitate opportunities for human beings to realise their natural talents and act to the extent that their desires intersect their capacities. For the "reform liberals" of the Age of Reason, the society that so provided would be just.

As regards the second fiction of classical liberalism, i.e. that majority rule delivers justice, there was the evident fact that the majority could err (whether by their direct voices or indirectly through their representatives) and there was the truth that, for any particular issue, the majority did not genuinely reflect the will of the minority. While these truths could be somewhat suppressed as long as the body of political participants remained small and the complexity of government remained limited, the technological and popular revolutions of the late eighteenth century demanded their resolution: the more the participants, the greater the possibility of error by the majority, and the greater in number and complexity the decisions, the greater the number and variety of minorities. Above all, the nonsense of uniformity was exposed: with a separation of church and state and a separation of powers, society could be the plurality that Aristotle had long before recognized it was in nature. However, to accommodate pluralism required tolerance.

The idea of tolerance in Western thought has several roots, but it is largely tied to the matter of religion and followed from the separation of church and state.[38] Laissez-faire economics also required tolerance of new ideas and methods. Expanding trade and the effects of mass production in the nineteenth century added yet more need for tolerance as large movements of people accompanied movements of goods and ideas. *To have been intolerant would have been to turn away the fruits of progress (at least in a material sense) in most fields of science. Within the polity, this required, above all, the freedom to "be different," i.e. to think differently and act differently.* Such freedom led naturally to the formation of innumerable associations based on common philosophies, trades, commercial interests, pass-times and so forth. In other words, there was an explosion of compacts within the compact of the polity with all subsidiary compacts being dependent upon their conformity with the first or higher social compact of membership of the polity. In truth, philosophers to this point had not much thought about the origin of the polity and philosophers even to the present have largely taken it for granted. *Nevertheless, in the terms of the first social compact were to be found the limitations on all subsidiary compacts. In a general sense, then, the idea of tolerance is the sum of liberty which does not contradict the higher compact irrespective of majority rule where uniformity is not required.* Accordingly, tolerance would apply to the behavior of human beings in their nature, i.e. both individually and in groups. As for the obligations of government, the classical liberal notion was merely permissive. But, for the reasons explained by the reform liberals, the positive actions of government would also be necessary to materially facilitate differentness whether of the individual or the group.

In addition to accommodating the fact of plurality in society, the structure of the polity had to develop to accommodate an ever-enlarging breadth of participation which, in turn, compounded the complexity of relations in the order; according to Herbert Spencer (1820-1903), this movement reflected "evolution" which, in his words, is the 'advance from the simple to the complex". Evolutionary or not, this expanding democracy was effectively dictated by the requirements of expanding economic liberalization inasmuch as the commercial, property-owning middle class acquired an increasing responsibility for the wealth of society. *As economic decision-making was less and less centralized, so political decision-making would have to follow. This argument was strengthened by the additional fact that industrial and, much more so, post-industrial society required increasingly educated, able and even mobile human resources. To secure these needs, the philosophy of the reform liberals was succeeded by that of the "social democrats" who argued (for other reasons) for the social reforms which were realised in the legislation of complex protections for the disadvantaged.* Soon thereafter, devices such as "universal suffrage" were employed in ever-widening applications in order to really bring the people into the matrix of participatory government. The room for discord similarly expanded.

With the monarchs stripped of their divine rights and the body politic having expanded considerably in breadth and complexity, tensions within the polity mounted as legitimacy of government dangled amid a widening body of competing interests. Forces uniting the polity at the level of the first compact were tested by other interests and contracts, some of which even spanned frontiers. *However, through the melding of historical residues and rising national competitiveness, the polity of the state found new strength in the social compact that congealed around nationalism.* This nineteenth century period of so-called "nation-building" featured the creation of new and larger polities formed both by conquest and contract (although many of the latter were also achieved under duress). Interestingly, the popular philosophy of the time combined both the idea of natural rights for citizens of the "nation-state" (sometimes including an expanding measure of tolerance for a certain differentness within the state, at least for individuals and/or religious groups) and an increasingly intense intolerance for "foreigners" who were viewed as threatening or simply disliked. At the same time, this "we versus they" mentality made for good citizen-soldiers—of whose need there was an increasing likelihood. *For the essence of nationalism is the myth of purity which demands the rejection of human equality: nationalism is "a political programme"[39] based on the conviction that "those like me" should be united because it is "good" that like be with like and unlike be apart. Of course, the really ominous element of nationalism is the implication of superiority and inferiority.[40] Consequently, nationalism, especially combined with chauvinism, is inherently conflict-oriented as it pits "we" against "they" in a test of superiority inevitably based on might. Commenting upon the devastation subsequently wrought by nationalism in Europe, Clement Atlee was moved to characterize nationalism as "egotism writ large".*[41]

Unfortunately, despite the massive loss of life and property that was experienced in The Great War at the beginning of the twentieth century, there was a remarkable failure to recognize the essential cause. Rather than respond directly to the problem of nationalism, the victors (themselves, of course, nationalists) simply endeavoured to contain the problem by sorting out the nationalities with the hypothesis that monolithic nations coincident with state would allow peaceful relations between these states. *This logic inspired the "principle of nationalities" which was applied in the peace treaties ending the First World War. The principle of nationalities had two elements: first, it aimed at fulfilling the object of "one nation, one State" through a new territorial partition of Europe and, second, it aimed at quelling supposedly frustrated national aspirations by guaranteeing protections for "national minorities" who "still remain incorporated in spite of themselves, in spite of their national feelings, in states which are not in sympathy with their national feelings".* [42] The need for the application of this new principle was the widely held feeling that Europe remained "profoundly troubled and upset: treaties have ended the hostilities, but profound unrest remains".[43] That the underlying problem was located in the very idea of "nationalities" and nationalism apparently struck very few writers as the cause of the War was blamed not on nationalism per se but on the excessive nationalism of imperialism spurred on by "a spirit of animosity among the nations" relating to economic inequalities and "unjustified [economic] discriminations" combined with the interests of the militarists who profited from "a profound feeling of insecurity".[44] With the same logic, it was thought that internationalism would be served by the application of the principle of nationalities since the decided causes of the War were also "the forces most hostile to international spirit".[45]

It is perhaps one of the great tragedies of modern history that the survivors of the First World War failed to recognize or appropriately deal with the problem of nationalism. *Clearly, the inherent problem with nationalism is that it relies on the premise of differentness and requires discrimination in the application of policies of separation or assimilation. Nationalism also assumed uniformity of being in the sense of homogeneity of "nations" and uniformity of behaviour in the sense of homogeneity of aspirations, tastes and desires among members of "the nation"*, even where unnecessary As noted by many,[46] it was this same egotistic and intolerant "we/they" philosophy that provided popular legitimacy for the even more perverse ideas that generated the Second World War as efforts are made to systematically separate and "purify" the nations along racist lines. Only after these horrific endeavours had run some bloody course and been defeated in a bloodier war was some large part of their false premises rejected.

With the experience of the Second World War, the founders of the United Nations rediscovered the universalism of the Stoics and humanists in asserting human rights.[47] *This rediscovery and the impetus for it are clearly stated in both the Preamble of the United Nations Charter (hereafter, Charter) and the Universal Declaration of Human Rights (UDHR). Specifically, the Charter begins, after stating its primary objective of saving "succeeding generations from the scourge of war", with a reaffirmation of "faith... in the dignity and worth of the human person". The UDHR is even clearer in its "recognition of the inherent dignity and of the equal and inalienable rights of all members of the human family" and, more simply put in Article 1, the assertion that "all human beings are born free and equal in dignity and rights." These affirmations and assertions are followed, logically, with proscription against discrimination: in other words, following the liberal philosophy of natural rights and reason, the first premise of equality gave rise to the first principle of non-discrimination. Perverse ideas of inequality, purity, superiority and inferiority had been rejected out of hand.*

Having agreed upon the first premise and established the first principle of a new order, the States Parties to the Charter went about further specifying the various rights and freedoms which gave substantive meaning to the first premise with the objective of securing dignity. In relation to individual rights and freedoms, these could be articulated with a good degree of specificity and frequently with little disagreement. *However, when it came to articulating rights and freedoms for man in his social dimension, i.e. in groups, there was considerable disagreement even over the idea that man has natural social rights. This disagreement reflected the clash of prevailing ideologies between, primarily, American individualism epitomized by Thoreau's "Walden Pond" and the socialist/communist philosophy of Marxist-Leninism. Despite this clash (which was formulated in mistaken "either/or" and "chicken or the egg" dichotomies), the experience of the first half of the twentieth century had made it clear that certain groups existed who had to be protected both for humanitarian reasons and lest their frustrations give rise to new conflicts.* Consequently, the idea of protection of minorities (essentially in the sense of nationalist ideas) was agreed upon and given institutional life in the creation of a Sub-commission of the United Nations Commission on Human Rights.

The structure of society[48] espoused by the Charter and the UDHR was responsive to the horrors of recent experience. Thus, after attempting to guarantee the peace by outlawing the use of force, it emphasized protections in the form of minimum rights and freedoms. *What it did not do was clearly establish the processes of evolution in the "just society" either within the state or for the international community. In other words, there were insufficient rules or procedures to deal with the underlying conflicts which gave rise to violence. However, some idea of how the evolutionary movement was to take place within the state was provided in the principle of non-discrimination and the prescription of democracy that was somewhat articulated in Article 21 of the UDHR. What was being confronted, of course, was no less than the same concern that inspired* The Social Contract: *as Rousseau formulated it, "the problem is to find a form of association which will defend and protect with the whole common force the person and goods of each associate, and in which each, while uniting himself with all, may still obey himself alone, and remain as free as before".[49] Adding the fact that "the associate" may also unite with some (rather than all) for various purposes, this formulation of the problem is the continuing challenge of democracy in the just [multinational] society.*

Sorting out the democratic puzzle

Evolution in the just society is generated by the fundamental principles of democracy: non-discrimination in the formation and application of the laws (i.e. equal participation and due obedience), and the majority rule. As Thomas Jefferson observed in his assertion of the "two truths" he held to be "self-evident" (i.e. that all men have inalienable rights and that governments derive just powers from the consent of the governed), the second principle follows the first. *In other words, the logic is linear such that before there may be said to be an issue relating to the majority rule, it must be established that the principle of non-discrimination in the enjoyment of inalienable rights has been properly applied. If the first principle is not properly applied, then "the issue" probably resides in this stage; if the issue remains after the proper application of the fist principle, then it resides in the application of the second principle.*

Before going any further, it is perhaps necessary to clarify that, according to human rights philosophy, "democracy" is not an end in itself but a means to an end, i.e. the enjoyment of human dignity through the fulfillment of the self or, in Stoical terms, the "attainment of complete selfhood". Moreover, democracy is not a singular notion, but rather a composite of principles and subsidiary rules as mentioned above. Thus, it should be understood that "democracy" does not exist outside, beside or intertwined with human rights,[50] *but, as a term, is really an abbreviation for a certain collection of human rights relating to participation in the polity and facilitating control over one's own destiny. This understanding explains, inter alia, why "democracy" does not have a "generally established meaning" unto itself;*[51] *it is a composite. It also explains why there is no 'right to democracy' per se: there are rights to various other entitlements which, together, would amount in practice to what is generally referred to as democracy.*

Participation in the evolution of the polity towards the attainment of fulfillment for all is, again, the composite idea of democracy. That the rights of participation effecting a say over one's life are human rights may be contested by some[52] with the argument that one is not born with a right to vote, but insofar as the philosophy of human rights is that all humans are born with a similar essence including the endowments of reason and tastes, the need to have a say over one's life is equally human. The issue of how much say one may have over one's life has natural limitations; increasing the extent of that say is the object of the social compact. Nature, therefore, dictates a certain hierarchy of rights deriving from the social compact, e.g. beginning with the right to life itself. Only subsequent to the attainment of these rudimentary rights pertaining to existence do the rights pertaining to the structure and functioning of the polity have meaning, or, put the other way, the rights of participation in the formation and application of the laws lose their meaning in the absence of the enjoyment of the other rudimentary rights. *In this sense, the logic of participatory rights is also linear such that before it may be said that there is an issue relating to participation, it must be established that there is no issue relating to enjoyment of the rudimentary rights:* participatory rights, or as some call them "political rights", "presuppose civil rights and liberties and certain basic social rights".[53]

In human rights philosophy, founded on the first premise of equality, the term "minority" does not arise but in the context of democracy and in relation to the majority rule.[54] *As the majority rule is necessarily issue-oriented, so is the constitution of any minority. The problem with the majority rule as devised by Locke is that it is inherently flawed and, without considerable moderation in the form of tolerance and specific application, tends towards tyranny.*[55] This tendency is exacerbated the less there is tolerance in the form of protections and facilitations for alternatives where uniformity is not required and the further one gets from specific application.

The problem of specific application arises particularly with the institution of representative government which replaces participation relating to specific decisions with participation only in the selection of representatives who, as agents of the people, are charged with the responsibility of formulating and applying the laws. Since such an institution detaches the people from the laws through the introduction of intermediaries, this idea was rejected by Rousseau. Nevertheless, larger and complex polities necessitated the development of the institution of representative government inasmuch as the direct participation of the whole population in every decision was simply not feasible. *Consequently, the risk of a tyranny of the majority is even further enlarged in the institution of representative government insofar as the people are not asked to express their desires so much in relation to issues as they are asked to express their desires in relation to the appointment of persons who will make the laws, i.e. legislators.* Moreover, despite the insistence of philosophers like Burke that the representatives are to act for all, there is the likelihood that the successful candidates will act more for the interests of those who selected them (i.e. the majority or plurality, depending on the method of selection) either because they personally share these interests or because they feel bound by an implied contract with the voters selecting them. This reality adds fuel to the fire of fear in the democratic state that the majority (especially constituted through their representatives) will not take into account the specific needs of minorities.[56]

Accepting that there are things about social organization in the polity that require uniformity (such as the rule that everyone drives his or her car on the same side of the road) and accepting that complex society requires at least some large degree of representative government, *the challenge of democracy is to enable the greatest fulfillment of selves on the widest scale. Hence, where uniformity is required, the majority may dictate the convention, but where uniformity is not required, the plurality of desires should be accommodated so far as is feasible.* Feasibility, in turn, is determined by reason such that, for example, the state composed of groups desiring the use of three different languages may reasonably accommodate all desires in trilingual institutions of government and public affairs, whereas the state composed of groups desiring the use of hundreds of different languages may reasonably choose the use of the most common for institutions of government and public affairs; other outcomes could also be envisaged such as variations of institutional languages according to geographic concentrations of the groups. Obviously, no specific formulation may be devised as a rule since everything depends upon the composition of desires relating to the issue at hand in the specific circumstances. *Of course, it is to be reiterated that the application of the majority rule is never to conflict with the enjoyment of the more rudimentary rights.*

Focusing on the determinative value of the relative need for uniformity leads to two other comments on the working of democracy. First, the more important the issue that requires uniformity, the greater the degree of accord would be necessary since the desire of minorities could not, by definition, be accommodated and the resultant frustration may give rise to instability and violence. Thus, one may begin with the requirement of absolute accord in the very formation of the policy. Past this most basic issue, it would be desirable that a high degree of accord be obtained for other constitutional issues. To calculate such accord, it may also be desirable to place the most important issues before the entire population in plebiscites rather than leave them to representatives. In fact, these ideas are found in several democratic states which require, for example, an expression of popular consent in plebiscites or two-thirds majorities of representatives for constitutional changes.[57]

The second comment relates to those issues which do not require uniformity. In deciding how these affairs shall be regulated, a variety of formulae may be devised depending upon the issues. *For example, some affairs are by nature conducive to regulation in a horizontal fashion such as large parts of the content and administration of family law or education. Recognizing this fact, and in having to administer a large empire with diverse groups, the Ottomans employed a "millet" system of minority control over "their" issues.*[58] While this system was hardly based on any recognition of "human rights," its application is most compatible with the philosophy of human rights. In the first place, the idea of horizontal regulation gives

> meaning to permissiveness for social behaviour which is not required to be uniform. It also raises the issue of facilities which relates further to the question of "What rights of the minority may be exercisable against the majority?" Essential to this system, however, is the idea that the minority decides for itself the system it wishes to apply for these identified concerns.

John Packer does not note the possibility that the existence and experiences of ethnic minorities in multi-ethnic empires may have played a key role in the eventual popular emergence of the nation-state concept. He seems to ascribe this emergence to the failure of liberal theory and the growing complexity of societal development. However, to fully understand the extent and breadth of Mr. Packer's contribution to the minority rights dialogue, we refer the reader to his recent article, "On the Content of Minority Rights," where he indicates:

> That possibilities may be afforded in theory does not mean they have been actualized in terms of international standards adopted by States in contemporary international relations. It is thus with a view to clarifying the actuality of minority rights that we move from an examination of what could be "possible" to what "is".[59]

Similar analysis and discussions based on empirical experiences concerning the nature of democracy in multinational states took place at international conferences attended by scholars and statesmen of various cultures and socio-political and economic circumstances. One of the most salient series of such conferences was that of the before-mentioned Project on Ethnic Relations (PER), which consisted of a series of conferences held over the period 1991-1995 between representatives of Eastern European and American governments and human service representatives, undertaken with the cooperation of the Committee on Human Rights and Democratic Institutions of the Organization for Security and Cooperation in Europe (OSCE) and the Ford Foundation.

Our observation of the output from such conferences suggests that the comments and opinions expressed are significantly influenced by pragmatic political and economic considerations, actual minority conflicts or potential conflicts in the region of interest to the presenter as well as by the historical philosophical orientation of the region and/or presenter towards democracy. Our observation suggests that political as well as philosophic orientation in relation to the problematic of recognizing minorities for the purpose of international protection and implementing a concept of democracy in multinational states differs significantly from region to region and culture to culture, and seems to be significantly influenced by differing objective historical factors which any proposed concept of minority rights (within the context of implementing democracy) should be able to navigate in order to be both acceptable and feasible. As such, these comments and opinions reflect empirical experiences influenced by the complex socio-political and economic circumstances of real world situations. The following quotes are examples of recorded comments and opinions expressed at the PER conferences in relation to the search for democracy in multinational states.[60] Note that all additions for clarification which we have made have been placed in square brackets.

Moscow, January 20-21, 1995

"Cultural pluralism [as required for democracy in multinational states (MNS)] would also require a reexamination and redefinition of the term "minorities" as it is applied in Eastern Europe and the former Soviet Union. Minorities in this region differ from those in North America, which have their origins in immigration. In contrast, most European ethnic communities are groups of people living in their historical territories. Also, there needs to be a shift away from traditional definitions of the term that focus upon their relatively small proportions in the population. Instead, a country's minorities should be thought of as equal communities or partner groups [democracy in MNS requires this]. No ethnic community should aim for the status of a titular nation or nationality, since this almost invariably leads to other ethnic groups being placed in an inferior position..."

"... the crisis in Chechnya involves not only Chechen nationalism but also Russian nationalism. [The nationalism of the majority ethnie should be considered no more acceptable for democracy in MNS than the nationalism of the minorities]... The war in Chechnya causes concern about the future of democracy in Russia, said one Western observer, because the decision to intervene ran counter to the logic of democratic development on several grounds. First, the intervention did not rely on any sizable public support... Second, the war has proved to be extremely costly, further aggravating economic anxieties..."

"...the notion of a "post-Communist vacuum" did not accurately describe the situation. There was a much stronger vacuum under Communism by virtue of the restrictions on freedom of thought and the absence of democratic rights... By contrast, the region today is experiencing what could well be described as a "chaos of ideas." While there was widespread agreement that democracy was the only acceptable form of political rule, the actual practices and content of democracy varied and did not necessarily resemble the practices and content of democracy as understood in the West. Until a consensus on the nature of the democratic order was reached, there would continue to be disagreement about political fundamentals, and different interpretations of democracy would be in competition, with potentially destabilizing effects. In this situation, ethnic loyalty could be a source of stability. [The role and influence on SHCSD of national minorities cannot be superseded by ideology in democratic MNS]... Since 1991, not only the power institutions but the whole structure of Russian society has collapsed..."

"In democracies, the legitimization of statehood is much more complicated than in other polities because it requires citizenship rather than ethnicity to act as the unifying force. From this perspective, the Chechnya crisis was an example of the failure to promote civic identities in the Russian Federation, because the Chechens had not developed a sense of loyalty toward Russia..." [Democracy in MNS demands that minorities have a responsibility to develop loyalty not only to their group, but also to the state in which they live.]

"... politicians in Moscow failed from the outset to recognize the fact that Soviet-style federalism was not a sharing of power between the center and its territorial units, but rather a number of ethnically based entities subordinated to a totalitarian center." [Federalism can be used in MNS to provide minorities with institutional self-determination. However, this is only true if democracy, not totalitarianism, is the guiding ideology.]

Washington, D.C., June 13-14, 1995.

"The government must recognize that Slovakia is a multinational state. Too many attempts are being made to portray the

Hungarian minority and the opposition parties as the "enemy." Violence against Hungarians has broken out for the first time in thirty years..." [As noted in the next chapter, official recognition of the existence of a minority is one of the first recommendations of the minority rights dialogue to maintain state peace and unity.]

3) New York, September 27-28, 1993

"The process of identity-building may well take years, given the specific configuration and state of Serbian society. The socio-economic structure of this society today is characterized by the almost complete disappearance of both upper and middle classes, which elsewhere form the core of a civil society...The delay of privatization and of a transition to the market economy has also helped to preserve ethnic solidarity, which might otherwise have been to a great extent diluted by market relations based on private interests..." [In democratic MNS, the existence of national minorities must be officially and pragmatically recognized in order to discourage demonization of or violence against the national minority.]

"... Since real and invented histories and arguments for the uniqueness of this or that group of people are being used in political struggles, it would not be productive to raise objections to the foundations for demands made by these groups. The approach rather should be to seek a balance between respect for the human rights of all individuals and accommodation of group rights. Otherwise, the concept of "collective rights," which underlies most ethnically based claims and demands, will, by its intrinsic rigidity, block any road to compromise...In each case, the objective is to give minorities access to governing their affairs, rather than isolating them from power through majoritarian electoral arrangements..." [Democracy in MNS requires the recognition of collective minority rights, and consociational electoral arrangements where necessary to avoid isolating the national minority or preventing it from sharing power. This comment also suggests that economic conditions permitting the emergence of a middle and upper class is also a requirement for democracy in MNS.]

"...a political identity for the Serbian community in Croatia has yet to be created, and that is a precondition for positive cooperation with the democratic opposition forces inside Serbia as well as in the Croatian political arena. The current situation of the Serbian community in Croatia is worsened, according to another participant, by various forms of discrimination... many Croatian Serbs are forced to give up their ethnic identity to preserve their jobs and social status..." [Non-discrimination is a prerequisite for democracy in a MNS as well as the creation of a political identity for those national minorities who have none but desire and need one.]

"...a specific form for the participation of the Serbian minority in the Croatian political process that was suggested as long ago as the end of 1990: a consultative "Serbian Assembly" elected by the Serbian community and attached to the Croatian parliament to advise on policies and legislation in ethnically sensitive fields, such as education, language rights, and culture. If dialogue and cooperation between the state authorities and Serb representatives are assured, it would then become possible to negotiate and implement solutions acceptable to the Serbs in Croatia..." [Consultative minority assemblies attached to the national congress or parliament or assembly is one method of providing for democratic expression in MNS.]

"... The frequent failures of ethnic politics demonstrate clearly the fallacy of the notion of self-determination, which amounts to a demand for a separate state for each ethnic group. Such "monoethnic" states, particularly if they emerge in an environment of hostility or intolerance, might well become legitimized tools of genocide or racism. The solution proposed was to separate the concepts of sovereignty and territorial integrity which have been inseparable throughout modern history... a concept of "transparent sovereignty" [was put forth] in which states could perform a number of government functions for communities of their co-ethnics living on the territories of other states... " [To encourage democratic SHCSD in MNS the concept of self-determination must be understood, appropriately separated from that of political independence, and viewed according to its international legal denotation. Also, the concept of *"transparent sovereignty"* can be used to meet certain minority needs if suitable in a particular case.]

"American participants found themselves arguing about the limits of the means available to outside actors and about the applicability of essentially Western models of institution-building and the legal protection of minority rights... A Serbian participant argued that the international community should not shrink from pushing for a "constitutional consensus" ensuring the adequate protection of minority rights. The European Community failed to do so in Bosnia and left the issue open in Croatia." [Strengthening the role of international organizations to intervene in the protection of minorities in MNS will serve the interests of democracy.]

Stupava, Czechoslovakia, April 30-May 2, 1992

"The Roma are a unique group in Europe. As Gheorghe[61] pointed out, they are a people in diaspora who have no homeland. The Roma do not consider India, whence they began their migrations centuries ago, as a homeland; indeed, they reject the notion of a homeland altogether. This lack of a territorial base has had a profound effect on the perception of the Roma by host societies. As Helena Klimova[62] noted, the ownership of a historical territory is closely associated with the idea of permanence and stability. A transnational group, lacking a geographical homeland or political territory, is perceived as unstable and, hence, untrustworthy..." [Giving special attention to unique national minorities who may have no homeland or may be dispersed throughout the MNS can help to prevent discrimination and thus promote SHCSD and democracy.]

"...while claiming and desiring to be democratic states, most European nations remain ethnic states and, in the midst of transition, they continue to drive towards ethnic homogeneity. Another serious problem for the future of the Roma is that the emergence of [majoritarian] democratic principles has in some cases actually reduced their access to advantageous treatment. Under the Communist regime, the Roma were allowed and even pressured to enter secondary school. Now, however, there is a completely different attitude. For instance, in school admissions in the Czech lands and Slovakia the Roma must compete on an equal footing with all other candidates, and the results are determined by computer. The principle of ethnic equality, and the unpleasant memory of granting rewards and exceptions to persons of the "working class" often lead governments to prohibit quotas and the treatment of an ethnic minority as socially disadvantaged." [The achievement of democracy in MNS requires states to drop the ideal of the nation-state homogeneity in favor of MNS cultural pluralism, as well as to provide for affirmative action where required.]

"...the necessary judicial framework in Czechoslovakia, especially the declaration on human rights that recognized the

Roma as a nationality group, was an important achievement and deserves the thanks of the Roma; nevertheless the Roma are now like children who are still unable to walk on their own. As Hancock[65] put it, the Roma have not yet escaped the "cycle of despair." *The needs are to instill belief in self, to teach new skills, and to provide opportunities.* As Hochschild[66] explained, there are two strategies for dealing with such "estranged poor." The first is to enable them to enter mainstream society, and the second is to provide a satisfying alternative. In the first strategy, the teaching of skills must be accompanied by a restoration of faith if it is to be effective..." [Democratic SHCSD demands that each MNS must find the democratic model that fits its specific situation. Democratic models are not cross-culturally portable. Also, minority education must often be tailored to their special needs in order to enable their socio-economic development.]

Bucharest, June 17-18, 1991

"... the American interest in East European ethnic problems was based on an understanding that the processes of democracy were complex and could be imperiled by destructive ethnic conflict. At the same time, ethnic accord would benefit Europe, and the United States has an important stake in a peaceful Europe. However, America could only bring to the symposium a friendly, neutral and sympathetic ear, for it had no answers and continues to seek solutions to its own ethnic problems..." [Stronger states should not attempt to impose their minority protection models on other states.]

"The lack of a common terminology, and the differences in perceptions held by Romanian and American participants, immediately became apparent in discussions of the nature and definition of ethnic relations in Romania. The phraseology used by American participants was one of ethnic "majorities and minorities." Their approach was pragmatic: the need to prevent social instability and ethnic violence. Priorities were implicitly assigned to the several minorities according to their size; their potential for involvement in serious, especially violent, ethnic conflict; and to their presumed capacity for formating, articulating, mobilizing in support of, and achieving their demands *vis-à-vis* the majority-controlled state. From a human rights perspective, all minorities were recognized as equally important. However, from the perspective of contemporary political realities, the problems presented for the state by large minority populations were considered potentially greater and therefore, to require more immediate attention. Following this logic, Istvan Deak[63] proposed that the conference focus on the problems of the Hungarian, Rom (Gypsy), Jewish and German ethnic minorities. This point of view was immediately, and rather sharply, rejected by the participants from the Romanian Academy and by many of the ethnic group representatives for two reasons; the first stemming from the nature of their approach, which considered conciliation possible only if based on the equal and similar treatment of all ethnic groups regardless of their size; the second resulting from what appeared to some U.S. participants as to be hyper-sensitivity concerning national identity and ethnic Romanian (majority) rights. In the first instance, the terminology of "majority-minority" was considered by participants as inherently and unnecessarily political, whereas "ethnic group" desensitized the issue and better allowed for sober discussion and identification of common interests. This point of view was shared by Academy researchers, such as Carmen and Dragos Seuleanu, with researchers of non-Romanian ethnicity, such as the Hungarian sociologist Zoltan Rostas, who noted that political and academic discourse were not compatible." [The confusion of terminology denotation and varying conotations tends to impede the minority rights democracy dialogue across cultures as well as across professions and academic disciplines. There is a need to assist this dialogue by adapting meanings to international legal definitions from which the dialogue first originated.]

"A second line of criticism levelled against this terminology by the ethnic Hungarian, German, Russian and Albanian participants, as well as by members of the Academy, was that "minority" referred to a quantity rather than a quality. This was interpreted as a reduction in ethnic group status. As Paul Phillipi[67] complained, while the Saxon community had played a very important political and economic role in Romania state building in the past, because of post-war emigration, the community would now be considered negligible were state-centered American criteria to be applied. Other ethnic group representatives also objected to being characterized as insignificant merely because of small numbers. Efforts by some, such as Dinu Giurescu,[68]to explain that, juridically, all non-ethnic Romanians are "minorities" had very little impact on the discussion..." [The discussion indicated that democracy in MNS was enhanced by providing equal status to all national minorities regardless of size or perceived objective importance.]

Table 5:
Number of Formal Democracies, 1974, 1990-95

Year	Number of Democracies	Number of Countries	Democracies as a % of All Countries
1974	39	142	27.5%
1990	76	165	46.1%
1991	91	183	49.7%
1992	99	186	53.2%
1993	108	190	56.8%
1994	114	191	59.7%
1995	117	191	61.3%

Sources: Data from Freedom House, *Freedom in the World: The Annual Survey of Political Rights and Civil Liberties, 1990-91, 1991-92, 1992-93, 1993-94, 1994-95* (New York: Freedom House, 1991 and years following); and *Freedom Review* 27 (January-February 1996).

Table 6:
Formal and Liberal Democracies, 1990-95

Year	Number of Formal Democracies	**Number of** Free States (Liberal Democracies)	Free States as a % of Formal Democracies	Total
1990	76 (46.1%)	65 (39.4%)	85.5%	165
1991	91 (49.7%)	76 (41.5%)	83.5%	183
1992	99 (53.2%)	75 (40.3%)	75.8%	186
1993	108 (56.8%)	72 (37.9%)	66.7%	190
1994	114 (59.7%)	76 (39.8%)	66.7%	191
1995	117 (61.3%)	76 (39.8%)	65.0%	191

Sources: See Table 5.

> "...the Yugoslav experience, after World War II, when the government dropped the concept of minority rights for individual ones, and added that of self-determination, led to a series of territorial states in which individual rights proved to be insufficient for most ethnic groups who continued to push for group rights for the purposes of education, etc. Several of the minority participants, referring to this perceived need, argued that the goal of the state should be unity in diversity. Jowitt[68] countered that, while the notion of unity and diversity presented a nice ideal, the typical result was a Tower of Babel, where Hungarians are Hungarians, Romanians are Romanians, Rom are Rom, etc. The question arises: what, if anything, will they have in common? The solution, according to Jowitt, is neither to make ethnic identity all-important, nor eliminate ethnic identity, but to relativize it. Jowitt contested the assertion that naming itself, unconnected with a change in social relations, was that important. He argued that the alternation of "nigger," "colored," "Afro-American," "Black," and now, "African-American" had not changed the fundamental reality of racial discrimination in the United States..." [Also, individual rights are necessary but not sufficient. One cannot encourage democracy in MNS by changing how a minority is called or calls itself without changing relative socio-economic and political relationships.]

Our content analysis suggests that these comments and opinions lend support to the major assertions of this chapter: that there are fundamentally differing views and orientations related to culture as to how to accommodate minority rights in the democratic state, as well as to the operational nature of democracy itself; that these views also tend to vary in relation to region, economic and political situations, as well as historical circumstances; that the present North American orientation is one view in competition and in interaction with others, having its own dark antecedents and bright future ideals, etc.. However, despite the conceptual disorder among scholars as to the definition and meaning of democracy in abstract and democracy in multinational states, the global popularity of democracy, as defined in this research, among minorities and others[70] continues to increase. Thus the impact of this popularity coupled with the impact of the technological revolution on public education, assures that multinational states cannot avoid their minority populations' enthusiasm for democratic participation, and in turn, the implications of democracy in relation to minority rights. For example, in examining the situation in the Palestinian West Bank elections, Ziad Abu Amr states that despite restrictive Israeli policies, "The heavy turnout also reflected a popular desire for political participation, power sharing, and the establishment of democratic order."[71] Similarly, an elderly Chechen, during the seizure of Grozny by the new Russian democratic government, is reported by Syed Shihabuddin Ahmed, editor of *The Messenger,* to have said: "Fifty years ago, I was shot at by the fascists, and now these so-called democrats shoot at me. I have lived long enough now to know [that they are not democrats.]"[72]

Perhaps the best précis of the problematics and recommendations exposed in this chapter to generate a peaceful search for democracy and SHCSD in multinational states was offered by the UN Special Rapporteur on Minority Rights when he provided the following prudent advice:

> States should increasingly replace coercive power with responsibility and accountability, which is the essence of democracy. This should be done by accommodating all groups on a basis of equal respect for their identity, allowing for effective participation, and ensuring consultation whenever their interests are affected by decisions made at the center. Accommodation does not mean anarchy. There is a need to maintain order throughout the transition period. Territorial integrity and basic political stability should be ensured through a process of inclusion and adaptation by which all groups are given the possibility to be equally at home in the common state.[73]

---

1 While many writers refer to early Greece as the source of democratic concepts, the combining of these concepts with the concept of the nation-state seems to have occurred under the influence of such writers as J.J. Rousseau, John Stuart Mill, John Locke, Thomas Hobbes, etc..

2 See Appendix V. Multinational states are not viewed the same as multicultural ones in which immigrant minorities continue to remain in their culture while in the process of assimilation or integration into the dominant culture, the major politico-legal difference being that in multinational states, the founding groups are not expected to assimilate, but rather to integrate politically, and perhaps experience "fusion." While this is the term used by the UN, we see fusion as a form of natural assimilation which nonetheless acknowledges the principle of the right of self-determination. Also, in relation to the prerequisites for the continuous

development of democracy, the most important prerequisite seems to be that democracy does not develop in a manner which permits it to be used as a pretext for the domination of a stronger group over a weaker one. Other prerequisites can be seen in the recommendations for successful minority / majority relations in multinational states (see Chapter IV, "Social Proclivity to Conflict").

3 See Chapter Two graphs illustrating ethnic distribution in multinational states. Source *Map 'N' Facts World Atlas 1994, supra..*

4 For example, see Charles L Taylor and David A. Jodice, *World Handbook of Political and Social indicators*, 3d ed., Yale University Press, Princeton,1983.

5 Special Rights in international law are associated with collective or minority rights (usually resulting from a treaty, convention or a constitutional-legal negotiated agreement) wherein a group or minority are extended rights which apply exclusively to them and not necessarily to other citizens. It is related to *Jus Aequum*. Concerning special rights, Professor Antonis Bredimas of the University of Athens calls attention to the most problematic aspect of their application: " Les mesures speciales en faveur des groupes minoritaires constitutent l'un des aspects les plus épineux de la protection internationale des minorités. Elles se trouvent en effet à l'intersection de deux contradictions fondamentales. D'une part, elles subissent la tension qui exist entre la conception individualiste et universaliste des droits de l'homme et les conception inverse, celle qui voit une protection plus adequate des minorités dans les droits collectif. D'autre part, les mesures specials sont conditionnées, à des degres certes variables, par la tension qui se manifeste entre la souverainété étatique et la perspective d'une eventuelle secession de la minorité nationale."

6 See specifically the scholars presented *in Nations et Nationalism, La découverte, Les dossiers de L'état du monde,* Paris, 1995 and *New Forms of Discrimination* earlier mentioned, as well as the bibliography for this research. While there is little direct writing on the definition of national minorities (see chapter on the definition of the term 'minority'), our empirical survey revealed whenever the term national minority was used, its usage accorded with the empirically derived definition mentioned above.

7 Antonis Bredimas, "Les Mésures Speciales en faveur des Minorités," *New Forms of Discrimination , supra.,* p . 285.

8 See Appendix. V.

9 See Wolfgang Friedman, *supra.*

10 These statistical were verified by calculations of data obtained from *Map 'N' Facts World Atlas 1994.*

11 See Alvin Toffler, M. Kaplan, S. Huntington, Alain Minc, *supra.* We disagree with the predictions in relation to the degree of nation-state disintegration into disorder, because we do not feel that appropriate consideration was given to the potential of human rights and particularly minority rights as a tool to maintain state unity.

12 See Amitai Etzioni, "The Evils of Self-Determination: Taking Sides ," in John Rourke, ed., *World Politics Sixth Edition,* 1995 p. 338. Also see S. P. Huntington, *supra.* and K. Deutsch, *Nation Building and National Development,* Athernton Press, New York, 1963.

13 E. Balibari and I. Wallerstein, *Race, Nation, Classe, Les identités Ambiques,* La Découverte, Paris, 1988. Particularly see Gil Delannoi's article,"Le

Nationalism et Catalyse Ideologique"in *Nation et Nationalisms, supra.*, p. 39.

14 This definition results from listing perceived cross-cultural demand for effective and efficient functioning as ascertained from the analysis in Chapter IV of this research entitled "Human Service in the Multinational Village," the recommendations indicated during the Project on Ethnic Relations conferences, *supra.*, and from John M. Packer and Kristian Mytti, eds., *The Protection of Ethnic and Linguistic Minorities in Europe, supra.*, then inducing a definition that seems to meet all minimum requirements or at minimuim did not conflict with any requirement.

15 Larry Diamond, "Is the Third Wave Over?" *Journal of Democracy*, Vol. 7, No. 7, July 1996, pp. 21-35.

16 Terry Lynn Karl, "Imposing Consent? Electoralism versus Democratization in El Salvador," in Paul Drake and Eduardo Silva, eds., *Elections and Democratization in Latin America, 1980-1985*, Center for Iberian and Latin American Studies, San Diego, 1986, pp. 9-36.

17 See Larry Diamond, *supra.*, p. 22.

18 Larry Diamond, *supra.*, p. 23.

19 See Manheim and Rich, *supra.*

20 See Ziad Abu-Amr *et al*, "Pluralism and the Palestinians," in *Journal of Democracy, supra.*, p. 89.

21 Lahouari Addi, "Algeria's Tragic Contradictions," in *Journal of Democracy, supra.*, p. 94.

22 Themba Sono, "'Democracy' as an Instrument of National and International Domination," in Hans Koechler, ed., *Democracy and an Alternative World Order*, Jamahir Society for Culture and Philosophy, Vienna, 1996.

23 Michael Binyon, "Gorbachev issues warning against Nato expansion, *The Times*, October 30, 1996.

24 See Allan Rosas, "Democracy and Human Rights," in Allan Rosas and Jan Helgesen (eds), *Human Rights in a Changing East-West Perspective*, London, Pinter Printers, 1990, p. 17.

25 A. Buchanan, *Secession: the Morality of Political Divorce*, Westview Press, Boulder, 1991.

26 H. Arendt, *The Origins of Totalitarianism*, Harcourt, Brace, Jovanovich, New York, 1973, p. 275.

27 J. Plamennatz, "Two Types of Nationalism," in E. Kamenka, *The Nature and Evolution of An Idea*, London, 1973, p. 301.

28 L. Dumont, "Nationalism et Communalisme," in *Homo hierarchicus. Le systeme des castes et ses implications*, Gallimard, Paris , 1966, p. 377.

29 See Minc and Kaplan, *supra.*.

30 Asbjorn Eide, *supra.*

31 John Packer, "On the Definition of Minorities," in John Packer and Kristian Mytti, eds., *Ethnic and Linguistic Minorities in Europe*, Abo Akademi University, Finland, 1993. All citations in the following excerpt are those of Mr. Packer. Emphasis has been added throughout this citation.

32 See John Packer, "On the Content of Minority Rights," in J. Räkkä, ed., *Do We Need Minority Rights?* Kluwer Law International, 1996, p. 121-178.

33 This inference is based on the comments and opinions presented by North American delegates to the various UN and other conferences concerning minority rights and democracy.

34 *Ibid.*, p. 144.

35 Although the articulation of these values reflects a dominant Western influence especially in the choice of terminology, legal philosophy and, indeed, legalism, it is submitted that the core of the reflected values finds expression in virtually all religions and philosophies of the world.

36 The calculation that "the more" is better than"the less" in the formulation of justice has been accepted by all liberal philosophers since Locke. Jeremy Bentham, proceeding from Immanuel Kant, formulated the calculation in his "utility principle": "everybody to count for one, nobody to count for more than one". The idea of this "counting" also found expression in John Stuart Mill's formulation that "One person's happiness assumed to be equal in degree to another person's is to be counted exactly the same." These formulations are recounted by Rawls (John Rawls, *A Theory of Justice*, Oxford, Oxford University Press, 1972, p. 182), who similarly subscribes to their essence (p. 77).

37 Vernon Van Dyke, "The Individual, The State and Ethnic Communities in Political Theory," in *World Politics*, Vol. XXIX, April, 1977, p. 343.

38 John Rawls, *supra*, p. 354.

39 Many scholars (e.g. Natan Lerner, *Group Rights and Discrimination in International Law*, Dordrecht, Martinus Nijhoff, 1991, p. 1) attribute the origin of modern international human rights law to the idea of tolerance found in the early attempts to protect religious minorities in Europe.

40 Daniel Warner, "Citizenship: East and West," paper to be presented to a colloquium of the same title, Graduate Institute of International Studies, 10-12 June 1993, Geneva, p. 8.

41 Commenting on the similar logic found in the "we/they" dichotomy of "ethnicity", Steiner characterizes the dichotomy as between 'good' and 'evil': "Demonization of 'the other' may become part of an ethnic group's credo and stamp out empathy". See Henry J. Steiner, "Ideals and Counter-Ideals in the Struggle Over Autonomy Regimes for Minorities," *Notre Dame Law Review*, Vol. 66, p. 1554.

42 William Ebenstein, *Great Political Thinkers: Plato to the Present*, Holt, Rinehart and Winston, 1951, p. 794.

43 Charles de Visscher, *The Stabilization of Europe*, University of Chicago Press, Chicago, 1924, p. 4.

44 *Ibid.*, p. 3.

45 *Ibid.*, p. 4-5.

46 *Ibid.*, p. 6.

47 e.g. R.N. Trivedi, "Protection of Ethnic Minorities," paper presented in conjunction with a course given at the International Institute of Human Rights, Strasbourg, July 8-10, 1985, p. 7, and prophetically, Ralph J. Bunche, *A World View of Race*, Kennikat Press, Port Washington, N.Y., 1936 (reprinted in 1968), *passim*.

48 While the notions expressed in the instruments developed by the United Nations reflected the views of the governments of the day, the ideas have also been rediscovered by contemporary philosophers. Among these stands out John Rawls, who, in *A Theory of Justice* (1972, pp. 60-61), sets forth two basic principles (to be applied in a serial order) for the just society: 1) that each should have the most extensive liberty compatible with the liberty of others; and 2) that inequalities should be arranged so as to everyone's advantage and in relation to positions and offices open to all.

[49] It may be noted here that, for contemporary philosophers like Rawls (1972, p. 7), concern for the "structure of society" as "the primary subject of justice" appears very similar to the composite of concerns addressed by international human rights law.

[50] Ebenstein, *supra*. p. 443.

[51] This conceptual error is made by several authors including, for example, Rosas (Allan Rosas, "Democracy, Human Rights, Good Government, Participatory Development: A Conceptual Framework," in Catarina Krause and Allan Rosas (eds), *Development Co-operation and Processes Towards Democracy*, Finnish Ministry for Foreign Affairs, Helsinki, 1991, p. 6, repeating his statement of 1990, p. 17) who, in an otherwise excellent recitation of some of the major factors and issues relating to democratic government, conceives of democracy and human rights as closely related but separate ideas in the form of "Siamese twins: they not only presuppose each other but are also genuinely intertwined."

[52] See Allan Rosas, "Democracy and Human Rights," in Allan Rosas and Jan Helgesen (eds), *Human Rights in a Changing East-West Perspective*, *supra.*, p. 17.

[53] Van Dyke, *supra*, p. 345.

[54] Allan Rosas, "Article 21" in Asbjorn Eide et al. (eds) *The Universal Declaration of Human Rights: A Commentary*, Scandinavian University Press, Oslo, 1992, p. 299.

[55] According to *The Compact Edition of the Oxford English Dictionary*, Vol. I, A-O, Oxford: Oxford University Press, 1971, p. 1805, the term "minority" in the context of political participation (democracy) first appeared in the writing of Ainsworth (1736) and was later employed in the writings of Edmund Burke (1774 and 1789).

[56] In the phraseology of Andrysek (Oldrich Andrysek, "Report on the Definition of Minorities," *SIM Special No. 8*, Netherlands Institute of Human Rights, Utrecht, 1989, p. 15), the real danger is that of "oppression."

[57] Louis B. Sohn,"The Rights of Minorities," in Louis Henkin (ed.), *The International Bill of Rights: the Covenant on Civil and Political Rights*, Columbia University Press, New York, 1981, p. 271.

[56] In an interesting analogy with corporate and commercial law, Hadden (1987, pp. 160-163) shows how the increasing seriousness of decisions should be accompanied by a broader consensus in the form of a parallel increase in the size of the required majority.

[57] Hurst Hannum, *Autonomy, Sovereignty, and Self-Determination: The Accommodation of Conflicting Rights*, University of Pennsylvania Press, Philadelphia, 1990, pp. 50-51.

[58] See the PER Conferences, *supra*. The additions to the following excerpts from PER conference reports, 1991-1995, result from a contextual analysis reflecting consideration of to whom, or to which comments, occasion or discussion the reported summation was directed. It should be remembered that these conferences were for the most part involving intellectual interaction between Americans and Eastern Europeans.

[59] Packer, "On the Rights of Minorities," *supra.*, p. 144.

[60] Nicolae Georghe, Institute of Sociology of the Romanian Academy.

[61] Helena Klimova, *supra*.

[62] PER listing for Hancock not available.

[63] PER listing for Hochschild not available.

[64] Istvan Deak, Columbia University.

[65] Paul Phillipi, *supra.*.

[66] Dinu Giurescu, University of Bucharest.

[67] Jowitt, *supra.*

[68] See the empirical analysis of democratic struggles in various states in Larry Diamond, "Is the Third Wave Over?", *supra.*, pp. 20, 22, 26, 31-2, 33, 35; Zaid Abu Amr, "Pluralism and the Palestinians," supra., p. 84; Foley & Edwards, "The Paradox of Civic Society," *supra.*, Crawford Young, "Africa: An Interim Balance Sheet," *supra.*, p. 59, 66; Ergun Ozbudun, "Turkey: How Far From Consolidation," *supra.*, p. 124, all in *The Journal of Democracy*, *supra.*.

[69] Ziad Abu-Amr, *supra.*, p. 84.

[70] Syed Shihabuddin Ahmed, Editor in Chief, *The Messenger*, Vol. 19, No. 9, February, 1995.

[71] Asbjorn Eide, *New Forms of Discrimination*, *supra.*, p. 233.

CHAPTER 4

Social Proclivity to Conflict

While it seems unlikely that the solution to the problematic of an international legal definition and classification of minorities is in our near future, actual multinational state conflicts with what, for all practical purposes, are national minorities, continue to increase, retarding societal development by demoralizing public law and order, disintegrating societal institutions and calling into question the impartiality of majoritarian democracy. Thus, more important than a legal minority definition or classification, effective and efficient social policy for future SHCSD requires that we give urgent attention to factors associated with manageable and unmanageable minority / state relations. The minority rights dialogue attempts to encourage just that. Following are examples of the factors we found to be most pertinent. The categories indicated by direct quotes have been selected from the 336 page work of Ervin Staub, *The Roots Of Evil: The Origin of Genocide and Other Group Violence*[1] which project what Dr Staub found were the chief psycho-cultural, historical and institutional factors predisposing societies to unmanageable minority / majority conflict [2] in MNS. Additional factors were derived from global observations and conclusions reached after a review of comments reported during the 1991-1995 Project on Ethnic Relations [PER] Conferences. When this is not the case, the appropriate comments are footnoted.

Psycho-Cultural factors

1. *Devaluation of a minority.* "A society that has long devalued a group and discriminated against its members, has strong respect for authority, and has an overly superior and / or vulnerable self-concept is more likely to turn against [minorities]." In relation to this concept of the effects of long term devaluation of groups, Claude Alvares, Editor of The Other India Press and Executive

Secretary of the Goa Foundation, the environmental watchdog for the state of Goa, expresses what he and many other third world scholars believe to be a widely held assumption among many Eurocentric scholars and others, serving to devalue First Nations and nonwestern European minorities, thereby facilitating discrimination against them:

> ..much academic knowledge in circulation in the Western world about the rest of the world, because it was the direct result of political overlording, was not only distorted but acutely contaminated by the ethnic concerns, goals, theories, obsessions, anxieties and peculiar assumptions and above all political goals of Western scholars and universities. It remains even today largely so defined, legitimized and decided by them irrespective of whether there is any concurrence from the objects of this discourse. But this is inevitable for it has been created specifically for the purposes of the West and for the exercise of its power and dominion and only incidentally for application elsewhere...
>
> This assumption ... was based on denying the existence of minds outside the West... The ruled were reckoned to be equipped with a mental ability of children, in need of complete direction and civilisational guidance.[3]

S.N. Nagarajan summed up this surisingly popular assertion in a short series made in 1987 in Penang, Malaysia, when he raised the question "What does the Western model really conclude about us?" then responded:

1. Your crafts are useless.
2. Your crops and plans are useless.
3. Your food is useless.
4. Your cropping patterns and agricultural patterns are useless.
5. Your houses are useless.
6. Your education is useless.
7. Your religion and ethics are absolutely useless.
8. Your culture is useless
9. Your soil is useless.
10. Your medical system is useless.
11. Your forests are useless.
12. Your irrigation system is useless.
13. Your administration is useless.
14. You are finally a useless fellow[4]

Devaluation of a minority viewed as a national subgroup helps to raise low self-esteem. "Initial acts that cause limited harm result in psychological changes that make further destructive actions possible. Victims are further devalued: for example, just-world thinking[5] may lead a majority in a MNS to believe that a minority's suffering is deserved. This furthers perpetrators' ability and willingness to act against victims, until "in the end people develop powerful commitment to genocide or to an ideology that supports it... Even bystanders who do not become perpetrators, if they passively observe as innocent people are victimized, will come to devalue the victims [to] justify their own passivity." Pointing to minorities as the cause of societal problems, however falsely, provides a facile avenue for problem resolution through concerted action against the scapegoat, and provides psychological reaffirmation for those banding together.

2. *"frustration, which results from interference with goal-directed behavior ."* The failure to fulfill goals and / or threat to life, material well-being, or self-esteem are factors predisposing members of a majority ethny in MNS to commit aggression against a national minority.

3. *Contradiction between reality and cultural ideals.* "Cultures can be characterized by their goals, explicit and implicit. In the United States, for example, according to one analysis, a basic goal is to maintain belief in equality of opportunity. The substantial inequalities of wealth, status and power are often explained by either hereditary differences in ability or differences in effort. These are genuine influences, but exclusive emphasis on them [when accounting for the minority's disproportionate representation among the poor, the imprisoned, etc.] obscures the extent to which inequality is due to a social organization that enables some people to maintain unearned privileges and limits opportunity for others..." Another consequence is devaluation of minorities and the poor as a whole, who are seen as incompetent or lazy, and who may also see themselves this way, which may keep them passive and accepting of their situation.

4. *Aggression as a cultural ideal.* "Some cultures (and individuals) idealize aggression. American television programs and films attest to some idealization." This cultural factor, of course, facilitates minority / majority conflict.

5. *Unconscious projection.* "The unconscious is another source of motivation for harming others. Self doubt, sexual feelings, anger

and the desire to hurt and even the experience of suffering can become unacceptable to people because of messages from their environment, especially their parents. These desires and feelings cause anxiety and must be defended against. The feelings and related thoughts are repressed, or denied. They become unavailable to consciousness. Later they may be projected onto other people. Anger may be displaced from parents onto [minorities] who are acceptable targets of anger. One characteristic of the authoritarian personality is such displacement and projection."

6. *An extreme incapacity for empathy*. This speaks for itself, in combination with hardship conditions and long-term devaluation.

7. *A poor self-concept and world view.* A poor or shaky self-image, easily threatened, and a tendency to see the world, other people, or institutions as hostile may cause a constant need for self-defence and elevation of the self. People with such characteristics may be especially sensitive to life problems and predisposed to discrimination against minorities.

8. *Subservience to authority.* Certain people are inclined to obey authority and to act punitively toward people not in authority. This is an aspect of what some psychologists call "authoritarian personalities."

9. *Obedience to authority and the authoritarianism of culture.* "Stanley Milgram's research[6] on obedience to authority showed that many ordinary people can be induced, even by someone with limited authority, to administer what they believe to be extremely painful and life-threatening electric shocks. Milgram suggested that people can enter an "agentic" mode in which they relinquish individual responsibility and act as agents of authority." Thus, the more the institutions of the majority ethny in a MNS foster authoritarianism, the more that state is predisposed to minority / majority conflict. The lack of minorities in roles of power can lead to 'us' and 'them' separation, devaluation and cruelty, particularly when the powerless are degraded.

Institutional factors

1. *Disempowerment of a minority* in MNS through the rule of majoritarian democracy. Inherent in the logic of the concept of democracy is the premise that the more directly people are able to participate in political decision making about things that affect

their lives, the more those decisions will be acceptable to their needs, values, culture and environmental situation. Thus, implementation of such decisions (having a broadly based support in both majority and minority needs, culture and societal values) receives maximum popular support. It is upon the simple genius and credibility of this assumption that the democratic concept wins, not only the hearts and souls of the majority of citizens in most states, but also the endorsement (if not the allegiance) of most political leaders.

If we accept this democratic premise (no matter in what cultural form), then we must accept that its reversal would be a move towards increasing disorder, confusion and chaos. Also if we accept that such a reversal (disempowerment) would impact similarly on any community, group, or citizen, then it stands to reason that, given the higher likelihood of greater value differences and consequently greater unique needs among societal groups called minorities, they would likely be more affected by their access or lack of access to effective democratic processes that recognize the existence of their collective interests. The minority rights approach, by confronting the dilemma often posed by 'majoritarian' democracy in MNS therefore endorses the empowerment tool of minority rights and assists in the conceptualization of structural and philosophical requirements for realizing multinational democracy, SHCSD, and conflict avoidance or management.[7]

2. *A mass media dominated by and essentially responsive to, the interest, culture, history, and circumstances of only the dominant group.* There has emerged, over the past few decades, an international consensus among third world and now most progressive scholars, political leaders, and activists, that the news media plays a key role in psychologically and sociologically conditioning societal attitudes towards minorities.[8] Consequently biased media-animated attitudes are often represented in socio-political policy and policy delivery, facilitating discrimination and encouraging, through negative imagery, stereotyping and victimization of minorities.

The question of assuring objective non-biased news coverage in multinational states poses a difficult challenge to liberal democratic MNS where the philosophical question of what is meant by "freedom of the press" in relation to hate literature is yet to be satisfactorily resolved. Despite the international legal interdiction against hate literature," and unlike Canada and most of western Europe, some important multinational states like the U.S. continue to permit the publication of such literature under the banner of a constitutional right to 'freedom of speech'. This is true although the international law of the *International Covenant on Civil and Political Rights* (ICCPR), to which the U.S. is a party, clearly rejects this position.[9]

Scholars on the effects of news media reporting in MNS[10] all call attention to the sad fact that truth and objectivity quickly fall victim to intense bias when "devalued" or "demonized" ethnies seek minority rights from a MNS unreceptive to their implementation. They call attention to the need for the media to be proactive at all times in maintaining the type of programming that gives equal respect to the human rights and dignity of minorities. In short, the news media, similar to human services and law enforcement in multinational states are faced with the problematic of cognitizing, conceptualizing and implementing the meaning of "consociation," news coverage, and entertainment programming.[11]

3. *Segregation in housing*. It can be argued that the policy of segregation in the U.S. led to the riots and insurrections in all U.S. major cities during the 1960's. "Discrimination is also served by poverty and persistent differences in social status, together with institutions that limit social mobility." It is also facilitated when the minority can be easily identified physically.

4. *Organizations capable of carrying out mistreatment.* "Motivation for mistreating a group is not enough; the capacity to fulfill it must be present. Often the motivation does not even fully arise until there is belief in the capacity to fulfill it." Inferior material circumstances and easy visual identification can facilitate discrimination or aggression against a minority, making it vulnerable and unable to practice self-defence. Being in such a position often encourages aggression.

5. *Groupthink.* "[This exists where] decision-making groups engage in "groupthink" and members are reluctant to contradict each other. Once an idea has gained any support, especially by the leader, members refrain from criticism or the introduction of new ideas, which limits alternatives."

6. *Compartmentalization and integration.* One may avoid facing the fact that minority persecution is taking place by concentrating on the immediate task, ignoring ethics and long-term consequences.

"Many Nazi doctors focused on medical 'achievements' in their cruel experiments. Camp commanders focused on efficiency. Bureaucrats prepared regulations and train schedules for transporting victims. Over time, internal changes will increasingly diminish the need to compartmentalize."

7. *The institutionalization of a rule-centered morality.* This focuses on norms, conventions and the maintenance of the status quo, unlike a human-centered orientation, which prioritizes the well-being of individuals or the group to social procedures in place. Thus the rule-centered institutional and systemic focus is more predisposed to facilitate discrimination against minorities. "The greater the systemic and institutional demands a group makes on its members and the more it guides their lives, the more completely the members can relinquish their burdensome identity and assume a group identity." This facilitates majority / minority conflict because submerging oneself in a group makes it difficult to maintain independent judgment where its use may block anti-minority activities.

8. *Social customs, rules, and standards.* "Many customs and rules are second nature to us; we 'automatically' follow them, without awareness. They may even define for us when to become angry and how to express our anger. They define our modes of interaction with others, including the respect (or lack of respect) we show others." Minorities, who frequently fill certain devalued positions in society, are thus confronted with vicious circles such as: they are janitors because they are discriminated against / they are discriminated against because they are janitors.

Ideological factors

1. *Destructive ideology.* "[Any] ideology with a destructive potential can become a guiding force, overriding contrary elements in the culture of the society. However, an ideology has to fit [the existing, historically-generated cultural institutions] if it is to be adopted... socialization of the young will create individuals whose personal values and conduct accord with those of the [ideological] system. It is unlikely that Roman soldiers who killed enemies defeated in battle experienced remorse: their socialization and experience made killing defeated enemies and enslaving women and children normal operating procedures..."

2. *Conceptualizing the state as an organization with interests of its own.* In this conceptualization, the state is viewed as needing to survive in a world of competing and often hostile (or perceived as hostile) nation-states. "[T]o maintain its power, to bring about obedience, and to unite the group, some states [feel it is right to] commit genocide." This is often seen not only as impeding the minority rights approach, but also one of the major reasons for the international protection of minorities.

3. *The fanatic as perpetrator.* "The personalities of many would-be perpetrators and decision makers predispose them not necessarily to violence but to fanaticism... Fanatics are under the influence of a system of beliefs to which they subordinate everything else. They interpret and evaluate reality from the perspective of this system. Any means to fulfill the ideology's overriding goals come to seem acceptable" even if it involves minority victimization.

4. *The designation of racism as the sole cause of minority conflicts.* Apart from the obvious superficiality of such an approach, it facilitates conflict because it focuses good-will civic action, social policy attention and societal resources on only one aspect of the problematic: *the attitudes of private individuals or small marginal groups.* All the factors mentioned in this chapter and many more could be considered components of racism or the reasons for racism. The convergence of all good-will civic activity and socio-political policy around the changing of attitudes, if accompanied by a failure to de-mystify the substantive reasons these attitudes exist, leads only to the frustration of civic good will, which is often apparent in what is popularly referred to as a societal backlash against minority rights. Changing societal attitudes may well require a focus on restructuring societal institutions; rethinking the rationalization of mass media programming, the contents of the education system, and the concept of justice guiding the output of our judicial systems; the reconceptualization of the goals of law enforcement, etc.. Indeed, once the meaning of racism is appropriately associated with the general problematic of SHCSD, we may come to conclude that ending racism means giving the ending of racism second priority to the protection of individuals and groups against *its negative effects* on their daily lives and socio-psychological formation, just as providing emergency food to the starving takes precedence over showing them how to produce food for

themselves. Such a paradigm shift in itself would go a long way in creating the type of conditions that would, in themselves, reduce attitudinal racism and provide the psychic space and security required for "fusion" (natural assimilation) to occur within the context of a multinational SHCSD.

It is the suspicion of some scholars that race or racism has been emphasized as a "catch-all" explanation for the suffering of non-Europeans to the poor of Europe because it suggests to them that such inequality is related to race, not to the policies and politico-economic system globally in place. Viewing the world from this relative advantage, they then fail to recognize or associate the reasons for their own suffering as being the same as that of others under the same global politico-economic system. In "The Metamorphoses of Colonialism," Jeremy Seabrook writes:

> The colonised people of the West have been so deeply installed within its compulsions that they can no longer name it, or recognize it for what it is. They have been the minor beneficiaries of an imperial project upon which they have become so dependent, and by which they have been so depowered, that they are unable to identify with resistances and freedom struggles that occur elsewhere in the world. *The serviceable distraction of racism acts as a further impermeable barrier to recognition, to perceiving the sameness of the processes which unroll globally, as they once unfolded domestically within any one of the so-called metropolitcan countries.*
>
> This colonialism, like any other, involves an abridgement of freedoms, an undermining of autonomy; but since these things do not acknowledge themselves, all the protests at it come out in deviant, symbolic and involuted ways - like crime, "mindless' or arbitrary violence, addiction, social and emotional dislocation. All these can be ascribed to defective or faulty individuals, and are not properly located in the economic and social processes [thus] are no longer... susceptible to human intervention.[12]

However, making appropriate changes in the orientation of institutions (bringing them up to date)[13] will be difficult, and depends on our moral and political will to retool and recreate our ideals of democracy as they relate to MNS in the global village of the post-industrial information age.[14]

Historical factors

1. *The minority had originally been forced into political union* through military conquest or the threat of military conquest (e.g. Quebec in Canada, the Chicanos of Texas and California in the United States, the Lithuanians of the USSR, the Irish of the United Kingdom, the Kurds of Turkey, the Tutsi of Uganda, the Ibo of Nigeria).

2. *The existence of an extraordinary degree of cultural incompatibility* between the culture of the state and that of the minority (e.g. the Amero-Liberians of Liberia, the Palestinians of Israel).

3. *The original purpose of political union was to facilitate socio-economic exploitation* and was not politically amenable to corrections (e.g. French Algeria).

4. *An untenable demographic situation of the minority*, for military, economic or political reasons, made political unity impossible, although the state concerned calls for that unity. This is seen when minorities such as the Kurds of Iraq, Iran and Turkey find what they consider one nation divided by several states. A similar but much less potentially problematic situation exists in relation to the Inuit of Northern Canada and Denmark. International law justifies the consideration of size, potential size and internal density of population in relation to the type of self-determination rights legally available. Such considerations are in conformity with the maintenance of the international peace directive of international law.

5. *The state in the past provided for minority rights, then became unwilling or unable to do so.* This was probably the case withThe Slovak Republic before the "velvet divorce" in Czechoslovakia.

6. *A history of use of aggression to deal with conflict.* Like individuals, cultures carry blueprints for dealing with minority problems. Repeated use of aggression to deal with conflict makes it acceptable. Aggressive plans and strategies are developed, the aggressor becomes competent in the use of aggression, and renewed aggression is more likely. Thus, a history of aggression makes it more "available." It was the case in every unmanageable minority/state conflict situation studied, that the minority or minorities involved expressed the opinion that the circumstances and/or arrangements leading to their past integration into the MNS were unjust and that the resulting institutions of the state favored the majority ethny or alliance of ethnies. They usually indicated that some form of restorative justice was required,

including a renegotiation of the MNS constitutions, nondiscrimination, political autonomy, etc.. Even in the rare cases where minorities were also ethno-nationalist and were not reacting essentially to perceived oppression but rather aspiring to achieve political, religious or socio-cultural ideals or racist mythology, historical circumstance was still an important factor. For example, to understand the current attitudes in the conflict between the Serbs and Bosnians ("the search for the greater Serbia"), it seems necessary to revisit the 1389 AD battle of Kosovo which frustrated, perhaps forever, the Serbian ideal of consolidating their dominance in the Balkans, by enabling more than five centuries of Turkish Islamic dominance in the region. The 'field of Blackbirds'[15] and Kosovo Polje are celebrated almost as Serbian cults.[16] Similarly among non-ethno-nationalist minorities, we find that past events, usually involving conquest and perceived oppression, are re-animated to influence their presents and futures.

We feel that it was this realization by sincere statesmen of the embrace of the present and future by the past that led to the advent, after the horrors of World War II, of the new international law of peace and cooperation which condemned the older rules condoning the right to conquest. Perhaps they came to believe that all events have consequences and perhaps in relation to the conquest of nations, there is seldom if ever, in fact, a *'fait accompli'* — witness, in relation to Quebec, the recurring theme of *'Les plaines d'Abraham'*; of *'the land and their treaty right to it;'* in relation to indigenous peoples; of *'the conquest of New Mexico'* in relation to the Chicano, and so on.

Moral-spiritual factors

1. *The desire for material gain or power.* "North and South American Indians were killed mainly because others wanted their land. In Paraguay, for example, roads were built into the jungle, greatly increasing land values, and the Ache Indians became 'inconvenient.' In such cases of *'internal colonialization,'* cultural preconditions include profound devaluation and a history of discrimination — the victims were often excluded from participation in society — and at times a history of conflict and mistreatment."

2. *The in-group / out-group societal moral orientation.* "Sparta subordinated individual dignity and freedom to the interests of the state; Athens elevated individual freedom, dignity, human

reason and creativity. The institution of slavery in Athens demonstrates that dominant value orientations need not apply to those outside the boundaries of the ingroup. Indians and blacks in America, Jews in many places, Armenians in Turkey, and those defined as enemies by ideology or other criteria have been traditionally excluded from the domain of dominant moral orientations; otherwise unacceptable acts become acceptable when directed at them.. Recent research in psychology has shown that human beings have a tendency to divide the world into 'us' and 'them.' They use seemingly trivial information to create ingroups and outgroups and then discriminate against members of the outgroup." This is often seen in relation to some religious groupings.

3. *The tendency to hide feelings in public.* "People tend to inhibit expressions of feeling in public. In an emergency, the fact that all bystanders are hiding their feelings may lead them all to believe that there is no need for concern and nothing need be done. Hiding [moral] reactions is also common when suffering is inflicted by agents of society on members of a minority." The expression of moral indignation by even one bystander can cause the others to express themselves.

The minority rights dialogue and the promotion of peace

The purpose of this section is to demonstrate that the factors important to the minority rights dialogue were recognized in the issues facing decision makers in real world situations such as those facing the countries of eastern Europe in the process of reinstitutionalization following the collapse of the USSR, as reflected in the reports of the Project on Ethnic Relations (PER) conferences which were conducted on a yearly basis thereafter, bringing together government officials, intellectuals, political figures and activists to address contemporary developments in eastern Europe. The following direct quotes indicate factors that were considered, in these real world situations, to have demonstrated a facility for negative consequences:[17]

1. Prague, Czech Republic - March, 1994

Prominent among the forces that shape public opinion and thus the growth or containment of ethnonationalism are the media

> of mass communication. Observers have been struck by the often destructive part the media play in creating or exacerbating interethnic tensions... It is also impossible to disassociate the media from the political conflicts in eastern Europe and Eurasia. Elites battling for supremacy view control of the media as a cornerstone of their bid for, or retention of, power... A study of the press by *Vreme* in March 1991 found that a media "war" had already begun well before the outbreak of hostilities between Serbs and Croats... Another, related problem is a lack of "moral criteria."... Political elites have a vested interest in promoting ethnic divisions and nationalism through subtle messages and pressure on the media... A low level of professionalism, inexperience, lack of knowledge about ethnic groups, and a strong inclination toward self-censorship among working journalists also contribute to a poor job of covering interethnic relations.[18]

This statement corroborates our earlier theoretical emphasis on the media as of major importance in facilitating conflict or peaceful SHCSD in MNS.

2. Moscow, Russia, 1992

> Throughout the conference, participants debated a number of basic issues that by now are familiar in post-communist societies: whether to adopt a civic or an ethnic orientation; whether to focus on the individual or the collective; whether to place priority on redressing past injustices against ethnic minorities or on achieving democratic transformation; whether to promote the distinctiveness and cultural renaissance of various ethnic groups within their own territories or to focus on measures to strengthen the Federation...

These comments indicated that the factors important to the minority rights dialogue were recognized in the issues facing decision-makers at the Moscow Conference.

> The civic orientation emphasizes the danger of current tensions between ethnic groups and the long-term implications of socio-political instability. This approach implicitly defines two priorities for policy makers in the Russian Federation: first, the avoidance of violent and deadly conflicts, and second, the stabilization of social, political, and economic life. Both are seen as prerequisites for a successful transition to democracy. This

orientation was emphasized by the Americans, the East Europeans, and a number of Russian Federation participants (primarily those connected with GOSKOMNATS and other state organizations)...The other orientation emphasizes the preservation of ethnic cultures and encompasses pleas for support in recovering traditions and aspects of culture which had been forbidden, obtaining compensation for past repressions, and gaining preferential access to economic resources and state power in the future. Those embracing this orientation generally make demands on the central state authority either for "affirmative" distribution of resources or for broadly defined rights of self determination, including independent statehood. The principal concern of this group is the improvement of their demographic, territorial and societal status. Underlying this position is a strongly felt sense of entitlement to compensation for gross injustices, in particular the suppression of ethnic culture and forced assimilation under the former Communist regime.

This conference comment suggests that the civic model emphasized by the U.S. does not encompass the minority rights model as seen by non-American delegates, who add the notion of the need for cultural recovery, and for compensation in relation to the gross injustice of past suppression of ethnic identity, while the civic model speaks instead to the rights of citizens, i.e. the rights of the majority.

The inherently ambiguous nature of terms such as autonomy and self-determination, which can range in meaning from concessions to local self-administration to full sovereignty, has added to the prevailing uncertainty and insecurity. This ambiguity is amplified by the full range of conflicting interpretations currently in use among both central authorities and ethnic groups...The problem of secession was the focus of much discussion, with most participants expressing pessimism about the future. As Bokaev[19] explained, though his republic favored continuing the Russian Federation, ethnic Russians were pushing them toward advocating separate statehood because of the Russians' continued domination of non-Russian peoples. This, in turn, has led to fears, expressed by one Russian representative, that ethnic Russians living on the territory of a seceding republic would be discriminated against in their own "motherland".[20]

This conference discussion also falls within the purview of the minority rights dialogue as expressed by decision makers in real world situations. It also indicates the need to overcome terminological confusion (earlier noted in the Preface to this research), and an awareness of the tendency of former minorities, once free, to abuse the right of self-determination by victimizing other groups who become minorities as a result of this action, thus violating their international legal responsibilities.

3. Belgrade, June, 1995

> The most frequently cited causes of the [Serbian-Bosnian] war were: (1) The habit of using force [a psycho-cultural factor earlier cited from the work of Ervin Staub] and the widespread feeling that "if we're not capable of producing well, at least we're capable of fighting." (2) Intensification of the politics of ethnicity and of warnings about "foreign threats," in an effort to avoid democratization... (3) The "delirium of sovereignty"—the revival of the concept of sovereignty as absolute power over subjects [note the significance in relation to the earlier quotes by John Saul concerning the role of the citizen]. (4) Failures of the international community — its acquiescence...

Here we see spokespeople involved in resolving a real world situation explaining its causes in terms of psycho-cultural factors. The failure of the international community and the delirium of sovereignty are added to the factors already mentioned.

> One view was that, since the Federal Republic of Yugoslavia was established against the wishes of an important part of its population (a reference primarily to the Albanians of Kosovo) and under conditions that rendered its establishment legally dubious, it was unreasonable to expect popular support for political pluralism in the country...The high degree of territorial concentration of Albanians in Kosovo and that province's location adjacent to Albania and to Albanian-majority regions of Macedonia make Albanian-Serbian relations especially problematic ...

> ...all minorities in the former Yugoslavia face problems that include the attitudes of majoritarian ruling parties, discrimination on individual and group levels, efforts to promote assimilation, and, ultimately and most tragically, attempts to

> change the demographic profiles of certain regions... there can be no peace or stability in the country unless ethnic problems are addressed. They can be dealt with in part at the level of protection of the rights of the individual citizen, but they must also be dealt with by recognition of the rights of minority groups.[21]

These observations and opinions corroborate that the theoretical, historical, circumstantial and demographic factors earlier presented are important to real world conflicts. In emphasizing the need for minority rights, it also corroborates a weakening of majoritarian democracy in MNS seeking SHCSD.

4. Slovakia (in Washington), June, 1995

> There were two problems that contributed to the breakup of Czechoslovakia. First, the Czechs were operating on the "civic principle"; Slovaks said they agreed with this approach but that they also had specific Slovak needs. Second, Czechs and Slovaks lacked a common vision of the future. Both of these problems can now be seen in Slovakia. Slovakia is building a state based upon civic principles; the Hungarians agree for the most part but insist that there are also specific issues that have to be addressed for the Hungarian community. Slovaks and Hungarians are talking on two different levels and do not understand each other...Slovakia lacks opportunities for dialogue... the constitution states that minorities are entitled to participate in decision-making on affairs that concern them, yet there is no legislation to implement this right. When the government was developing its proposals on bilingual education and budget restructuring, the minorities were not consulted...

This comment is an excellent example of the factors called to our attention from the 1992 Moscow conference comments about former minorities discriminating against other minorities once they become a majority. This may be due to the fact that even when minorities struggle to achieve statehood and succeed, the minority rights idea itself has never been well-understood or popular. The comment also questions the suitability of the civic minority protection model for the attainment of MNS unity, peace and security within the context of SHCSD in a democracy.

... A problem arises in explaining such positions to voters in northern and central Slovakia, where there are relatively few Hungarians. These voters perceive the Hungarians [minority] as incessantly "demanding things."[22]

This quote from the PER Conference report suggests the failure of the mass media to communicate the Hungarian demands without bias.

The above reflections on the psycho-cultural, institutional, historical and moral-spiritual factors associated with unmanageable minority-state conflict and counter to the spirit, principles and standards of international minority rights law, [23] provide sufficient insight to adequately contemplate "what's hot and what's not" (which type of social policy or state practices in relation to minorities may facilitate manageable minority-majority relations and consequently promote the spiritual and political will to achieve SHCSD, and which do not).[24] The UN Sub-Commission and the High Commissioner on National Minorities of the OSCE recommended the same principles expounded in this section to multinational states. Recommendations from the High Commissioner should be of special interest since they are recommendations being given to states in the process of attempting to resolve current real world minority conflicts. For some examples, see Appendix II.

In reviewing the logic in this reflection on factors that facilitate discrimination and conflict, we suggest the following are factors that should promote nondiscrimination and manageable minority-majority relations within the context of encouraging state unity, security, tolerance and SHCSD:

1. *Where appropriately demanded and internationally legal, states should accept to provide minorities with special measures* (such as affirmative action) or special rights (i.e. appropriate control over their societal institutions, territorial autonomy etc.) or if absolutely necessary and feasible, political independence (internal or complete).

2. *The constitutional recognition of the national minority and its rights and obligations.* Providing a desirable legal identity for the minority at the constitutional level is not only convincing in relation to attesting to the political will of the state to meet its responsibilities in regard to the institution of minority rights, but also enables, facilitates and encourages all societal institutions to do the same.

3. *The establishment of an appropriate human service social and delivery policy* that is structurally, ideologically, and educationally attuned to the society's diversity and multinationalism / multiculturalism so that governments' multinational political policies can be appropriately translated into social and social delivery policies at the sub-national levels. The interdependency between national political policies and subnational social policies is obvious, if not easy to realize. See Annex A for an example of what might represent an instance of the difficulty of sub-national delivery of national social policy in the City of Regina. This concerns the city's difficulty in facilitation of The Circle Project, a service organization which views itself as coordinating federal First Nations self-government policy with local needs. Annex B provides an essay *on the characteristics and qualities which seem necessary for successful human service work in multinational/multicultural environments* prepared for this research by a human services worker with fifteen years of experience working in Montreal with Quebec's multicultural and English communities.[25]

4. *Requiring minorities to give appropriate attention to their international-legal responsibilities* concerning demographic, national security, natural resources and national economic development priorities of the state in which they live, in their search for equal status through the realization of minority rights. This point was well made by Elsa Stamatopoulou-Robbins of the UN Human Rights Center in a Briefing delivered on 8 November, 1991 at the Dag Hammarskjold Library, UN, New York to representatives of minority organizations from the U.S. and elsewhere, facilitated by the International Human Rights Association of American Minorities (IHRAAM). This is often reiterated in statements and writing by most UN officials and scholars engaged in the minority rights dialogue.[26]

5. *States should strive to avoid environmental destruction* in all cases but particularly where it threatens the survival of a minority. This recommendation especially concerns the First Nations and indigenous peoples. Most of the (potentially) unmanageable conflicts in Canada involving First Nations' rights also involved the question of land rights and environmental issues in relation to perceived First Nations' survival needs.

6. *Multinational states would benefit from broader use of more direct democratic procedures* such as the plebiscite to poll minorities on issues of particular concern to them. Plebiscites and referenda are

often used in Switzerland in matters related to important minority issues. It seems to be a successful way of providing for democratic participation in decisions concerning issues of special significance, when regular democratic structures or processes are not available and where popular cooperation is viewed as important.

7. *Providing for minorities' politico-legal right to self determination* with the understanding that this does not mean political independence except as a last resort. An action such as this by states provides a better basis not only for maintaining peaceful relations but also for resolving conflicts when they arise. This is probable because it clearly suggests that the state has no hidden agenda in relation to the minority concerned and that it is willing to deal or negotiate on a equal status basis. In addition, it adds dimension and flexibility to democracy and provides a potential for greater societal creativity.[27]

As earlier mentioned, while the extreme of every nation or minority seeking a state is absurd and definitely not a goal of the minority rights dialogue, the opposite extreme of a commitment to maintain state political unity at whatever cost to human lives and well being is equally unacceptable and also leads to violence, destruction and chaos.[28] The answer seems to rest in finding a balance between these extremes.

8. *Where a minority in the state suffers from past gross violations of human rights, the state should be willing to remedy* by compensation, restoration, reconciliation or satisfaction. This forms a part of states' responsibility in international law.[29]

9. *Ways should be sought to ensure that the media in multinational states is responsive to their multinational societal responsibilities* as it concerns the minority rights dialogue. On this important point, the following liberal democratic comment is on record from a PER Conference:

> For democracy to take root successfully in eastern Europe, the media of the region must begin to act as a neutral forum to air opposing political views on ethnicity and nationalism... standards for reporting on interethnic relations must come from within the journalistic community itself. Politicians who exploit nationalist feelings will not change their behavior until they see that it is politically expeditious to do so. The media can play a role in this process... Anonymous pejorative quotes are no longer printed in the *New York Times*, for example. On the other hand, attributed hate speech is not suppressed but is published, so

> that it can be answered in letters to the editor, editorial columns, and radio and television talk shows. If hate speech is not answered, a newspaper often will criticize those individuals or institutions it believes should have responded. [Interestingly, the work by Elvin Staub suggests that this approach encourages rather than discourages racism, because it may give the impression that it's all right to hate or attack ethnic groups, that same is a normal conversational controversy in that society]... Participants agreed that journalists had to be trained in nonpolitical professionalism...The democratic task of the journalist is to make the straightforward communication of opinions possible without playing a partisan role in the delivery of factual information... it [is] essential for journalists to identify and contact civic groups that both study minorities and defend their rights...[so that] journalists [become aware] of interethnic relations and problems, what is published and what is omitted in stories about ethnic groups and ethnically based violence, the percentage of news dealing with interethnic relations, linguistic usages in stories about ethnic groups, and minority access to the media..[30]

Ervin Staub's study adds the suggestion that the application of truly democratic and pragmatic structures and processes in a climate of caring for human needs, where citizens feel and enjoy their individual freedom to be different and speak out against discriminations as well as exert sufficient collective control over societal political decision making processes, establishes a societal proclivity towards peaceful, cooperative and productive minority / state relations. For example, he writes:

> Active opposition by bystanders can reactivate the perpetrators' moral values and also cause them to be concerned about retaliation... Democratic societies with different racial and ethnic and religious groups free to express their differences are necessarily pluralistic, especially when these ethnic subcultures enter the mainstream. *As a result, children conform less to authority. Moral development is advanced by cultural pluralism, because it requires people to resolve conflicting standards and expectations..*[Italics added]...Deep-seated hostilities may be maintained by ongoing cultural arrangements that conflict with conscious values. Sometimes social movements arise when discrepancies come to the surface. In America, the civil rights movement of the 1960s arose when discrepancies between long-held ideals and national reality became a powerful motivation for change... Social reality

> can be even more strongly affected by the views of others. *The way some people define the meaning of events powerfully influences other bystanders' reactions to emergencies. Even what people regard as sounds of distress and how they react to distress depends on what other people say... psychological research shows that a single deviation from group behavior can greatly diminish conformity.* [Italics added]... When a society begins to mistreat some of its members, resistance by bystanders, in words and action, will influence others and inhibit the personal changes that would result from passivity.[31]

In concluding this section, we note that an analysis of the recommendations made raises questions about the sufficiency of the civic model for minority protection and conflict resolution in multinational states, since it does not encourage the need for special rights and measures as a part of the democratic process. By focusing on the achievement of mono-cultural civic conformity, will the democracy it produces also be flexible enough and sufficiently conceptually endowed to successfully process the demands and needs of national minorities? The concept of minority rights and obligations in a real sense represents a reiteration of the social contract theory at the collective level where the essential questions remain: why, under what conditions, and for what moral and politico-social reasons should groups enter into a political relationship under the authority of a state? In short, what are the rights and responsibilities of each and how will this political union benefit each within the context of encouraging SHCSD?

A response to these questions will require a minority rights model that responds to key socio-political problematics experienced by or within the multinational state:

1. *The partiality of the apparatus of the state's government.* Frequently state institutions come to be viewed by the minority as being not only under the control of but (un)balanced in favor of the majority in such a manner as to stifle the minorities' politico-economic, social or cultural development.[32]

2. *An excessive and disproportionate use of force* (police, military, etc.) *à propos* the minority for what, in the final analysis, could be described as attempts to re-establish the state's moral and legal authority in situations where, in the view of the minority, the state monopoly of legal and moral authority is doubtful, often leaving it with only an indisputable monopoly of force.[33]

3. *Disproportionate numbers of minority members in prisons*, on welfare, suffering from chronic health problems, etc.[34]

4. *Ethno-nationalism or chauvinism* on the part of the minority or majority.[35]

5. *The threat of outside intervention or the actual intervention* in behalf of the minority by a foreign state.[36]

6. *The insistence of a multinational state on acting as a nation-state* accompanied by attempts at forced assimilation.[37]

7. *Constitutional-legal denial of the right of a minority* to self-determination.[38]

8. *An attempt by the minority to seize control, through secession or self-determination, of natural resources* essential to the survival of the national economy, or an attempt by the state to deny a minority appropriate benefits from natural resources in areas where it is demographically dominant and/or has historical claims.[39]

9. *The creation of social policy* and delivery of human services without appropriate consideration given to cultural diversity.[40] In a state such as Canada, for example, this creates an unacceptable gap between the government's proclaimed minority policies recognizing First Nations inherent right to self-determination and its actual capacity to deliver, through the lack of appropriate transformation of social policy.

10. *Environmental destruction* in situations wherein a minority's survival is dependent on the maintenance of that environment.[41]

11. *Politically inappropriate or internationally illegal demands by a minority* for political independence.[42]

12. *Denial by the state or its institutions of a minority's democratically chosen identity.*[43]

13. *A biased news and communications media's failure* to avoid creating, or conscious efforts to create negative images of minorities.[44]

14. *A failure of commitment by minorities to international legal responsibilities* as well as rights. Minorities should be aware of their international legal responsibility to respect, protect and promote the human rights of all, as well as their responsibility to the state in which they live.

---

1 Ervin Staub, *The Roots Of Evil: The Origin of Genocide and Other Group Violence*, Cambridge University Press, 1993.

[2] Note that we have occasionally added what we felt to be equivalent terminology for the purpose of increasing clarity as it concerns the minority rights dialogue.

[3] Claude Alvares, "Resisting the West's Intellectual Discourse," in *Dominance of the West Over the Rest, supra..*

[4] Cited in Alvares, *supra.*

[5] "According to the just-world hypothesis, which has received substantial experimental support, people tend to assume that victims have earned their suffering by their actions or character... Those whose belief is strong denigrate poor people, underprivileged groups, or minorities. Strong belief in a just world is associated with rigid application of social rules and belief in the importance of convention, as opposed to empathy and concern with human welfare. People do not devalue victims whose innocence is clearly and definitely established. But how often can that be done? How can Jews or blacks, communists or anticommunists be cleared of misdeeds, evil intentions or defaults viewed as inherent in their nature, particularly in a climate of prejudice?...To avoid empathy, people distance themselves from victims. This can be accomplished by devaluation. Under difficult life conditions, concern about the self also diminishes concern about others' suffering." Staub, *supra.*

[6] S. Miligram, *Obedience to Authority: An Experimental View,* Harper & Row, New York, 1974.

[7] Reports from the PER Conferences clearly indicate that national minorities in unmanageable conflict with MNS felt that they do not have enough say in the decisions and institutions which affect their lives.

[8] See PER conference report, *The Media of Eastern Europe and the Former Soviet Union*. Prague, The Czech Republic, March 3-6, 1994, pp.10-12. For a more extensive view of the importance of the media in Canada and the U.S., see Jack Fuller, *New Values,* University of Chicago Press 1996 and Carl Jensen, *Censored,* Seven Stories Press, 1996. "The complaint in a nutshell, is that the media have ceased to be bulwarks of democracy and are now active agents in its frustration ...they divert attention from the real issues to which any mature collectivity should attend..." in review by Christopher Kornan, May 25, 1996 issue of *The Globe& Mail*. Also note the UN discussions leading to the recognition by most states of the need for a New Information Order.

[9] See the case of the Alberta pin, Records of the Human Rights Committee, 1992.

[10] See PER reports, *Roots of Evil* bibliography, and Jan Nederveen Pieterse, *White on Black, supra.* A sample of the more than 200 scholars they cite or refer to in their reseach (particularly those who spoke on impact of the new media on societal attitudes in relation to minorities, particularly the Jewish minority in Hilter's Germany) suggests that societies where the dominant group controls the news media are more likely to succumb to bias in favor of the dominant group in times of domestic conflicts. In reviewing the history of the western mass media's view of others from the pre-colonial period until modern times, Jan Nederveen Pieterse demonstrates this probability in *White On Black* and documents a history involving western media bais in relation to minorities of non-European origin. Although he deals only with minorities of biological racial differences in relation to what he refers to as Europeans or whites, this book, with its graphic illistrations,

seems by far the most comprehensive and researched book of its type availlable.

11 Here we are suggesting that human service should conceptualize consociated social policy and delivery methods; universities should conceptualize the impact of establishing consociated democracy in education; law enforcement must evaluate its consequences for social control and policing, etc., and the mass media should do likewise.

12 Jeremy Seabrook, "The Metamorphosis of Colonialism," in *Dominance of the West Over the Rest, supra.*

13 Bringing them up to date refers to their integration into new social and economic theory that is in tune with the technological revolution and our new production capacities and requirements. The post-industrial society has altered the relationship among the factors of prodution in such a manner as to render older social theory obsolete.

14 In this context, globalization does not refer to the globalization of capitalism or the free market, but to the decolonisation of history and the metamorphosis of colonialism under the impact of the technological revolution and resultant information explosion.

15 The battlefield on which Serbian Tsar Lazar and his Knights fell to the 27,000 strong army of the Ottoman Sultan Murat I. In the Serbian epic,Tsar Lazar chose martyrdom when offered the choice of an earthly Kingdom or a heavenly throne. Some scholars also suggest that ironically, current Serb anger against the Bosnian Muslims is misplaced since it was they who were largely responsible for guaranteeing the independence of the Serbian Orthodox church and thus the survival of the cult of Kosovo Polje.

16 Mujeeb R. Khan, "The Other in the Balkans,"in *The Journal of Muslim Minority Affairs*, vol 16, no. 1, Jan. 1996, Insitiute of Muslim Minority Affairs, pp. 49-52.

17 These factors were selected from an analysis of statements made by representatives to the before-mentioned PER conferences.

18 Project on Ethnic Relations Report, *The Media of Eastern Europe and the Former Soviet Union: Reporting on Interethnic Relations*, Prague, The Czech Republic, March 3-6, 1996.

19 Pyotr Dzorzhievich Bokaev, Department of Inter-Ethnic Relations, Council of Ministers, Kalmyk Republic.

20 Project on Ethnic Relations Report, *Nationality Policy in the Russian Federation*, Moscow, September 22-24, 1992.

21 Project on Ethnic Relations, *Democratic Processes and Ethnic Relations in Yugoslavia*, Belgrade, June 23-24, 1995.

22 Project on Ethnic Relations, *Slovakia Roundtable in the United States*, Washgton, D.C., June 13-15, 1995.

23 See Appendix I.

24 Increasingly, international fora are expressing the importance of the spiritual dimension for democratic human centered development. See *The Ethical And Spiritual Dimensions of Social Progress*, The World Summit for Social Development, 6-12 March, 1995 Copenhagen, UN Pub. sales no.95.iv2. ISBN 92-1-030037-8.

25 Provision of greater democracy (as defined in this research) in society is today almost universally accepted as a means of increasing general creative productivity. Note the decline of the Soviet state, its inablility to legislate or ideologically compel sufficiently competitive production initiatives, the

adaptation of democratic structures and processes in communist China and consequent increase in GNP, creative arts, spirituality (as seen in increased church attendence, etc.). Even with small groups such as astronauts orbiting beyond the earth, it has been demonstrated that the more a group can be involved in the decision making process as it relates to issues of significance to them, the greater will be its general productivity. (See ***Scientific American***, June 1995, p. 70.)

26 If the minority concerned sees or chooses self-determination in the form of self- government, then international minority rights law would also consider self-government for that minority as a form of self-determination.

27 Concerning political and moral responsibility, see Fernando Henrique Cardosa, "In Praise of the Art of Politics," pp. 10-19 and Lahouari Addi, "Algeria's Tragic Contradictions," p. 96, in *The Journal of Democracy, supra*..

28 Note the cases of Rwanda, Bosnia-Herzegovena, the U.S.S.R., Czecho-slovakia, Liberia, etc.

29 Yussuf Kly," Dances With Affirmative Action," *The Canadian Journal of Native Studies*, vol.14 no. 1, 1994.

30 Project on Ethnic Relations, *The Media of Eastern Europe and the Former Soviet Union: Reporting on Interethnic Relations*, Prague, The Czech Republic, 1994, pp. 2, 4, 7, 8,11, 12.

31 Ervin Staub, *The Roots of Evil, supra*., pp. 5, 63-65, 87.

32 The remainder of these opinions also result from a summary of the researcher's intuitive and deductive analysis of the materials already presented. For example, this can be deduced from the PER discussion on democracy in multinational states or from the UN Special Rapporteur's observations or recommendations earlier presented, etc.

33 *Ibid*. This can be deduced from the PER discussion on democracy in multinational states or from the UN Special Rapporteur's observations or recommendations earlier presented. Also it is suggested in the UN document entitled *Guiding principles for Crime Prevention and Criminal Justice in the context of development and a New International Order*, etc.

34 See B. Singh Bolaria and Rosemary Bolaria, *Racial Minorities, Medicine and Health*, Fernwood Publishing, Halifax, 1994.

35 This was discussed in one form or another at almost all occasions recorded during the PER, the discussions at the UN Sub-Commission, the sessions on minorities held by the OSCE, and most scholars on minority rights reviewed.

36 This is particularly true if the foreign state is perceived as a traditional enemy. This was often suggested in the works of international legal scholars such as Eide, Bravan, Alfredsson, etc..

37 Can be inferred from comments made at the PER Conferences, etc.. Also see statement by UN Special Rapporteur advising states against the institution of forced assimilation. See Asbjorn Eide, *New Forms of Discrimination, supra*.

38 Although the right to self-determination is not usually viewed as automatically meaning the right to secession, it is important to grant this right without conditions since its denial leads minorities to feel unable to negotiate in good faith, and thus may set the stage for charges of violation of fundamental human rights which in turn may provide international legal cause for demands for political independence. Our observations of minority

conflicts suggest that minorities often seek greater autonomy because they feel that the dominant groups are not willing to deal with them on the basis of legal or political equal status.

[39] The reason for this opinion is rather obvious, and the real world situation does not lack empirical evidence as to its existence, e.g. Biafra in Nigeria, Katanga in Congo, etc..

[40] Suggested from observation of the UN human service activities in a multinational / multicultural environment (see next chapter). Also see the work prepared by the International Association of Social Workers, and the Council of Europe entitled respectively, *Human Rights* and *Social Workers* and *Human Rights and the Police*, Strasbourg, Council of Europe publishing and documentation services, reprinted 1992.

[41] This was deduced from our observation of the situation and resistance of the aboriginal minorities in the Brazilian Amazon rain forest as well as our Vienna discussions with human rights representatives of the Massai minority in Kenya. Also note the situation of numerous First Nations conflicts in Canada, particularly that of the First Nations in Labrador in environmental confrontation with the air force training flights over the lands on which they depend for survival, of the Nauhaux Nation in B.C. resisting the encroachment of logging companies.

[42] Both the Bosnian Serbs as well as the Bosnian Muslims demand of political independence appears to be politically inappropriate in that it led to destruction and unmanageable international conflict.

[43] From discussions at the OSCE and the PER Conferences concerning the Roma, it appears to this researcher that the efforts to not accept the Roma definition of themselves as other than a social minority facilitated greater conflict, etc. and serves as an example of how such policies may act to increase anti-minority conflict. On the other hand, the acceptance by Spain of the Catalonian identity seems to have prevented conflict and may lead to greater SHCSD.

[44] This point was often made by statesmen and minority rights representatives at meetings of the Working Group on Minorities of the UN Sub-Commission, as well as scholars throughout the research.

CHAPTER 5

Human Service in the Multinational Village

The UN is most often spoken of as if it is an international organization aspiring to become a world government,[1] or a system for world government that does not work because of the role played by power politics within the international legal framework of 'the sovereign equality of states'. Further, in *Global Survival*, Benjamin B. Ferencz writes:

> If our present structure of international society is not changed so that it can cope effectively with problems that can only be resolved globally, the existing global institutions will become irrelevant anachronisms. Humankind will either seek and find new pragmatic solutions and working modalities which will, of necessity, be invented to resolve regional and global problems — or it will destroy itself.[2]

However, our observations in the context of the minority rights dialogue suggest a more pragmatic way of viewing the UN that not only permits us to better understand its limitations, but also, until such limitations are overcome, offers the UN as a model for human service policies and delivery in multinational states, if only to elaborate, for human service didactic purposes, the generic problematic of service intervention in a multinational milieu.

The UN has designated inequality as being the number one global problematic and most explosive division in the history of humankind.[3] However, since inequality is viewed chiefly as a distribution problem rather than one of production, the question arises as to how such inequality could increase between 1960-1996, at a time when the UN claimed to be promoting macro-level economic and social policies leading to socio-economic equality and equalization, etc. An adequate response to this question requires a retake of the situation and socio-economic role of the United Nations in the global village.

Figure 3:

Global economic disparities. Distribution on economic activity, 1989 (percentage of world total; quintiles of population ranked by income)

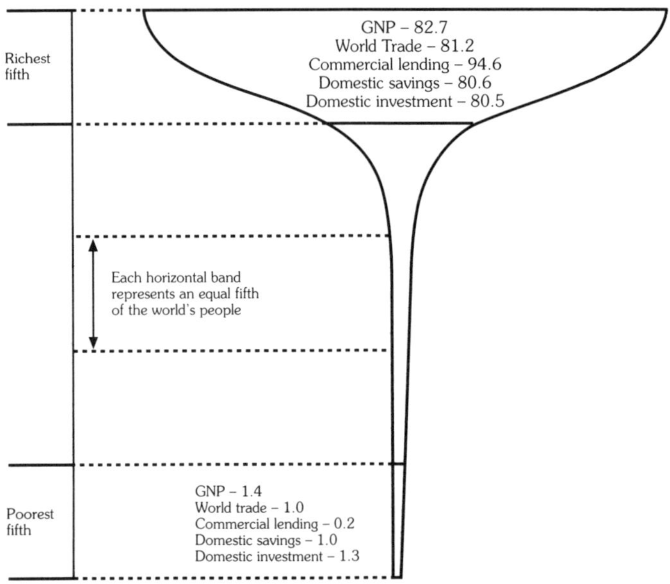

Source: Human Development Report 1992, UNDP, New York, 1992

When we revisit the UN Charter, we are first struck by the magnanimity of its equality concepts. It appears to provide what might be the first social contract for the global village. When the UN came into existence in 1945, the General Assembly was founded on the basis of one state, one vote (article 18). At that time, no one was forecasting decolonization even within the century — although the UN Charter opened the door to this possibility and probably envisioned its occurrence in the future. The founders of the UN were advised in 1947 to make plans for expansion up to as few as 70 members.[4] Although decolonization occurred earlier than envisioned, the UN Charter provided for a means by which the World War II victors would continue to act as if they represented the global majority. History provides us with few, if any, examples of world military powers voluntarily surrendering that power or sharing it equitably. This seems to have held true in relation to the willingness of the big five war time victors to share or surrender their hegemony over socio-economic and military decision making with the UN. As Erskine Childers points out:

> After perfect democratic preambular language and provisions for the world community's legislative body, suddenly we find that 5 out of the original 51 (and now 184) members of the polity:
> — can veto the admission of any new member (Article 4);
> — can veto choice of the chief public servant (Article 97);
> — are permanent, un-elected members of the organ charged with peace and security in the community; (Article 23)
> — can veto any proposed police action to protect the community or enforce its laws (Chapter VII);
> — can deny the full community the right to make recommendations on a threat to its own security (Article 12);
> — can prevent (and have by non-implementation, for nearly fifty years so far) the establishment of a community system for the regulation of weapons (Article 26);
> — and as if this were not enough, can veto any *amendment* to the Charter (Article 108, 109).[5]

The effects of such undemocratic instruments, along with the economic weaknesses of the south,[6] the opportunist reinterpretation of the word'economic' in the Charter responsibilities of ECOSOC,[7] etc. mean the UN is constantly being pushed toward the original idea of the World War II allies: to become an organization chiefly responsible for implementing their policies for peace and security. The *travaux preparatoires* to the documents mentioned in the footnotes suggests that it was the smaller states, socialist and third world states that obliged the UN agenda to recognize the importance of dealing with socio-economic problems such as inequality, etc., in order to make possible the search for peace, democracy and security. The potential clash in the UN between these two priority orientations has created a situation wherein the North (led by the World War II allies) often uses its wealth and special UN status to frustrate the efforts of the smaller and developing states to deal with the issues of socio-economic inequality. As Erskine Childers writes:

> — In the 1970s, the North accepted the Declaration of a New International Economic Order and then demonstrated that they had absolutely no intention of agreeing to implement it;
> — The North converted the IMF from its original role as the world's central bank, intervening equitably in both surplus and deficit countries, to being the dictator of highly destructive economic and social policies in developing countries;
> — The North steadily increased the staff of the World Bank, at salaries up to 35 per cent higher than the UN's, while imposing an actual cut of 13 per cent in UN staff;
> — the North arranged for the crippling of the Office of the UN Director-General, established by the majority in the General Assembly to give the UN high-calibre macro-economic leadership on North-South issues (finally Mr. Boutros-Ghali just abolished it);
> — the promotion of other international organizations such as GATT and Bretton Woods (under the control of the big five) for global economic policy making;
> — the North largely ignored UNCTAD resolutions for nearly 30 years and then set about its evisceration, more or less completed at Cartagena in 1992 and
> — in the same year got Mr. Boutros-Ghali to abolish the UN Centre on Transnational Corporations and to abandon any further attempt to establish a Code of Conduct for such corporations.
>
> The gist of all this seems to be that the UN, which was indeed supposed to initiate and coordinate macro-economic studies and policies (Article 58), not just activities (Article 63) of its specialized agencies and become the centerpiece in the formulation of economic macro-policy for the global village, seems reduced to essentially an agency for implementing socio-economic policies.[8]

Given the above-mentioned political situation in which the UN finds itself, as well as the priority it gives to socio-economic and ecological well-being for the achievement or maintenance of world peace and security,[9] the United Nations can, for the foreseeable future, be viewed equally, if only for pragmatic purposes, as a global human service organization operating in the ultimate multinational environment to promote global SHCSD. Accordingly, the evaluation of its structures, methods, policies, etc. should be of assistance to social policy decision-makers in multinational states dealing with their domestic minorities.

In observing the crystallization of the post World War II international system that gave birth to the United Nations, we note that the most salient and definitive impetus was the desire to eliminate the type of conditions in Europe (if not in the whole world) which led to the enormous destruction caused by World Wars I and II. The UN establishment of an Economic and Social Council, a General Assembly, a Security Council, and eventually Specialized Agencies, etc. with their respective mandates and increasing NGO connections serves as tangible evidence that it institutionalized its role as one of providing *ecologically sustainable political and socio-economic* human services[10] to states existing in theoretical sovereign equality, who were also responsible for the international law legitimizing its creation and operation. It is thus, necessarily, these states acting in concert whose sovereign powers the UN recognizes, and who must finance its programs, even as it serves as the chief institution though which sovereign state powers may be curtailed and channeled towards goals compatible with SHCSD, a requirement for world peace and security.[11] Regardless of the political nature of some of the human services it provides, or of the hopes, expectations and rhetoric of many scholars and statesmen, we must bear in mind that the UN was established essentially *as an agent of aggregated state powers*[12] for the purpose of providing an enormous range of human services, including political as well as social, economic and environmental services, to states under unique circumstances, and more recently, with the advent of human rights treaties, to their citizens and sub-national units.

Quite different from the situation of legislators in a state parliament or congress where each is legally, politically and functionally constrained to adhere to the decisions of the majority, states at the UN can legally opt out of implementing decisions reached by the majority in the UN's General Assembly, and particularly its most powerful political organ, the Security Council. Further, majority positions in the Security Council can be defeated by the veto opinion of one state. Even in other UN political organs, a state can refuse to become a party to a convention or treaty which the majority of states have approved. This is so often the case with both major and smaller states that it has become one of the popular reasons cited for viewing the UN as an ineffective world government or, more appropriately, organization.Thus the UN, like domestic human service agencies, depends for its existence on states, not the other way around. This is most demonstrably true in relation to such non-political fundamentals as finances. State dependency on the UN is visibly limited to its being a "good office" through which foreign policy and aid is conducted or enhanced, and facilitating a legitimate, peaceful and secure global order in which daily international transactions can take place.

Perhaps the major difference in the relationship between domestic human service agencies and their government, and that between the UN and states, is in the degree of policy dependency and interdependency. Different from domestic human service agencies, the UN provides political and diplomatic human services as an important aspect of its mandate. Its decisions influence and shape states' socio-political policies directly. Therefore between the UN on which states depend for international services, and the states upon whose decisions the UN in turn depends, there is greater social policy decision making interdependency. The Boards of Directors of domestic human service institutions are not usually composed of independent government representatives. Domestic social and human service policy is more closely tied to the feedback loop to the political agenda of a single government determining social policy. Thus domestic human service agencies enjoy less instrumentality than the UN to adapt social policy to societal needs and demands. However, the policies they follow, having been formulated by government, are more easily physically enforced than those of the UN. Equally important in understanding the uniqueness of the UN as a human service provider is the fact that different from any single domestic human service provider, the continuous existence of the UN is considered by many as essential to the international well-being or growth of the states' socio-economic and military power and states' ability to benefit through various forms of international cooperation. It is the significant degree of responsibility for the development of global law which UN politico-legal services maintain, that permits states to be recognized by other states and to carry on the greater part of their daily transactions and international commercial operations under conditions of law and order.[13]

The ongoing daily need for the UN as well as the essence of the human service problematic it faces can, in large part, be summarized in the popular maxim: *There can be no peace without justice and no justice without peace.* Faced with the justice end of this maxim and pressed by states towards improving global cooperation and security within the context of the present world order, the UN has increasingly, over the past few decades, augmented its social, human-centered developmental and environmental roles in order to effectively deal with the justice aspect of its prime directive of achieving or maintaining global peace. Its recent re-engagement with the sticky and emotion-laden minority problematic is an example of this augmentation and of the realization by the UN of the serious effects that neglect of such problems may hold for future societal development.[14] This renewed attention attests to the UN recognition that fulfillment of its panoply of goals — sustainable human centered development, environmental protection, the elimination of poverty, rights for the child, the enjoyment of civic, political, economic and social rights, etc. — requires that such special problematics as that posed by minorities in MNS be resolved.[15]

Today more than 95% of all UN activities[16] involve social and environmental services to states, sub-national groups, and citizens of states.[17] Similar to domestic social work agencies, more than 80% of the UN's work concerns the poorer, underdeveloped and underprivileged sectors of the global village.[18] The UN system employs approximately 53,000 international civic servants of whom more than two thirds are assigned to human service positions in The Human Rights Center, UN programs, UN secretariats, and UN specialized agencies and other departments and organs.[19] Apart from its charter, purposes, structure and predominant activities, perhaps the most convincing evidence of the existence of the UN's dependency on state governments, in this period of what domestic human service agencies refer to as retrenchment (cut-backs in social funding), is its financial situation and the reasons it gives for this situation. Similar to domestic agencies which blame government for inadequate funding to properly provide their services, so too the UN blames the states not only for inadequate funding, but for failure to pay already agreed-upon assessments.

> Money shortages are nothing new at the United Nations. It has been plagued by them since its founding 51 years ago. Many member countries fail to pay their dues on time for a variety of reasons, ranging from budgetary technicalities to simple poverty.

> Others have withheld payments as a pressure tactic or to make a political point. The current financial crisis includes all of these elements. But it is unlike any other in UN history. Its magnitude is unprecedented. It threatens not only the UN's ability to fulfil the mandates given it by member countries, but the Organization's very existence... The U.S. and other countries pushed hard for these cuts in the General Assembly — but now decline to fund the very austerity budget they approved.[20]

However, whereas in the domestic situation, blame for inadequate financing of human service agencies falls upon the government as a whole, which has complete discretionary powers over its budget, in the UN situation, individual states may fail to appropriately carry their share of the financial burden, leaving the remainder of the aggregate of states to suffer from the reduced capacity of the UN to fulfill its mandate.

Viewing the UN from the perspective of a human service organization permits a unique understanding of its reality and circumstances as well as its numerous accomplishments, and potential contributions to a more holistic understanding of SHCSD in relation to the major issues of today, particularly the minority rights problematic. The work of the UN is invaluable for providing the data-bases and conceptual frameworks for pragmatic knowledge of the association between minority rights and other major issues (i.e. sustainability, poverty, effective and efficient policing, democracy, etc., in short, SHCSD). However it is the UN as a model of a successfully functioning human service organization in the most extensive multinational/multicultural milieu,[20] that is of direct importance to understanding the problems involved in implementing minority rights in multinational states.

Human service in a multinational environment

In its efforts to service the global village, the UN is politically, legally and pragmatically obligated to recognize the equal status of all states and indirectly, to a lesser degree, the nations or groups within multinational states called national minorities. This means that, when creating socio-political and service delivery policy, the UN is required to be sufficiently cognizant of, and willing and able to give appropriate equal consideration to, the culture (ideals, values, socio-political institutions, socio-economic and legal circumstances, etc.) of all international personalities of the global village.[22] Providing services in a multinational global milieu has occasioned the UN to develop macro-level attributes (structures and policies) which contribute to its operational success. Some of these, we feel, are informative for micro-level domestic human service organizations and political decision makers in multinational states who are confronted with the minority rights problematic.

Political Attributes[23]

1. *Policy and Structural "Relative Neutrality".* While the ideal of neutrality is viewed in the UN as an organizational goal or attribute, judged by its structural functional organization and resulting policies, the UN's concept of neutrality assumes the necessity to relate to or incorporate the significance of relevant power configurations. This is usually achieved through a policy of structuring real world power configurations into the make-up of its organs, etc.. Its creation of the Security Council's veto is an example of this orientation. We have chosen to call this "policy and structure relative neutrality." This means that if the power configuration in the milieu changes (for whatever reason) before the structures of UN institutions and policies are able to reflect that change, operational success decreases. This premise seems to account for the present UN difficulties after the collapse of the Soviet Union and the advent of "the new world order"[24] as well as its present drive for structural and policy reforms. Present UN structures and policies are not in sync with changes in the international power configuration. In relation to domestic human services, a similar situation occurs when societal theory and structures for social policy decision making is out of sync with changed societal circumstances, needs and demands.

2. *Transactions on the Basis of Common or Universal Values.* The UN efforts to include a concern for human rights and international law in all of its policies and activities can be seen as an effort to promote common values which facilitate its successful operations as well as international relations and cooperation in general. But most important is its exclusive use of international law as the only legitimate basis of transactions, operations, enforcements and agreements. *The significance of this is that, in a multinational milieu, successful operation requires that only values*

or agreements common to the parties concerned[25] *should be applied as law or social policy, in the public domain, to all parties.* Such a conclusion was reached by Professor Haas, who noted, following his empirical analysis in relation to conflict resolution between states, that: " Success is easier to achieve if the contending parties are members of the same cold war bloc."[26] The recommendations to multinational states of the OSCE High Commissioner on National Minorities never fail to reiterate this principle.

3. *The Structurization of Multinational Policy and other Decision making.* While many organizations recognize the need for multinational education and experiences for their personnel, multinationalism of UN personnel is practically a condition of the UN's capacity to operate.[27] Multinationalism/multiculturalism is imposed on it by the differing cultures and civilizations in its multinational milieu. The UN method of multinationalization of personnel seems both unique and highly informative. Finding itself in a position where it must engage personnel at all levels, not only in relation to knowledge and skills, but also in relation to proportional regional representation (e.g. the regional rotation of the position of the secretary general, etc.),[28] UN policy and other decisions are made in what is often referred to by observers as a condition of chaos. However, our own observation leads us to view this condition (to the extent to which it produces pragmatic and effective decisions and policy) as a *necessary and constructive chaos*[29] which is in actuality required for successful operations, i.e. a chaos resulting from the exercise of a mode of organization where the structures and processes of no one culture, civilization or state is permitted or enabled to dominate during any fixed period of time—although many states attempt to dominate particular UN organs or agencies, etc., sometimes succeeding to a large degree, sometimes failing completely and often compromising in order to remain influential. Who dominates at any point in time is heavily dependent on issues and intensity of interest in a particular issue, and continual alterations in the relevant general power configuration. Thus power does not shift smoothly from one istate or group of states to another according to predetermined, well-known and openly stated criteria, but rather usually involves the interplay of many other less visible or calculable cultural, political, etc., factors — similar to the flutter of the butterfly wing's role in the creation of weather conditions. This aspect of the UN is unique to international organizations, but practically unknown to domestic

organizations wherein positions of power in organization change in a more perceptable fashion, e.g. established procedure criteria, ideology, performance criteria, etc..[30] This means that structures, institutions and processes resulting from UN decision making must, by the logic of structural functionalism, embrace multiculturalism and multinationalism. These structures, institutions and policies can thus be argued to represent the maximum that the different states and nations involved can, under the circumstances of that period, agree to accept. At the domestic level, the nearest equivalent would be *constructive disorder* for pedagogic purposes, for example, the establishment of sections of human service training institutions without any congressional or parliamentary structure where neither the majority nor the minority institutions or values, etc. are able, continuously over time, to dominate any structures involved in decision or policy making. This may also be reflected in certain multinational environments in which individuals are compelled, by the nature of this environment, to give significant consideration to the values, etc., of both the majority and the national minority in the process of the formation of their own values, beliefs, behaviors, and so forth.

4. *The Promotion of Inter-Ethnic Dialogue at all Levels.* The UN's approach to this task is so successful that many observers, unaware of the necessity for multinational consensus building and frustrated by inaction on crucial issues, often refer to the UN as a debating society. Our observations suggest rather that, given the anarchical nature of the international system in general, this seemingly tedious, endless and useless process of the UN is fundamental to achieving the common multinational understandings and commonly created conceptualizations required to animate a political environment permitting cooperative constructive actions. Concerning this kind of process, the *OSCE Newsletter* similarly observed, in relation to the Bosnian minority problematic, that: "the OSCE's and other organizations' sustained program of promoting inter-ethnic dialogue among various strata of society, represent steps in the direction of a more normal political environment."[31]

5. *Organizational Flexibility.* As suggested above, the role that dialogue for consensus building and compromise plays in successful multinational operations requires organizational and individual flexibility that strikes an appropriate balance between

being rule centered and human centered. This also implies being nonjudgmental on the sub-universal cultural level.[32]

6. *The Knowledge of the Relevant Major Issues.* In order for the UN to successfully render social or political services, its personnel (operating under the general international standard that democracy, the will of the people, is the sole basis for legitimate government), must be aware of the international, national and local issues that their service efforts will implicate, as well as the interconnections between these issues as it relates to objectives, policies and resources, etc.. For example, in operating in less developed international regions (similar to performing social services in poorer sectors, domestically), UN personnel are faced with the salience of issues which may be less important in the wealthier states, and vice versa. Thus, personnel must not only know what the issues are but also their relative degree of salience in relation to issues less popular but crucial to the achievement of societal goals. While for richer states (like richer areas within states) the most salient issue for the UN may be the maintenance of peace, the facilitation of the free market economy, etc., for the poorer states (similar to the poorer areas within states), the most salient issues may be the encouragement of economic and social development, health care and access to other primary public services, etc.. Statistical analysis suggests that while a situation or the resolution of a problem may be "popularly" viewed as important, focus on this basis of salience does not predict success. Conflicts in eastern Europe (the Muslim-Serb minorities, Hungarians in The Slovak Republic, etc.), western Europe (Turkish-Greek conflict, Irish-English, Catalans and Basques in Spain); Africa (Tutsi and Hutu in Rwanda), Asia (Tamils and Sinhalese in Sri Lanka), North America (the Quebec referendum, U.S. riots during the '60's) are striking examples where the popular demand for socio-economic development lost priority to the minority / state conflicts. Finding itself unable to effectively assist the free market economy or socio-economic development in the presence of minority-state conflict, the UN may decide to give priority to a minority rights approach.

Acquiring this political attribute of creating policies in light of pertinent issues, although necessary for both, is immensely more difficult for the UN than for domestic human service agencies. Global issues are more comprehensive than domestic ones and tend to impact and focus public scrutiny on UN human service efforts directly, while domestic human service organizations are sheltered to a significant degree by governments' responsibility for social policy, etc..

The most important global issues currently confronting citizens and nations of the global village, and consequently UN human service efforts, should be indicated to a significant degree by issues of most concern to delegates and participants of such international and national conferences as the Beijing Conference on Women's Rights and Development, the North African Conference on Alternatives to the Present World Order, conferences of the Canadian Anti-Poverty Organization, the1995 UN New York NGO conference, the Organization for Security and Cooperation in Europe (OSCE) 1995 Netherlands' and Ottawa Conferences, the 1995 and 1996 Meeting of the UN Human Rights Commission, the 1996 Conference on Democracy and Terrorism of the International Institute for Non-Aligned Studies, New Delhi, India, etc.. The following list of issues were observed or reported to be most frequently mentioned during the above mentioned conferences:

1. ***The use of human rights, and minority rights in particular, by major powers to achieve foreign policy or political objectives***. Chandra Muzaffar expresses this concern most eloquently:

> The determination, even obduracy that the west [U.S.] displays when it comes to preserving and enhancing its global dominance far surpasses its concern for human rights. There is perhaps no better proof of this than the west's [U.S.'s] lack of genuine commitment to the protection of human rights and human lives in Bosnia-Herzegovina... *In fact, the U.S. and its allies heralded the end of the cold war with a new— the Gulf War—which revealed once more all the hypocrisy about human rights... it is obvious from the outset that their primary objective was to restore western [U.S.]..]control over the oil-taps."* [33]

This view of the use of human rights in the Gulf War is not only held by Third World representatives but also by high government officials in such advanced states as France.[34]

2. ***The expansion of the role of NATO after the economic, political and social collapse of the USSR.*** The issue here seems to evolve around the U.S. role in NATO and whether or not it is being used to increase the U.S.'s political and socio-economic influence in both western and eastern Europe. This point is often

expressed by Russian government officials, and was highlighted at the North African Conference on an Alternative World Order:

> Mr. Andrew Hood (Britain) of the Campaign for Non-Alignment, [in] examin[ing] the role of NATO, [saw it] as an instrument of U.S. foreign policy... He [viewed] NATO as an undemocratic institution ... which hinders democratic accountability and scrutiny. Mr. Hood said NATO has supported undemocratic regimes [and is often] used to legitimize U.S. aggression... Mr. Hood [felt that] NATO, along with the European Union, International Monetary Fund and European Bank for Reconstruction and Development are helping to promote the reconstruction of Europe along lines favourable to Western capitalism.[35]

While Mr. Hood is not from the developing world, his opinion was similar to that voiced by the majority of Third World participants encountered. NATO was equally at issue in the PER 1995 Slovakia U.S. roundtable. However, here several delegates came to its defence. For example:

> ...an official of the [U.S.] National Security Council also discussed the redefinition of NATO as a security organization of the democratic community. He explained that NATO is more than a military alliance; it represents the underpinnings of the global democratic community... He also emphasized that NATO is not anti-Russian and should not be viewed as a military alliance directed against other countries. The choice is not between NATO and Russia.... Equally important is the fact that the U.S. views the ethnic issue no longer as only a human-rights issue, but also as a security issue... Bosnia has confirmed this point of view. U.S. interest in ethnic issues [according to this spokesman] does not mean partisan support for every minority cause, issue, or group, however. Officially, the U.S. believes not in group rights but rather in individual rights. These officials [of the U.S. Security Council] agreed that, ultimately, the resolution of internal problems, including ethnic conflicts, is a practical matter. If a government has to show more tolerance than that demonstrated by other European nations, so be it. The U.S. is concerned that governments avoid political foolishness and the exacerbation of problems by retracting previously granted rights — e.g. revoking the use of already existing bilingual signs.[36]

3. ***Sustainable human centered development.*** In general, the most important political issue raised in relation to sustainability

was whether the present economic/industrial system acts to destroy the environment. Edward Goldsmith, author and co-editor of *The Ecologist*, suggests that we consider that:

> ... modern man now co-opts for his own purposes some 40% of the net biological product of photosynthesis occurring in terrestrial ecosystems... In addition he now produces massive amounts of synthetic organic chemicals such as PCBs, CFCs and nearly all modern pesticides which being totally foreign to the natural world (xenobiotic), cannot be recycled within it and can only accumulate — or break down into decay products that are often equally unrecyclable...
>
> ... our agricultural lands are losing some 26 billion tons of topsoil every year... In addition, though it is now accepted that our destructive economic activities are leading to the rapid destabilisation of world climate... which could well render much of this planet uninhabitable... governments are [not] doing anything about it.
>
> ... measures required to assure our survival on this planet cannot, in the aberrant society we have created, be undertaken because they are not "economic". This implies that if we are to survive on this planet we shall have to create a very different sort of society — one in which economic activities can once again be brought under social control...[37]

4. ***The empowerment of women.*** Far from being confined to the conferences on the rights of women to equality, this issue has become of salience to most major world problems: development, the rights of the child, minority rights, sustainable human centered development, etc.. John C. Raines, a professor of religion at Temple University, provides what he calls a post-modernist analysis of the situation of women in most societies. He writes:

> From Latin American liberation theology we have learned about the category of "invisibility." To be invisible, we have learned, is to have no voice, to gain no recognition. To be forced into invisibility is to be dominated, to be oppressed and marginalised. And to be made *invisible* is the routine experience of powerless persons and powerless groups. It is how they learn about and often internalise who owns and controls the means of visibility.

But now comes a crucial interpretive move. What if it is not simply enforced invisibility, but also *enforced visibility* that dominates and subjugates, that causes one to doubt one's claim and competence?... One pattern, striking in its pervasiveness, [is]... subjecting the women to continuous scrutiny...

Hunter ... turns to the French post-modernist Michel Foucault and uses his analysis of the prison built by Jeremy Bentham, a prison called the Panopticon. Bentham designed this 19th century prison around a central guard tower shrouded in darkness and surrounded by back-lit, one-person cells. The system of control operated upon the prisoners by isolating them, and then subjecting each to pervasive surveillance by a guard they cannot see but know may be watching, a guard having power to reward or to punish. The ingenious part of all this, as Bentham and Foucault both recognised was, to quote Hunter:

> when an individual is subjected to a gaze that *could* always be watching, but is not *necessarily* watching at any given moment, that individual internalizes the power relation and [quoting Foucault] "becomes the principle of his own subjection."

The one who is subjected to the ubiquitous gaze of another who has power to reward or to punish *internalises the power of that gaze*. Such a person then becomes the everywhere present self-monitor of how they look, of how they appear to this other, even when the other is not looking. The prison works almost automatically, not because of the presence of walls, but because of their absence.

[Hunter] argues that the conditions of control used upon battered women, the continuous surveillance their batterers impose, is not an exception but is instead *the generalized life-condition of all women living inside patriarchal societies.* [38]

5. ***The New World Order***. The issue here is whether the tenets of the so-called "new international order" prevent the development of the third world states and whether this term should be considered an epithet for the presumed victory of global capitalism over social democracy and socialism. T.M. Duffy writes:

The idea of the 'end of history' has been utilized to demobilize people. This is in addition to the destruction of the environment

> and the marginalized role of the opposition and the absence of an independent choice for the citizens... Popular movements should undertake the task of protecting the environment, emphasize the importance of diversity, autonomy, consensus-building, emotional and intellectual awareness. Solidarity should take the place of competition. In that regard, decision-making should be conducted at the bottom level, i.e. as local as possible. Horizontal relationships must prevail and ecology and human needs must be harmonized.[39]

The chief problematic paradigm is that both capitalism and communism seem to have been unable to produce sustainable human centered development and that market forces alone are unable to provide for appropriate attention to human, spiritual and cultural needs. A radical representation of what appears to have become a global fear (particularly in third world states) is presented by the British author and journalist, Jeremy Seabrook, who writes:

> The industrialised world has for 200 years subjected its own peoples to a long and persistent development that has taken a single direction: the extirpation of all previous ways of answering need and its supersession by the market...
>
> For the development of this alien culture leads to a paradox: which is that the process that robs and removes from our own grasp our capacity to do and make and answer need for ourselves and each other itself becomes a culture in the end; and what is more, one that now seeks to extend its imperium once more, in what it calls a single global economy...
>
> For the West, by the relentless projection of its affluence and wealth around the world, has now induced the countries of the south to AUTOCOLONISE in its interests. The GATT agreement merely formalises what has long been an established reality: the governments of the South are ready to police their own people in the interests of the global possessing classes... To autocolonise means to impose upon one's own country an economic model imported from elsewhere, a model that is not in the interests of a majority of the people...This is how the West is now ready for its next major assault on a backward, impoverished, helpless, depowered, dependent, corrupt, venal Third World...[40]

6. ***Global terrorism and other such politically orientated criminal activities.*** Here the main issue concerns the effects of the use of terrorism as a political tool on democratic development.[41] An important functional concern from the UN perspective is the effort to pragmatically determine which parties to a political dispute (which includes the clandestine use of force by both parties) might be regarded as terrorist, and under what conditions, etc.. Other issues of pragmatic importance to successful UN human service operations in relation to terrorism include the difficulty of establishing international criminal courts, achieving jurisdiction over the accused, and finally providing for adequate sanctions or punishments, etc.. For instance, the success of the UN's international criminal court proceeding in The Hague is crucial to the UN's social and political operational success, if not its capacity to operate at all, in Bosnia-Herzegovinia.

7. ***The international refugee and immigrant crisis***. These international issues are most closely related, in international human rights and humanitarian law, with issues of population, health care, poverty, discrimination and other socio-political problematics. We will deal with socio-political issues in the next section of this chapter.

8. ***Increasing criticism of the western model of democracy.*** What is of greatest importance for future UN human service efforts is not the criticism of democracy *per se*, but the tendency to confuse the western, or more correctly, the U.S. model of democracy with the UN's universal concept of democracy as englobed in human rights and international law, and the concommitant use of that confusion by some anti-demoocratic elites to discredit the actions and behavior of western states, particularly the U.S., as a means of discrediting the universal democratic concept. However, most critics of the U.S. and western models, while presenting a serious challenge to its present dominant model, see and accept democracy as universally applicable. The gist of their orientation can be seen in the following:

> The crisis of democracy can be attributed to many factors, which can, in turn, be classified in two categories:
> First: objective causes. The most important of these causes are:
> (a) modern ideologies and philosophical systems;
> (b) specific political concepts;
> (c) parliamentary representation.

(a) The first cause is related to the philosophical origin upon which some modern ideologies are established. The liberal ideology is established on the contradiction between authority and freedom and states that freedom cannot be guaranteed unless authority is limited. In this context, liberal democracy became a mediating instrument between a guarantee of freedom and the establishment of authority in political society... The struggle between these two poles triggered:

- a trend supporting individual freedom and preventing authority from obstructing this freedom;
- a trend defending authority and urging it to protect individual freedom so as to organize society, lift the status of the underprivileged and eliminate social deprivation...The totalitarian societies attempted to limit freedom in the name of state authority and based their endeavors on the "right" or "obligation" to defend public freedom and interest. The community of citizens was oppressed by the ruling [elites] and by the state ownership of the means of production...

b) The second cause for the crisis of modern democracy lies in the conceptualization of freedom and equality. The "[liberal]" definition of freedom contained a serious flaw since it considered the protection of the individual from the interference of the state authority (or from the necessity to interfere in the name of the community) to be the essence of freedom. In the liberal and totalitarian schools, the above-mentioned rights [to equality, freedom and ownership] therefore became meaningless [because without guarantees of the individual's continuing involvement in the decision making of the state, and thus state involvement in guaranteeing this and other rights, there can be no human rights.].. The individuals would take part in the banquet of freedom but would be unable to sit at its table."... Thus it [is] confirmed that these rights (equality, freedom, ownership) [are] only worthless formal rights [unless they can be owned by the citizen through their ownership of government]...

c) The third cause is related to the representative system of governing, which was adopted as a means of expressing public will... decisions were exercised authoritatively by a particular minority which had monopolized for itself the right to decide, explain and determine and thus, deprived the majority of the right to participate in the decision-making process...The members of parliaments practically sever their ties to their

> voters and to the people as soon as they win a parliamentary seat. The people's representatives turn out to be seekers of power, although they still claim to act in the name of the people and the nation.[42]

9. ***UN reform***. Perhaps the most perplexing political issues for the UN and greatest challenge to its ability to continue successful operations results from the often contradictory demands emanating from all regions of the global village, mostly between the so-called developed world and developing states. The developed states, led by the U.S., are demanding a structural adjustment policy for the UN, the same policy applied globally as well as domestically which has yet to demonstrate that when applied in a package, it produces desirable SHCSD. On the other hand, in the search for a *new international economic, communicatons and social order*, developing states have been demanding more democratic UN structures and procedures. From the NGO level, demands are being made for greater participation in UN decision making processes in order to encourage greater UN efforts in areas such as human rights, social spending for the poor, protection of the environment, the elimination of discrimination against women, minority rights, etc.. Different from domestic governmental human service bureaucracy but similar to domestic politicians during an election, the UN seems to have sought to embrace all of the principal challenges presented in order to continue successful operations. Whether it will be able to adequately process these demands for policy, structural and procedural changes remains to be seen. The Independent Working Group on the Future of the United Nations made the following observations :

> Fifty years ago, the United Nations was created, brought into being by the vision, the hope and the determination of men and women who had seen at first hand the dangers of rampant nationalism, of economic depression, of freedom lost, and war unbridled... But it has not come through these fifty years unscathed. Like any good vessel, it needs refitting, weak timbers replaced, compasses reset. This is the objective that underlies the present report...
>
> The economic and social problems that confront [the UN as well as domestic human service agencies] are by no means limited to the most disadvantaged countries. Varied societies are

challenged by debilitating debt, by the volatility of the international financial system, by unemployment and persistent poverty, and by increasingly destructive crime and corruption. A profligate consumption of resources in developed countries, and a similar trend in developing countries, is undermining the health of large ecosystems... The breakdown of bipolar control has lifted restrictions on long-simmering civic, ethnic, and territorial disputes. Of the nearly 100 armed conflicts in the world since 1989, all but five were, or are, internal....

These [like the disorder in inner cities] are the disparate circumstances in which the United Nations must pursue the goal of international security in the coming years. In this pursuit, security must be seen as encompassing the political, the economic, and the social conditions within which people and nations exist...

The fear that a sweeping human rights agenda would intrude upon national sovereignty will have given way to the recognition that societies are better protected, and their prospects for sustained human development improved, by systems of representative government whereby the rights of individuals and groups are assured...

The social agenda of the UN [needs to] be tackled through a much improved coordination of agencies, as well as through active cooperation with the nongovernmental and private sector...

...the Security Council [should] be expanded from its present membership of 15 to a total of approximately 23 Members, of whom not more than five would be new Permanent Members... At the same time, the veto would be applicable only to peacekeeping and enforcement measures... if there is an increase in the number of Members accorded veto rights — necessarily by Charter revision — as a complementary measure, an amendment restricting the scope of the veto for all Permanent Members would be desirable.

Since many of today's conflicts stem from social or economic causes, the assessment office must develop knowledge of internal economic and social developments as well as of the state of political or international relations...

The imposition of economic sanctions offers the principal non-military means of responding to breaches of the peace... But their use must also be weighed against the possible suffering of innocent people, economic losses by participating countries, and strains suffered by third-party states affected by sanctions...

...we [recommend that] the functions of ECOSOC be taken over by two UN bodies that will fulfill the Charter's original purposes, but with a very different structure, authority, mandate and membership. These bodies [would] be a new Economic Council and a new Social Council...[They would then come together to] constitute the Global Alliance for Sustainable Development...

..*The Social Council should consider ways to strengthen and rationalize the Centre for Human Rights*...[emphasis added]

Assisting states undergoing crises in governance, or in the process of recovery from such crises, was not originally a concern of the UN's founders. The Charter does not provide guidance on these issues. Nevertheless, recent examples of Member States coming under acute social and political stress point to the need for the global community to offer assistance during critical times... [This recommendation appears similar to the welfare function in relation to individual citizens of states.][43]

While the above represent only instances reflecting the most important recommendations for change being presented, we feel that the most urgent will involve the rethinking of the Security Council to make it and the UN itself more democratic, bringing it into line with changing power relations in the global village.

As mentioned above, in order for the UN to achieve its political agenda, it has been constrained to confront a social agenda predetermined by global social issues and crisis. The magnitude and significance of the UN functions as a human service organization in a multinational milieu is reflected in the enormity and complexity of the social crises and problems it seeks to ameliorate or resolve. The following statistical overview should permit an adequate comparison of the scope of the UN's agencies with that of domestic human service agencies:

1. Service to refugees: In the decade preceding the 1990s, there was a 9 million increase in the number of refugees. The refugee population went from 8.5 million to approximately 19 million and this does not include those refugees directly under the mandate of the UN Relief and Works Agency for Palestinian refugees in the near East (UNRWA), according to the statistics reported by state governments to the UN High Commissioner for Refugees.

One of the added burdens for UN human service efforts is that most refugees are not only poor themselves but also are only able to achieve refugee status in the less developed states which are least able to provide for their basic human needs. In the developed states, which share only a small portion of the refugee burden, those refugees who are admitted are increasingly from the less developed world (particularly Asia) and tend to encounter discrimination to the extent that most become marginalized or a part of the underclasses. Their resistance to this discrimination often also involves the UN and its human rights anti-discrimination instrumentality. All this places UN human service agencies in the position of being called upon to assist refugees in their new settlement in the receiving state, in the provision of human needs, as well as in any efforts towards resettlement in their state of origin.[44] For example, several refugee populations in Africa have spent a long period outside their countries of origin. Refugee outflows from Angola, for instance, date from the 1970s, when the movement to secure independence from Portuguese rule was followed by internal conflict. By early 1991, most Angolan refugees found themselves in Zaire (308,000) and Zambia (99,000). The outflow of Rwandan refugees also started in the 1970s, as a result of ethnic conflict, which is one of the major causes for the increase in refugees, and consequent refugee problems, and therefore of high pertinence to the minority rights dialogue.

2. Global and National Family Planning Services: These UN services find their urgency in the increasing growth rate of the world's population and in the fact that a larger portion of that growth is taking place in the less developed states where it poses a threat to their already precarious economies and socio-political systems. The world population as of 1992 stood at between 5.4 and 5.5 billion. It is growing at the rate of 1.7 per cent per annum or 93 million per year. The increasing growth rate, of course, means that the period it takes to double decreases continally. For example, between 1950 and 1992, it more than doubled, growing from 2.5 billion to approx. 5.5 billion. By the end of the 20th century, it will increase by an additional 749 million and will reach 6.5 billion by the year 2025. Medium- ariant projections indicate that it will reach 8.5 billion.[45] This rapid rate of population growth has been of grave concern for three decades since the projection by the UN Club of Rome's systems dynamics report on population and future development.[46] Recently, due to its likely negative effects on states' potential for achieving sustainable human centered development and environmental protection, the June 1992 UN Conference on theEnvironment and Development in Rio de Janeiro refocused UN attention on the ecological limits to growth and the dangers posed by large and growing populations driven by poverty to irrevocably despoil the environment. Although political and economic disruptions are a main cause of the increasing migration, both within and between states, demograghic pressures and growing economic disparities create strong underlying forces for population movements. This growing movement of populations in itself threatens to become a serious source of international conflict.

The UN's key service role in this potential dilemma is and will likely remain one of providing technical, logistical, and educational support and encouragement to goverments and less developed communities in their efforts to institute family planning and family planning techniques. The continual demand for this UN educational role is indicated by the great difference in attitudes between the richer and poorer sectors of the global village in relation to the two chief determiners of family size: the use of effective contraceptives and the availability of abortion (see Table 5).[46] *Insofar as states' minorities often form a disproportionate percentage of the states' needy, this will require states to provide for minority rights and security in such a manner as to avoid minorities' likely suspicion (similar to that of less developed states confronting population planning demands from developed states) that family planning serves as little more than a convenient excuse for their relative underdevelopment.*

3. Services Providing for Basic Needs: While most scholars in the developed western states think of the world as moving from the industrial age into the information age, the UN human service agencies working among the poorer segment of the global village (similar to their domestic counterparts) find the world in which they function decades away from sharing either the benefits, liabilities or tenets of the information age. If we were to measure the stages of civilization in relation to the situation of the vast majority of nations and peoples, using Alvin Toffler's "wave theory" of civilizational development, we would be obliged to see most of the global village as still at the stage of the hoe.[48] A significant increase in this great inequality between the rich and poor occurred in the 1980s as a result of the slowing of the world economy and the new economic policies that were promoted by

Table 5:
Grounds on which abortion is permitted by level of development (percentage)

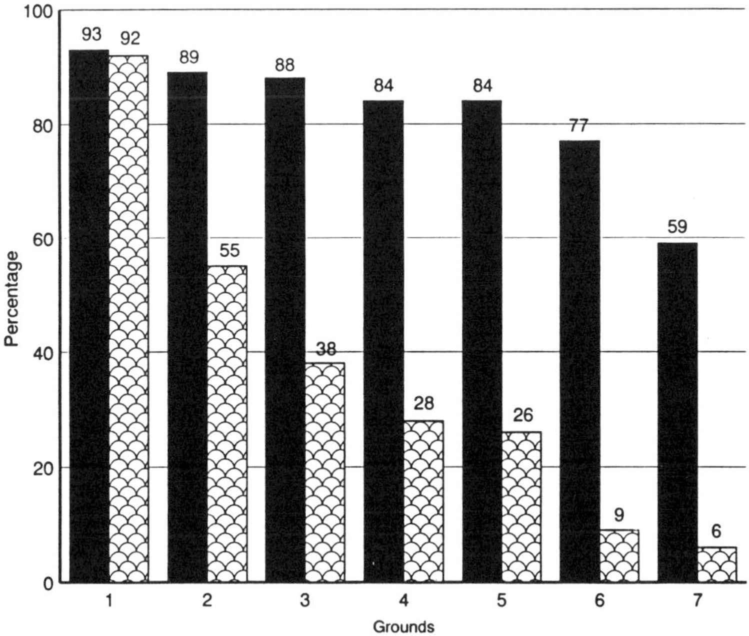

Developed countries
Developing countries

1. To save the life of the woman
2. To preserve physical health
3. To preserve mental health
4. Rape or incest
5. Foetal impairment
6. Economic or social reasons
7. Available on request

Source: Abortion Policies: A Global Review, vol. 1, *Afghanistan to France* (UN publication, Sales No. E.92.XIII.8); vol. II, *Gabon to Norway* (UN publication, Sales No. E.94.XIII.2); vol. III, *Oman to Zimbabwe* (forthcoming)

global institutions (particularly the structural adjustment policies of the International Monetary Fund and World Bank.)[49]

Our brief perusal of statistics immediately confirms the disparities between rich and poor, which as we noted in the Preface was recently cited by the UN as the major social dilemma facing humankind. Statistics of 1981 show that the developed states, with 17 per cent of the world's population, generated 72 per cent of world output. The developing states, while having 74 per cent of the world's population, had only 15 per cent of the world's output. These statistics indicate that the per capita output in developed states was 20 times higher than in developing states. In 1993, figures showed that output for developed states had increased and population in developing states had increased (see Table 6).

The statistics of 1990 show that the unemployed numbered 28 million people in the developed states, 7.5 million in eastern Europe and 70 million in developing states. These figures do not include discouraged workers, involuntary part-time workers or rural unemployment and underemployment, so they illustrate

Table 6:
Share of country groups in population and world GDP

	Share of GDP[a]		Share of population	
Country group	1981	1993[b]	1981	1993
Developed market economies	71.7	74.6	17.2	15.3
G-3[c]	44.8	48.1	9.1	8.3
Developing countries	15.2	18.5	74.3	77.3
Africa	1.7	1.7	10.1	11.9
Mediterranean	0.7	0.6	1.6	1.5
South and East Asia	5.4	9.4	53.3	54.1
Western Asia	2.6	2.4	1.2	1.4
Western hemisphere	4.8	4.5	8.2	8.4
Economies in transition[d]	13.1	6.9	8.4	6.9
Soviet Union	9.5	4.9	6.0	5.1
Memorandum items:				
15 heavily-indebted[e]	5.3	5.0	11.1	11.6
4 NICs[f]	1.3	2.4	-	-
China	1.3	3.2	22.4	21.6
Least developed countries	0.5	0.5	7.7	8.5
Sub-Saharan Africa (excl. Nigeria)	0.6	0.6	7.0	7.0
India	1.2	1.7	15.9	16.1

Source: United Nations/Department of Economic Information and Social Policy Analysis.

only a small portion of the dilemma facing UN efforts, which assume the right of all to employment. Both in terms of inequality and unemployment, national minorities which do not enjoy minority rights are likely to contribute disproportionately to these figures, because without appropriate political and social rights, national minorities will likely be unable to establish among their portion of the population those institutions which might be required to launch and support group development. Insofar as their existing inequalities propel further discrimination on the part of the dominant ethny, they are more likely to number among the unemployed, etc.. This means that the UN, in attemping to assist governments in confronting the problem of unemployment, must also promote the necessity for minority rights, and so, as we observe by the panoply of instruments in Appendix I, it endeavors to do.

Basic human needs are of most immediate concern to UN human service/humanitarian efforts — the supplying of food and shelter to the desperate poor. Contrary to the situation faced by domestic service agencies, where governments resist such needs of the poor, food and shelter are considered human rights by the UN, which is bound by its mandate to assist those who are without food or shelter in any way legal and feasible. Famine and homelessness (other than that caused by man-made and natural disasters) is seen by the UN as a product chiefly of a lack of purchasing power and thus more closely linked to inadequacies in economic systems and theory than to insufficiencies in production and supplies[50]— or indeed, to moral inadequacies or inherent incapabilities on the part of the deprived populations concerned. Social service agencies are confronted with the need to overcome the extensive misinformation and misunderstanding emanating largely from electoral processes which lead politicians (who then become legislators) to blame the poor in the interest of wealthier sectors of their electorates. The UN's human rights mandate, on the other hand, frees it to investigate appropriate and pragmatic responses to poverty situations. While it does not have to overcome the conceptual problems which derive from attitudinal influences of the electors in order to act, it does, however, require the cooperation of states and state resources which, as earlier noted, is often not forthcoming.

Of the 550 million people designated by UN statistics as being hungry (needing urgent humaniterian aid), 60 per cent were in

Asia, 30 per cent in Africa, 10 per cent in west Asia, Latin America and the Caribbean (see Table 5). In developing states, the 1987-89 dietary energy supply was 72 per cent less than that in developed states. A particularly unfair share of the burden falls on women and children. Thus, in attempting to service this problem the UN has found it necessary to call special attention to the rights of these two social minorities even when violations of their rights exist within the context of national minority demands.[51]

While in recent years the housing situation has worsened in developed states, the shortage of housing is a major concern in developing states because of rapid urbanization, uncontrolled settlements, overcrowding, insufficient drinking water, lack of sanitation and other public services, e.g. firefighting equipement, etc..[52] In developed states statistical indicators of housing conditions seem satisfactory in both qualitive and quanititative terms. A parity exists between household and standard dwelling numbers. However, these aggregate statistics mask differences in social access to adequate housing. Whereas in many developed states, almost the entire population, according to UN standards, is adequately housed, in these same states (especially those in which minority rights are not recognized or appropriately implemented, contributing to an otherwise general internal situation of social inequality), the rich are often over housed in relation to need, and the poor and vulnerable are often homeless. Homelessness increased rapidly in these countries during the past 10 years, due to insufficient new public housing construction, long-term unemployment, drug abuse, and in the case of Canada and the U.S. (where the homeless are estimated to number between 250,000 and 3 million), the de-institutionalization of many mentallly ill persons from hospitals without adequate out- patient followup treatment. Further, in the U.S., low income rental units have disappeared at the rate of half a million per year, while government housing allowances have failed to keep pace with rising rent.[53]

4. Health and Education Services: The situation confronting UN human service efforts in these sectors is equally challenging. In Asia and Africa, cholera and malaria have re-emerged. In Europe and North America, tuberculosis has made a comeback with a ferocity that resists the usual antibiotic cures. AIDS rages across Africa, and threatens Asia and Latin America as well as

Table 7:
Life expectancy at birth
1975-1990 (*in years*)

	1975-80	1980-85	1985-90
World	60.4	62.1	63.9
More developed regions	72.0	72.8	74.0
Less developed regions	57.4	59.4	61.4
Africa	47.9	49.6	52.0
Eastern Africa	47.1	47.9	50.6
Middle Africa	45.6	47.6	49.9
Northern Africa	53.9	56.6	59.1
Southern Africa	55.2	57.3	59.7
Western Africa	44.7	46.7	48.8
Asia	58.3	60.5	62.7
Eastern Asia	67.0	68.9	70.4
South-eastern Asia	54.1	57.9	60.9
Southern Asia	51.9	54.3	56.8
Western Asia	60.6	62.5	66.7
Latin America	63.3	65.2	66.7
Caribbean	66.2	67.7	69.0
Central America	63.4	65.6	67.6
South America	63.0	64.8	66.2
Europe	72.6	73.5	74.4
Eastern Europe	70.7	70.8	71.4
Northern Europe	73.3	74.5	75.5
Southern Europe	72.8	74.0	75.0
Western Europe	73.3	74.5	75.5
Northern America	73.3	74.7	75.6
Soviet Union (former)	67.9	67.9	70.0
Oceania	68.2	70.1	71.3

Source: World Population Prospects in 1990 (United Nations publication, Sales No. E.91.XIII.4).

Europe and North America. These and numerous other diseases strike poor states and the poor within developed states disproportionately, with those least able to obtain appropriate medical treatment. Again, unlike the situation of many domestic service agencies under the restraints of domestic laws and policy, the UN, functioning under the legality of international human rights law, recognizes the right to health care and is thus enabled to engage in the effort to secure this right to the best of its resources. Table 7 indicates that UN efforts (including those of encouraging technological/medical development and government provision of the human right to health care) may have met with a significant degree of success. However, the recent re-emergence of diseases thought to have been conquered along with an array of new ones, all at the same time that free market globalization is at its peak, indicates that what, in aggregate statistics, appears as improvements could be reversed by global budgetary cut-backs in health care services and other affiliated human services. In light of this possibility, we suggest that theUN should focus more on encouraging the establishment of programs of preventive and proactive health care and investigation into the effectiveness and usefulness of alternative medicines and treatments.

Our statistical observations indicate that the UN educational programs and services, particularly as it relates to literacy, may represent one of the most successful of UN human service efforts, and this is also true as it relates to women.[54] This improvement in education has not only benefitted global and domestic social integration, economic development, increased the value of labor, helped reduce poverty, affected demographic trends, affected population (by the decline of mortality and fertility rates, marriage patterns, and changes in the structure, size of composition of the family, etc.), but has also provided the unique vehicle permitting the technological communications revolution to impact on the peoples of the global village in such a manner as to begin the process of generating not only common expectations for a better material life, but equally, common aspirations for human rights and democracy.

When one focuses on the UN from the perspective of its being a human service organization, it becomes transparent that most of its human service projects, organs and agencies perform on the global level much of the same human services functions discharged by social or human services on the national and local levels, and that all of these UN services[55] are performed in the most culturally and politically diverse of multinational milieux. Quite different from the situation of the multinational state, there are no social or political contracts save for the very elusively worded and even more elusively understood International Covenants and other instruments forming the *jus consuetudinarium* of international law. Thus, it is logical to conclude that multicultural human services can be performed by domestic human service agencies in multinational societies (whether or not they are functioning as consociated democracies which recognize the full range of the minority rights concepts).[56] Areas of the UN human service policy (administrative or otherwise) that can be shown to operate successfully could serve as starting point models for analyzing the problematic of social policy creation for human serices delivery in multinational states such as Canada and the U.S..

In guise of concluding this chapter, we call attention to the need for future analysis of the UN-promoted model in relation to minority rights and societal development (see Appendix I) to discern the nature of the relationship between the implementation or nonimplementation of minority rights and government spending towards social welfare programs in multinational states. Our investigation of the minority rights dialogue as it parallels UN human service efforts in the global village suggests that when appropriate minority (or poorer state) rights are not recognized and implemented, forcing the minority (or poorer state) to become significantly disproportionately the clients of the social welfare systems (or international aid),[57] it becomes easier for the privileged and the opponents of social assistance (or international aid) to politically identify "the poor in general" with the demonized[58]minority (or poorer states) in the public consciousness. This may create a situation which increases public credulity in blaming the victim and thereby extricating the community, state and society from any responsibility for socio-economic conditions except as it concerns maintaining the economic and physical security of the rich and middle classes, and preventing government from encroaching upon the so-called civil and political rights of the poor. If an analysis of such UN generated statistics indicates that minorities' socio-economic well being is more proportionate to that of the majority when minority rights is implemented, then we can propose a direct link between social policy and minority rights in multinational states. In short, if SHCSD is dependent on social policy, then, perhaps worse for SHCSD, social policy can be held hostage to minority rights.

---

1 For example, Boutros Boutros-Ghali, in his article "Empowering the UN," writes: "The world is still in some ways in its middle ages when it comes

to international organizations and cooperation. Centuries were required before the struggle among monarchical and baronial forces was transformed into states capable of carrying out responsibilities in the fields of security, economy, and justice. There is no doubt that the institition of the UN system must travel such a path if chaos is to be avoided." See *World Politics Annual Editions 95/96* p. 235. Likewise, Francis Fukuyama in his article "Against the New Pessimism,"referred to the UN as if it was a superstate: "The UN, which many people hoped would become more effective after the cold war than it was in the days of the Soviet veto, has gotten overextended and is now presiding over policy failures in Bosnia, Somalia, and Haiti." See John T. Rourke, ed., *Taking Sides*, seventh edition, p.10.

2 Benjamin B. Ferencz, *Global Survival*, Oceana Publications, 1994, p.382.

3 See speech by James Gustave Speth, administrator of the UN Development Program (UNDP), reported by Reuters, Internet, July 16, 1996. Also see graph from *Population and the Environment: The Challenge Ahead*, UNFPA, New York, 1992.

4 UN Doc. N311, July, 1947.

5 Erskine Childers, "Demands for Equity and Equality: The North-South Divide in the United Nations," *International Democracy*, Jamahir Society for Culture & Philosophy, Vienna, 1995.

6 For example, see Erskine Childers, *ibid*, p. 25. In the 1991 session of the Economic and Social Council, the North, lead by the big five, only held 29% of the votes, but deployed 49% of total delegation strength. The South, representing the vast majority of humankind, due to financial weaknesses, held 71% of the votes but could only deploy 51%. Also see UN Doc. 861/ .IL/ 3/ 55(1)+1180(1) 1945.

7 Childers, *supra*.

8 *Ibid.*

9 In the Charter of the UN, this is mentioned as the third part of its purpose. However in practice, it was given first priority, because it is a real world priority; without the solution to socio-economic and ecological crises, global peace and security are probably impossible.

10 See Appendix IV.

11 Note that in the majority of UN conventions, declarations and resolutions, the principle of noninterference in the internal affairs of the state is reiterated. The principle of sovereign equality of states is restated and the fundamental principle that no state is bound by a treaty to which it is not a party is upheld. Also see art.4 of the Montevideo *Convention on the Rights and Duties of States*, 49 stat. 3097, 3 Bevans 145, 165 L.N.T.S. 19 (1933), and art. 2(1) of the UN Charter. The enforcement at the disposal of the UN is derived from such potent international legal, moral and political principles as "Promises must be kept,""*salus populi supreme lex*." Compare the similarity between the UN mission and the International Code of Ethics for Social Workers.

12 Differing state configurations at various times acting in concert so as to create international law or to legalize UN actions, etc.

13 Oscar Schachter, *Recueil Des Cours, Collected Courses of the Hague Academy Of International Law*, *supra*.

14 See Appendix I.

[15] In UN Doc. E/CN. 5/1995/100 In the elimination of poverty, minorities are economically and socially vulnerable as well as women, children, indigenous peoples, etc. See art. 23a. 23e, 23f . Other examples are art. 27 in the ICCPR and art. 3.5c in UN Doc.A/CONF.151/26 (Vol. I 12 August 1992).

[16] *A Guide to Information at the United Nations*. DPI/1444, 1995 New York ISBN 92-1-100542-6. See Appendix IV for example of data available in this text.

[17] See Appendix IV.

[18] *Ibid.*

[19] *A Guide to Information, supra.*. Note in Appendix IV that the majority of UN programs and agencies provide what can be viewed as human as opposed to governing or socio-political control services. Even the UN peacekeeping operations could be more accurately viewed more as an effort to render a human service than as enforcement. Was it not the UN human service approach to peacekeeping that was considered unsuitable for the enforcement operations in Bosnia? Here the enforcement operation was taken over by NATO until such time as 'there is a peace to keep'(until such time as enforcement can stimulate sufficient agreement between the parties in conflict and a desire for peace). For example, UNDPI 1993 Publication no. E.93.1.21 ISBN 92-1- 100515-9 p. 3, states: "The UN's role in peacekeeping is no longer limited to a military holding operation that permits diplomatic negotiations. Today, UN peacekeepers are engaged in a variety of activities. They supervise elections, disarm opposing factions, monitor human rights... providing humanitarian [welfare] asssistance, such as bringing food to the needy, repatriating and resettling refugees, building schools... providing medical help...", etc..

[20] United Nations Department of Public Information, DPI/1815/Rev.3 - 96-11806, May 1996.

[21] Ernst B. Haas, *The United Nations and Collective Management of International Conflict*, UNITAR, 1986 UN sales no. E.86.XV.ST/19. The statistics in this book clearly indicate that the UN services are global and that while conflict resolution has met with moderate success, areas such as social-economic and humanitarian services are far more successful. See Appendix IV. Professor Haas writes, p. 43: "The UN is no stronger than the collective will of the nations that support it. Of itself it can do nothing. It is a machinery through which the nations can cooperate. It can be used and developed... or it can be discarded and broken."

[22] This is true because the legality of the UN itself springs from international law and the rules by which it operates are products of international law as it pertains to the UN and other international organizations.

[23] These suggestions are derived from the following sources: intuitive analysis of first hand experiences and observation of the operation of the UN Human Rghts Center, the Human Rights Commission, Sub-Commission and its working groups, the various communications on OSCE institutions, efforts and policies particularly as it pertains to the minority problematic in eastern Europe (listserv@CC1.kuleuven. AC.BE), and the statistics provided by Ernst B. Haas in *The UN and Collective Management of International Conflicts, supra.*

[24] See the report of the independent working group on the future of the United Nations, Moeen Qureshi and Richard von Weizsacker co-chairs, *The United*

Nations in its second half-century, Office of Communications, Ford Foundation, 320 East 43rd Street, New York, NY 10017.

25 This concept of "common to all parties concerned" in the UN case may be limited to its political significance: the degree to which all parties concerned have agreed to accept or can agree to accept within the context of given power configurations. The public domain is taken from the international legal concept of the public domain and private or special domain. The public domain refers to the area of law that applies to all equal status parties, while the special domain refers to special law that affects only particular equal status parties. Law in the special domain is expected to operate without negatively affecting its operation in the public domain. Private international law and public international law are in principle an organized representation of this concept.

26 Haas, *supra*..

27 See Appendix III, Method of Recruitment.

28 *Ibid*

29 It is constructive in the sense that (like chaos theory) it provides for a natural, durable order where order is warranted. Thus we suggest that chaos is different from what is popularly meant by disorder.

30 The recent objection without explanation by the U.S. government concerning a second term for Boutros Boutros-Ghali as Secretary-General of the UN seems to have affected his chances, although the General Assembly has voted in his favor.

31 *OSCE Newsletter* vol. 3, no. 5, 1996.

52 Also note in "Reflection sur la pratique de l'intervention en milieu multi-ethnique" by Sylvie Riopelle that the author denotes a nonjudgmental approach and flexibility as key assets for social work in a multi-ethnic milieu. See Annex B. This point was also implied in the work of Ervin Staub, *supra*.

53 Chandra Muzaffar, "Human Rights and Hypocrisy in the International Order," in Chandra Muzaffar, ed. *Dominance of the West over the Rest, supra.*, pp. 91-97.

54 See *Au dela de l'horizon,* or any of the other major works of Jacques Attali, former adviser to French President Mitterand, 1981-91. In most of his major works, Attali views the U.S. as the leader of what he refers to as the *American economic zone* which is in economic competition with *the European zone led by France and Germany* and the *South-east Asian zone led by Japan.* In his analysis, control of the oil in the Middle East is a decisive factor which accounts for the pre-eminent position of the American zone.

55 *Towards an Alternative World Order,* Publication of Conference Proceedings, Jamahir Society for Culture and Philosophy, Vienna, 1995, p. 45.

56 The Slovakia Round Table in the United States, Washington, June 13-14, 1995.

57 Edward Goldsmith, "Economic Development and Environmental Destruction," in Chandra Muzaffar, ed., *Dominance of the West Over the Rest, supra.*, pp. 156-57.

58 James C. Raines, "Post-Modernism, Post-Colonialism and the Social Construction of Beauty," *ibid.*, pp. 37-39.

59 Dr. T. J. Duffy, *Towards an Alternative World Order, supra,* pp. 50-51.

60 Jeremy Seabrook, "The Metamorphoses of Colonialism," in *Dominance of the West Over the Rest, supra*.

[41] As an instance, the agenda of the Conference on Democracy and Terrorism is centered around the topics "Genesis of Terrorism and Its Transnational Character," and "Combating Terrorism to Ensure Right to Life."

[42] Miloud el Mahadby, "Democracy and People's Authority," in *Towards an Alternative World Order*, Publication of Conference Proceedings,, *supra*, pp. 21-25.

[43] The Independent Working Group on the Future of the United Nations, *The United Nations in its Second Half Century: The Report of the Independent Working Group on the Future of the United Nations*, Ford Foundation, 1995.

[44] An investigation of the UN volunteers' efforts in Latin Amerca and Cambodia is helpful in understanding the pragmatic nature and extent of UN Human Service efforts in relation to refugee problems.

[45] Table 3, *World Population Prospects: The 1992 Revision*, UN Publication Sales No. E.93.XIII.7.

[46] Jan Tinbergen, *The Limits to Growth*, Report to the Club of Rome, 1977.

[47] Table 6 provides a statistical representation of the type of differences that exist between the attitudes in the third world compared with those in the developed states.

[48] "Today, the lineup of the world civilizations is different. We are speeding towards a totally different structure of power that will create not a world cut in two but sharply divided into three contrasting and competing civilizations — the first still symbollized by the hoe; the second by the assembly line; and the third by the computer." See Alvin and Heidi Toffler, *supra.*, p 23.

[49] All UN publications reviewed held some version of this position. Also see Iqbal Asaria, "The World Bank: The Next Fifty Years," in *Dominance of the West over the Rest, supra.*

[50] Department of Economic and Social Information and Policy Analysis, Palais des Nations, 1211 Geneva 10 Switzerland UN Sales No. E.94.1V.4.

[51] The Lovelace Case is a classic example.

[52] See Assar Lindbeck, "Consequences of the Advanced Welfare State,"*The World Economy* (March 1988), pp 19-37.

[53] OECD, *Ageing Populations: The Social Policy Implications*, (Paris 1982), p.19 and OECD, *Lone-parent Families: The Economic Challenge*, OECD Social Policy Studies no. 8 (Paris, 1988), For other stats on housing, see: *Housing and Economic Adjustment* (UN publications, sales no. E.88.IV) p. 5; J. Breman,"Calcutta and the Urban Order in Asia ," *Development and Change*, vol.14, no. 2 (April 198390), pp. 157-158; S. Malpezzi, "Cost and benefit of rent control in Kumasi, Ghana;" M. Edwards, " Rental Housing and the Urban Poor" in P. Amis and P. Lloyd, eds., *Housing Africa's Poor* (Manchester University Press, 1990), pp. 253-272.

[53] See M. Edwards, *supra*.

[54] The array of UN human services are too vast to be truly represented within the limited scope of this Chapter. The UN is involved in every aspect of international life—from peace -keeping to the environment, from children's rights to air safety. The secretariat, one of the six principle organs of the UN, has ten separate departments and several operational programs. In addition to the secretariat, there are numerous specialized agencies and other affiliated bodies associated with the UN. See Appendix IV for a list of

the main areas of UN concern and the principle UN bodies dealing with them.

56 As earlier mentioned we limit these to those recognized in international law.

57 At the 1992 Moscow PER Conference, Mihail Ivanov, from the office of the President of the Bulgarian Government, noted: "After a period of ethnic calm and rapprochement following the extension of equal rights to Bulgaria's Turkish and Roma (Gypsy) minorities, the government now fears a dangerous situation as economic conflicts take on an ethnic coloration. At present Bulgaria is in deep recession. While high unemployment is a problem for all Bulgarians, it has hit the minority ethnic groups particularly hard: 80 percent of Romanies (Gypsies) and 48 percent of Turks are unemployed, compared with 14 to 15 percent of Bulgarians nationwide. The result has been increasing crime, xenophobia, and racist manifestations, phenomena also experienced in the Russian Federation."

58 Usually in situations of this nature, the mass media serves to perpetuate images of the minority so consistently negative as to make it almost impossible for the majority ethny to appreciate their cultural differences or to sympathetically identify with their situation or their problems. For the majority public, these people (at first the minority, then the poor, with whom they have come to be identified) are in the situation they are in "because, as a group, they are lazy, they have sub-normal intelligence, they do not value education, etc..

Conclusion

We began our efforts to familiarize our readers with the pertinent orientations of the dialogue concerning the relations between societal development and minority rights by a critique of the human rights approach itself, on which the international legal dialogue concerning minority rights in a democratic multinational state is based. We cited three aspects of these ongoing critiques as particularly helpful for removing many of the misapprehensions that bedazzle this dialogue and add to its popular inaccessibility. The first is of a technical politico-legal nature: that the lack of an agreed upon classification of minorities makes the search for agreement on an international legal definition and positive specification of legal rights almost impossible. Transposed into political logic, this implies that if it were possible to first achieve politico-legal agreement on a politically acceptable classification according to which different types of rights or needs could be delineated for each category, then agreement on a minority definition would be facilitated by the fact that political consensus would already have been created on how a minority legal definition might affect the socio-economic and political situation of each state concerned. Such a classification would permit minority rights to concur with minority needs, demands and responsibilities in the context of economic, historical and political circumstances of the states in which they live.

We responded to the first critique by highlighting the political nature of the impasse and proceeding to offer a classification (using the criteria set out in UN document E/CN.4/Sub.2/AC.5/WP.2 , 1 March 1996) of linguistic, ethnic or religious minorities into three politically determinable categories: *national minorities*, *immigrant minorities*, and *social minorities*. This categorization does not pretend to exhaust all possibilities, but it does seem to provide the general categories under which sub-classifications can be grouped with different degrees and types of rights according to need, circumstances, and political expedience.[1]

We also observed that of the three types of minorities, national minorities were most engaged in unmanageable conflicts with the state and for international legal purposes posed the greatest threat to national and global peace. We therefore focused our investigation on minority rights as it relates to national minorities. However, due to the lack of a clear distinction in international law between the rights of national minorities and other minorities, we often found it expedient, when source material made no distinction, to return to the generic term minorities which may or may not include all three categories, despite our view that international minority rights law, per se, uniquely applies to what we refer to as national minorities. Much of this legal confusion is created by the fact that, in order to give priority to the maintenance of peace, the UN and governments are being obliged to formulate minority rights policies and to justify these policies and decisions within the context of an international conventional law which itself is still in the early stages of formation and codification from international customary law and relatively recent treaty ratification and interpretation. In the most classical sense, they are being obliged, due to increasing minority rights demands, to place the cart before the horse.

The second critique was of a general political nature. There are widely held opinions suggesting that human rights in general (which include minority rights) are for all practical purposes hypocritical and only a sanctimonious means that governments and individual politicians employ to further national, group or self-interest. While not denying that human rights are often used in power politics,[2] we suggested, however, that this fact is irrelevant to the dialogue, because the reason why human rights serve as a useful tool for power politics is precisely *because* they are becoming universally accepted as minimum standards for the treatment of human beings, and whether or not they act politically or legally, or both politically and legally, to guide societal development is irrelevant. The question is, simply, whether or not human rights (and minority rights) should be included in any dialogue concerning the achievement of SHCSD. Our investigation suggests that the growing universal acceptance of human rights is an accomplishment and event in the societal development of humankind that merits our sincere attention, and provides a platform on which to stand in order to reach higher elevations of sustainable human centered societal development. Even the most severe critics of the human rights approach do not deny its contribution to the successful encouragement of common fundamental values and expectations in the global village. Indeed, perhaps the most eloquent critics in relation to its misuse by power politics are also some of the most eloquent supporters of human rights. For example, after criticizing the double standards the U.S. employed in its use of human rights in relation to Iraq, Libya, Cuba, etc., one such critic, Chandra Muzaffar,[3] goes on to list the numerous achievements of the human rights approach of the UN.

A third critique of special importance involved an attempt to correlate the definition of minorities to a democratic logic.[4] In essence, this critique called for an "associational approach" that, contrary to the present international minority rights orientation, would de-emphasize ethnic groups in favor of common interest based minority "associational groups," in which some or all individual members of the ethnic groups (national minorities) may or may not be included.

We feel that this approach, if it were acceptable to the inductive methodology of international law and the parties in conflict, would offer an excellent democratic solution because it seems to permit the search for democracy to achieve the highest degree of human rights. However, as pointed out, rationalization or deductive logic is not a primary source of international law whereas custom, treaties and state practice, etc., are. We emphasized that these international legal sources probably rendered definitions less serviceable to the abstract, formal and idealized search for democracy but more necessary in terms of the achievement and maintenance of domestic peace. Legal sources serve the interests of peace and democracy if we see peace as a necessary component of democracy, because they tend to limit *jus gentium* to *lex lata* which has developed from and reflects the realities of inter and intra-state politics and relations; such tested sources thus assure the viability of international legal development in what is still an anarchical international system. In short, we feel it is better to limit sources of law to commonly agreed-upon norms and standards by which states feel morally and legally constrained rather than to define legal norms on the basis of sources which are *extra legum*. While we agree with the democratic values and principles this critical orientation seeks to advance, we suggest that the creation of law through processes of deduction remains *lex ferenda* and should be encouraged primarily as legal advocacy. Since law is provisional and follows social development, such advocacy may serve to animate a comparative level of international socio-cultural development and thus new law. International law *(lex lata)* will remain, we feel, the chief catalyst accelerating this occurrence. To regard this legal confusion as it relates to minority definition as irresolvable within the context of international law is probably unjustified insofar as the present impasse simply reflects the actual socio-political stage of societal development: the lack of a sufficiently evolved public and governmental familiarity with the tenets of the international legal minority rights approach, particularly as it relates to national unity, security, the search for democracy, and sustainable human centered development.

We explored the minority rights dialogue as it relates to consociated democracy which provides equal status for minorities through restructuring democracy in MNS so as to recognize collective rights and the right to be different, as conceptualized by Arendt Lijphart and further articulated by UN Special Rapporteur, Asbjorn Eide, and other scholars.[5] We viewed their elucidations on consociation as a dialogue on the requirements in the search for democracy in multinational states, a re-application and reconceptualization of democracy and social contract theory in the context of the recent recognition of the MNS and its democratic need for collective rights.

Much of the historical evolution of western political philosophy as it relates to democratic societal political organization is predicated on inspirations which span human history from the ancient Athenian search for democracy and later, the individual and the nation-state (the social contract theorists, etc.), to the contemporary problematic of building democracy in multinational states. Until recently, there has been little political analysis of the rights and duties of nations or ethnic groups within states either toward each other or toward the state. Insofar as there has been a continuing tendency to confuse nation with state,[6] relations between nations under all circumstances were relegated, in keeping with the as yet unrealized ideal of the nation-state, to the realm of international relations and international law. The fact that intra-nation relations existed within states was generally ignored until the dialogue on the minority rights problematic as it relates to democracy first emerged among scholars of political science, international relations and international law. This may also go a great distance in explaining why governments, until recently, failed to functionally cognitize the multinational state, and politicians insisted on perpetuating the notion of the nation-state as the only viable alternative for socio-political organization, and its logical yet often unarticulated counterpart, the forced assimilation of national minorities.[7]

That American thinkers, in their search for individual freedom through majoritarian democracy, have paid little attention until recently to the cognition of the multinational state and its unique institutional and philosophical premises, suggests, as earlier implied: 1) that cognition and institutional elucidation of the multinational state is a relatively modern phenomena; 2) that the inspirational sources for American democracy — ancient Greece, the French and American revolutions — failed to cognitize the concept of democracy within the context of the multinational state; and 3) that as groups sought to escape from medieval or colonial empires, the state apparatus frequently served as the political instrument under which various groups united (albeit under the dominant among them) against the dominant center of the empire, seeking through this smaller more cohesive collective unit a greater participation in government decision making, and a greater emergence and empowerment of their own individual and group human rights than occurred within the previous politico-legal and often religious unit. This may be true although the new unit (the de facto multinational state) still encompassed groups other than that of the ethny itself.[8] Thus, the capability of the multinational state to achieve and maintain popular legitimacy as the unit of sovereignty in an environment idealizing the nation-state concept, depended on its genius in sheltering itself under the nation-state ideal.

We also presented empirical evidence, a selection of opinions and conclusions from various international conferences, that demonstrated that the minority rights dialogue occurs within the context of real world conflicts, and is influenced by international legal recommendations. The Moscow 1992 PER conference provides but one instance of this dialogue:

> Pyotr Bokaev[9] asserted... Had all nations united on equal terms, the union could have been preserved. Unfortunately, the union came into being through force — the destruction of statehoods, the suppression of ethnic identities, and the denial of individual human rights...

The problem now, according to Bronislaw Zadornovsky[10] of GOSKOMNATS, is to find a useful and acceptable model of federalism... The history of federalism in practice shows it to be a dynamic structure, a constant compromise between centralization and decentralization — between the conflicting aspirations of unification and separation. These compromises, which are more properly seen as processes than as final solutions, have been achieved either through agreements or constitutions... We therefore need a specific constitutional basis and new contractual forms... [also the right to self-determination has been wrongly understood to mean secession]... Unfortunately, [such] terms are used without precision by authorities on ethnic relations... In the case of the Russian Federation, the term self-determination is invoked with two contradictory aims in mind: to strengthen the Federation by providing the sovereignty necessary for a true federalism, and to provide the context for leaving the Federation altogether...

While Rasma Karklins[11] agreed that secession — and the extent to which it should be allowed — is a thorny issue, she maintained that it was extremely important to retain the possibility symbolically, since it appears that the only way to avoid secession is to accept it...

Stanovcic[12] proposed that, after so many years of living under models of domination, the region needed new models of accommodation such as consociational democracy as practiced in Switzerland.

We further indicated, as reported opinions and conclusions from the PER Conferences and other such international exchanges indicated,[13] that minority rights or the lack of same influenced the degree of socio-economic development, rule centered societal rigidity, violence, environmental degradation, the violation of women's and children's human rights, etc. — of SHCSD, in short. For example, it was noted at the 1995 Stupava PER conference that the insistence on classifying the Roma as a social rather than an ethnic minority had the effect of destroying institutional social controls which the Roma community required for positive socio-economic and cultural development. Likewise, the destruction of Roma social control without adequate replacement meant that much of the politico-social and cultural development and attitudes of the Roma youth became more accessible to an anti-social and anti-state orientation.

In addition to the environmental problems posed by the industrialization of land once under the protection of indigenous minorities, there is the fact that groups disproportionately subjected to poverty due to the effects of discrimination both leading to and stemming from their lack of minority rights, in their all-consuming effort to satisfy needs according to the socio-cultural norms dictated by the market and promoted by the mass media (TV), are frequently unable to establish sustainable consumption, land usage or environmental protection practices. The efforts of such groups, along with the other low wage earners, to satisfy market-generated needs further serves to support unbridled technological misproduction, overproduction, and environmental destruction. These tendencies contribute to urban blight and undevelopment, even in developed states.

We called attention to the aspect of the minority rights dialogue dealing with the psycho-cultural and other social proclivities of a society that predispose it to institutional discrimination and violence against a national minority, and highlighted the chief recommendations for proactive prevention and active management of minority / majority relations. Although these recommendations and opinions came from scholars independent of the UN effort as well as from statesmen and other responsible officials and individuals engaged in the *actual* management or resolution of *real world* minority / state conflicts, they all fell within the purview and intent of the minority rights dialogue in international human rights law, which is clearly summarized in the following statement by the Special Rapporteur of the UN Sub-Commission on the Prevention of Discrimination and Protection of Minorities:

> Many minority conflicts emerge from real or sometimes imagined discrimination, by the majority, against the minority. This is the primary subject matter addressed in the *International Convention on the Elimination of All Forms of Racial Discrimination* (hereafter CERD). Art. 1 of the convention defines "racial" to include also ethnic discrimination. *Less examined are the limits that have to be set for, and observed by, minorities and their members in order to safeguard the principle of equality.* The search for a separate existence and identity implies, to some extent, a request for diversity, which may be on collision course with equality but does not have to be so. Difficult issues do arise, however. What about access to employment? To land and property? *Can the*

minority reserve for itself preferential access in certain areas and at the same time require equal access in the larger society?

The 1992 Minority Declaration has addressed this issue. It is a significant step forward that Article 8 para. 3 states: *"measures taken by States to ensure the effective enjoyment of the rights set forth in this Declaration shall not prima facie be considered contrary to the principle of equality contained in the Universal Declaration of Human Rights."* Nevertheless, the issue has to be faced. When do measures intended to protect and promote the separate existence of groups violate the principle of equality? *Preferential measures (affirmative action) can be taken in order to create or restore equality in the common domain, where there has in the past been a policy or practice of discrimination which has deprived members of one group of equal opportunities. Such measures, however, are not intended and shall not have the effect of preserving differences; guidance on this point is found in CERD Article 1 para. 4:* they shall not "lead to the maintenance of separate rights for different racial groups" and "shall not be continued after the objectives for which they were taken have been achieved". *Such measures do not establish group rights under any sense of the word, but provide rights for individuals to be used in some contexts of competition. Transitional preferential treatment (affirmative action) is, therefore, entirely different from the measures envisaged under the Declaration of 1992, where the intention is to allow for a lasting manifestation of difference. Instead of transitional affirmative action we are under the Declaration addressing the rather different issue of special measures...*

The scope of "common concern" depends on what is taken out as "separate domain". Groups which are powerful by controlling resources, technology and organizational skill may want to limit the area of "common concern" in order to preserve privileges in what they consider separate domains, as has been done with the concept of "common affairs" in *apartheid* rhetoric.

In discussing the common domain, it must be recognized that every sovereign state is obliged to ensure to all its inhabitants, on a basis of equality, the enjoyment of the whole range of human rights as provided for in the *Universal Declaration of Human Rights*: civil, political, economic, social and cultural rights.

Whenever pluralist arrangements are contemplated, they must be limited in such a way so as not to prevent states from ensuring, without discrimination, the enjoyment of human rights to everyone under their jurisdiction.[14]

In international human rights law, both states and minorities have responsibilities and obligations to each other. One of the most damaging and misplaced criticisms often held by critics of the minority rights approach in international human rights law is that attempting to provide for international legal rights without ensuring that citizens have an adequate understanding of their responsibilities to the state and its government is superficial and impractical for engendering sustainable human centered development. While it is true that the minority rights approach, due to the imbalance of power between the state and the individual or minority, emphasizes rights instead of duties, it does not ignore or underestimate the importance of the minority's responsibilities to the state and others, including individuals and social minorities within the national minority.[15] The recognition of responsibilities is structured into the legal processes required for demanding or negotiating rights and in the general body of international law itself *(jus cogens)*. In general, as suggested in the last paragraph of the preceding quote, it is the responsibility of the minority as well as of the individual minority members to act or not act in such a manner as would deprive any other groups or individuals of the full protection of their human rights.[16]

Lastly, we presented a view of the UN as a human service organization chiefly responsible for providing human services in a multinational environment so as to call attention to the UN's unique response to unique demands placed on its social and service delivery policy in order to effectively operative in multinational environments, thus highlighting the probability that the social and human service delivery policy of MNS can effectively and efficiently be adapted to the demands of consociated democracy. The UN model requires the adoption of multinationalism in education, training, hiring, administration, social policy creation and delivery, and so forth.

In this chapter, we also suggested that the UN could serve as a guide to human service in MNS because its social focus in the global village parallels to a significant degree that of domestic social and human service in MNS:

> The issues that confront [developed and developing states] are almost identical to those facing [rich and poor] individuals and groups inside of states ... their significance to policy makers vary

> significantly... In the economies in transition [developing countries or the poor sectors of the developed state], poverty and unemployment have emerged as significant problems as they change from one set of institutional arrangements to another [in the case of the poorer sectors of developed countries, from the social democratic ideology regresses to 19th century free market policies]... In fact, larger inequalities in income and wealth are to be expected within the framework of new institutions and incentive structures, as [developing states] transform themselves into market economies [or as the poor in developed states are subjected to the ideology of the structural adjustment policies]... poverty remains a major economic and social problem... Demographic changes and growing restraints on public sector resources on the one hand, and persisting weaknesses in the delivery of social services on the other, posed new challenges to social [welfare and] security policies...
>
> [In the former developed Communist states], as international conflicts abated and societies became more liberal, ethnic and religious conflicts and civil wars among groups seeking to capture political power erupted... New nation states were formed and ethnic groups within nation states strove for self-determination...
>
> [In the developed western states] high levels of unemployment and the decline in the demand for unskilled labour in developed countries permitted the emergence of a class of long-term poor in these economies...
>
> The provision of [human] services has had to face several challenges during the last two years. The demand for social services in developed countries increased on account of continued high levels of unemployment, population aging and the growth of one parent families earning low or no incomes...
>
> In all groups of countries there has been dissatisfaction with social services provided by the public sector...[17]

If we give complete credence to the role of power, greed and short-sighted ethnic self-interest in shaping what states do as much as to common sense, the desire for justice, or enlightened self interest, then we may expect that the type of minority rights model multinational states will implement may depend solely on the future power configuration of the international politico-economic system, and that the power configuration of the system will not be significantly influenced by states' ability or willingness to provide for the human rights of their citizens. In such a view, one may conclude that the model accepted will result from the influence on the various states of the model(s) adopted and enforced by the most militarily powerful or economically influential.

On the other hand, as we have earlier suggested, global trends and crises may have converged in such a manner as to promote a systemic conditionality in which the functionality and perhaps even the continuous existence of a sovereign state-centered system itself depends increasingly on the state's ability to contribute to the resolution of global crises and to provide for the human rights of its citizens, the achievement of which will depend on the successful management of national minority/majority relations. No doubt this could be one of the least foreseen consequences of the global victory of democratic ideals and processes: that the maintenance of the authority of the state's apparatus becomes increasingly dependent not on power (its monopoly of violence, influence and resources) but on the state's successful management of internal issues including human rights, ethnic relations, and consequently sustainable human centered societal development.[18] Which type of minority system will be globally adopted seems, at this historical point, unanswerable. What does appear certain is that an effective system will have to be achieved if multinational states are to survive. The ideal of the nation-state must give way to the ideal of the multinational state. It is not unimaginable that this dilemma, pushing towards the impossibility of a system based on nation-states, may be resolved by the empowerment and superimposition of international organization.

We observed in relation to minority rights systems in place at the national level, that contemporary constitutional-legal models can be said to represent an interplay between the influences of the civic model represented in its extreme by the U.S. and the consociational model best represented in Switzerland.[19] It is often suggested that the disproportionate global influence of the civic model is due to the awesome politico-military and socio-economic power of the U.S., while the global influence of the consociational model is almost always attributed to Switzerland's perceived success in meeting the requirements of manageable ethnic relations.[20] Some states reviewed in our chapter on the definition of a minority have mixed aspects of the civic and consociated model or retain a consociational model established before World War II while in rhetoric or intentions they are moving toward the institution of the civic model. An example of this was observed in relation to the former Czechoslovakia, and was indicated as a reason for the "velvet divorce". During the PER Conferences, American government delegates cited the tendency of some MNS to withdraw minority rights after they were instituted as a threat to peace.

Several UN reports[21] attribute the popularity of the civic model for minority protection to the rise of the U.S. as a major power after World War II. This accords with our earlier observation in that most multinational states that were constituted after World War II rhetorically and constitutionally-legally adhere to the civic model.[22] Although this observation supports the power-politic orientation that the models used by the most politically powerful will exercise dominant influence on the policy of other multinational states whether or not the adopted model helps resolve the problematic of achieving SHCSD, past paradigms may, in the present turbulent systemic circumstances[23] be a less valid basis for future predictions.[24] It is particularly noteworthy, therefore, that the OSCE, in its efforts to ensure the harmonious transition of eastern European states from communist systems, has created a High Commissioner for National Minorities, whose mandate is defined, not in terms of advocacy for minority rights, but rather in terms of promotion of peace and social harmony (see Appendix II).

After observing the ongoing global dialogue on minority rights over the past year with particular attention to its ramifications in Canada (Sept. 1995- Sept. 1996), we are of the opinion that the future salience or success of this approach depends on:

1. The maintenance of the spiritual desire and political will to continue the search for a just community, just society and just world by all means necessary, including common sense.

2. The willingness of multinational states to offer politico-legal and constitutional recognition, with appropriate classification and delineation of rights, to their national minorities so as to promote an appropriate form of consociated democracy and equal status development.

3. In regard to Canada, the collective will to reach a political decision to be or not to be (that is, whether to influence the development of North America by creating appropriately independent socio-political policies in step with SHCSD, or to merge into the larger North American milieu without being in a position to significantly influence its socio-economic contours).

4. The successful encouragement of public education (the news media, particularly) to highlight the indispensable role of minority rights in facilitating sustainable human centered societal development and meaningful democracy in multinational states. This will involve promoting the understanding that because humankind is all essentially the same and equal, yet exhibits obvious differences, it is not necessary to have the same culture, values, physical appearance or political ideology in order to be equal. Humans are both different and equal, and have the right to be different and equal; racism, ethnocentrism, ethnocide, ethnic cleansing, genocide, etc., are undesirable by-products resulting essentially from the present subjective requirements for effecting human socio-psychological, political and material developmental needs within the context of a particular stage of development and the politico-socio-economic system presently in place. Therefore, one cannot eliminate negative social relations between groups without altering the processes and structure which causes them, any more than one can eliminate the depletion of the ozone layer without eliminating the manufacturing and production structures and processes which are responsible. Rather, we seek to prevent their ill effects on humans through seeking the socio-economic and political societal changes needed for their termination. This perspective better permits their control, demystification, eventual elimination and better protection of their potential victims through proactive measures such as minority rights. This necessarily includes the exposure of the public, through the use of the mass communications/entertainment and news media, to appropriate positive images of other cultures, which they would be able to positively receive. Sufficiently large sectors of the public must be simultaneously exposed so as to impact on collective norms as they concern the images of the other relevant cultures, and as it relates to strengthening and engaging the collective integrity, social control mechanisms and norms of national minorities in a commitment to mutual responsibility for SHCSD

and the consequent well being, security and political unity of the state.

5. It should be kept in mind that even a general policy recommendation may not apply to each specific group and specific situation. Each situation should be analysed within its own context and in relation to each group concerned. There are obvious situations where a positive and sincere attempt at assimilation (if desirable to all parties concerned) may be preferable to minority rights, if it is desired by neither group concerned. The point is that minority rights is just that: a right that should be implemented where needed and demanded.

6. In relation to *national minorities,* not just reactive but *constructive proactive* governmental and human service policies and delivery practices are required. Policies should make every effort to permit the auto-organization of national minority communities even when such auto-organization may appear unaccepting of certain majority norms, except in cases where such nonacceptance means an unwillingness to recognize the human rights of all parties concerned, including the weaker elements within the minority community. When appropriate to its circumstances, nonacceptance of majority norms, like their acceptance, may denote integrity, sincerity, honesty, courage, intelligence and above all, concern for human dignity and democracy. These are the same characteristics that states need to encourage in their search for SHCSD, national security and unity. Such groups should be engaged as a part of the societal body in a dialogue of economic, political, and social realism.[25] The history of such minorities suggests that to use state power otherwise will eventually lead to dishonest, unintelligent or uncaring individuals being placed in positions crucial to the social development of that minority as well as of the state. Needless to say, this would corrupt the system because it tends to deconstruct the democratic ideal and give priority to the consolidation and centralization of all power, regardless of societal developmental consequences, as well as to hinge governmental authority on ever-increasing societal control through the use of economic coercion and force. If exercised primarily in relation to the power to protect and punish, government becomes reduced to a protection racket.

7. The recognition of international law and the UN is vital to the ability of the state to create good will negotiations in minority-

state conflicts. Not only does this legitimize and facilitate the ability of the minority and the state to compare their positions with global legal standards, but by ostensibly ignoring the difference in power relations between the state and the minority, it provides for minority legal equal status by refusing the monopoly of legal authority by the state. Often it is only through international legal mechanisms that good will negotiations can take place and legal decisions can be mutually seen as just.

8. The political will to restrain free market economics to accommodate human rights. In the 1960s when the advanced states gave up their colonies abroad but maintained their economic orientation, institutions and socio-economic development theories, this led national investment to a greater focus on domestic human and natural resources in order to compete for economic dominance in the global market place which rendered domestic SHCSD secondary if not dysfunctional to capital accumulation for global investment. The net effect has been an increasing geographic equalization of investment for profit maximization, and the result of that, in turn, in what some scholars call the new world order and others view as global neocolonialism, has been cited as instigating the need for reduced social spending, the subjection of democracy to corporate interest, and the gradual deconstruction of the concept of SHCSD itself.

The special problem for national minorities posed by this tendency is the fact that, due to institutionalized discrimination over time, they, along with women and the poor, tend to number disproportionately among the weaker and consequently most vulnerable sectors inside the states in which they live, and are thus most susceptible to the worst aspects of structural adjustment program and its accompanying social policy.

9. The definition of minority, even when one is agreed upon, because of the human subjective factors and the commitment of international law to self-definition and democratic processes, should always be considered provisional. The natural law factors that minority rights are expected to facilitate must, by internal logic, encompass the possibility that a minority might, of its own free will, choose to redefine itself or to cease to exist as a separate nation, ethny or politico-legal identity. This also means that a multinational state's definition must also consequently be viewed as provisional.

In order to stimulate appropriate considerations of the factors mentioned above, perhaps *the most important task* will be that of engaging decision makers and citizens, at all levels and in all relevant areas of society and government, in or exposing them to, the minority rights dialogue in international law. This systemic vantage point will assist them in nurturing a more comprehensive perspective for a more just understanding of the international legal justice problem national minorities pose for SHCSD in multinational states. We hope that this exploration of the minority rights dialogue in international human rights law will contribute to this task.

---

1 For example, a sub-category of political pertinence mentioned during the 30 April-May 3, 1996 UN Working Group on Minorities is involuntary immigrant minorities of the Americas (formerly enslaved minorities) and *dispersed* or *geographically concentrated minorities*. Evidently, depending on whether the national, immigrant or social minority is concentrated in a geographical area where it forms the majority or dispersed throughout the territory of the state will affect its political disposition *vis-à-vis* the state, thus creating differing conditions for a political agreement on the nature of the rights (or lack of same) that can be instituted into law.

2 The world powers that compose the membership of NATO and OSCE are also members of the UN where they influence its human and minority policies through their domination of the Security Council and the sheer magnitude of their military and socio-economic power. Although the UN's involvement with the minority rights problematic is of a much longer duration and of a much broader scope, the members of the OSCE and NATO are usually participants in the major world crises involving minority rights facing the UN and vice-versa.

3 See Chandra Muzaffar, "Human Rights and Hypocrisy in the International Order," *supra*..

4 See John Packer, *supra*..

5 Such as Richard Falk, Yoram Dinstein, Patrick Thornberry, Hurst Hannum, Ian Brownlie, Gudmundur Alfredsson, etc..

6 While the Islamic civilization recognized minorities, in keeping with its religious orientation, it grouped all minorities, for the purpose of recognition, according to their confessional or religious identification. The effect and perhaps purpose of this was to encourage nation formation and identification on the basis of religious belief. No doubt this is a partial reason for the confusion existing in the definition of groups in the Bosnia-Herzegovina region of Eastern Europe where the cultures of Islamic and western civilization overlap — where Slavic groups (Serbs) are defined by ethny, while the Islamic group is defined by religion. Western European civilization, in keeping with its orientation towards the nation-state (a state

for each nation) encouraged identification around the ethnic group or nation, and since each ethnic group or nation was ideally to have a state, then state, nation and ethnic group seemed inextricable.

7 Note that international law does not disapprove of assimilation under appropriate circumstances and conditions largely relating to consent and self-definition of those so concerned. However, where this is not present, it attempts to mediate, though minority rights concepts, those conditions which have lead to natural, exploitative or abusive (non-equal status) assimilation.

8 While the problematic of empires and colonialism is less explored in terms of ethnic domination, modern research on the middle ages and the subsequent period preceding the emergence of the so-called nation-state gives us every reason to believe that lack of official empowerment of ethnic groups and recognition of their special needs, (discrimination against them) may have been one of the chief reasons for the emergence and popularity of the nation-state concept in the 19th century. The fact that the Marxist paradigm of class oppression became the popular progressive approach for the last seven decades, typically ignoring the ethnic interrelational problematic, served only to obscure a festering wound that would become re-inflamed in the late 20th century with volcanic fury to entrap societal development in a merry-go-round of violence, attempts at restorative/ recompensatory justice, backlashes, economic insecurity and increased policing and social controls.

9 Pyotr Dzorzhievich Bokaev, Department of Inter-Ethnic Relations, Council of Ministers, Kalmyk Republic.

10 Bronislav Bronislavovich Zardarnovsky, GOSKOMNATS.

11 Rasma Karklins, University of Illinois at Chicago..

12 Not available.

13 PER Conferences, Moscow, January 20-21, 1995; Washington, D.C., June 13-14, 1995; New York, September 27-28, 1993; Stupava, Czechoslovakia, April 30-May 2, 1992; Bucharest, June 17-18, 1991, *supra.*

14 Asbjorn Eide, UN Doc. E/CN.4/Sub.2/AC.5/1996/WP.2, *supra.* Emphasis added.

15 See the Human Rights Committee decision in the *Lovelace* case.

16 Bin Ch- Eng, "General Principles of the Law in the Concept of Responsibility: The Principle of Individual Responsibility," in *General Principles of Law as applied by International Courts and Tribunals.* London, 1953, pp. 208 ff.

17 Department of Economic Information and Social Policy Analysis, *World Social Situation in the 1990s*, UN Publication, New York, NY 10017, UN Sales No. E.94.IV.4.

18 According to scholars like Alain Minc, power depends increasingly on the control of the mass media, and in order to secure this type of control, internal relations and human needs must be up to standard. See Alain Minc, *supra.*

19 In a system that prevents any one national group or combination of groups from dominating the state apparatus, the use of the term minority to define any one of the national groups concerned appears inappropriate.

20 Note the discussion of the UK in relation to Northern Ireland. See Northern Ireland Discussion Paper 3, The Government of Northern Ireland, Northern Ireland Office HMSO, 1975, pp. 3-27.

21 See the reports of F. Caportorti, Asbjorne Eide, *supra.*

[22] It is well to note that many of these states in Africa and Asia find themselves with constitutions and government minority or civil rights policies that totally elude their social reality. The results are seen in the recent ethnic conflicts in Rwanda, Liberia, Nigeria, Sri Lanka, the 1960s effort to federate the West Indies, etc..

[23] The pace of technological change sharply accelerated during the last two decades. These changes were in three main areas: information technology, biotechnology and material sciences. These changes have affected virtually all aspects of everyday life and are therefore in parallel with the series of changes which brought about the Industrial Revolution some two hundred years ago. See *World Social Situation in the 1990s, supra.*

[24] Quebec's minority right to self-determination referendum policy is an example of how national minority internal demand in a democratic state is able to block external influence over certain state policies regardless of environmental power configurations, even when an ethnic majority accepts those policies. We may observe the recent and present situation of Canada and the U.S., operating as dyads wherein, through the concept of dyatic intensification of relations, the stronger more powerful state is expected to be able to obtain a larger measure of control over, if not dominate, the economic and socio-political policies of the weaker. (This premise is based on normative structural-functional axioms, and assumed to be true whether or not it is assumed to be good or bad for either of the states concerned and whether or not they enjoy friendly relations.) In the late 1970's, the Canadian political scientist C. Clarkson of the University of Toronto expressed this same notion as it relates to Canada and the U.S. as making Canadian policy under the circumstance of " sleeping in bed with an elephant".) Apart from the management of multicultural / multinational mega crises faced by all multinational states caused by the educational, technological and transportation revolutions and the resultant movement of populations to urban centers, Canada is faced with a special identify dilemma which increasingly paralyzes the system dynamic feedback loop between national policy and national demand (and of course needs as represented by demands) in relation to certain issues essential to the Canadian socio-cultural and political identity such as minority rights, independent literature, communications development, trade policies, health care and social welfare policies, etc. This paralysis seems to have reached a stage wherein a systemic breakup or complete merger with the larger North American system could occur. While it is not our intention to speculate on whether such an occurrence in relation to sustainable human centered democratic development would be good or bad, recognizing and deciding to accept or reject this "fusion" or merger should be a first order of the day for Canadian decision makers because without this collective political decision, it will remain increasingly difficult and perhaps eventually impossible to maintain indigenous Canadian socio-cultural and political policies sufficiently distinct from that of the rest of North America as to permit the maintenance of a separate Canadian socio-economic identity, (that is, policies adequately responsive to the Canadian historical, cultural and political circumstances and citizens' needs, as well as those of North America). While either choice, to reject or accept a "fusion," will allow Canada to break the chronic impasse, the choice will alter to a significant

degree the type of socio-economic and political policies available to Canadians. In addition, it will very likely affect the type of minority rights policies available to government for minority-state conflict management.

If due to sufficiently common heritage and sufficiently common socio-political philosophy, Canadians freely acquiesce to fusion, then in international legal terminology, it should be viewed as one of democratic self- determination. However, the problem or paralysis seems to arise from the possibility that there are salient differences between the heritage and socio-economic, etc. ideals and needs of the larger North American system [the majority] and the Canadian minority. If this is the case and an inappropriate socio-economic merger with the larger system is chosen, the consequences must of logical necessity engender minority and socio-economic policies inappropriate for the Canadian situation and circumstances, thus encouraging political dyfunctionality, national disunity, and perhaps a breakup into smaller subnational units. This may mean that the multinational state of Canada, like Czechoslovakia in a democratic system, was unable to adopt the policy influences of a powerful state due to the objection of a national minority. In the Canadian case, similar to that of Czechoslovakia, the systemic causes may be traced to the duality in North American development before and after the Second World War, coupled with the assimilationist demands of the present North American system in conflict with the objective multi-cultural internal demands of the Canadian system, as historically evolved.

After World War II, Canada inherited a socio-political and economic system that favored the structural-functional recognition of national minorities and consociated liberal democracy, while the majority in North America developed a more conservative and race restricted structural-functional democracy under the civic minority protection model, a model that served well to unite the races from Europe that had immigrated to North America and thus permit a less conflictual politico-economic development of North America. In this model, national minorities are given no special recognition; instead the multinational state strives to become a nation-state by assimilating all founding national groups into one nation. In North America, this meant assimilating all of the ethnic or racial groups into the stronger and larger dominant nation. This idea is popularly described as the 'American Dream'. Although the history and circumstances of Canada lend themselves less to the political need for realization of such ideals as it relates to minority rights, Canada's dyaic intense interactions on all levels with the U.S. appears to have influenced the appearance of the practicality, politico-economic advantages, and popularity of the US minority rights civic model in Canada. Of course, the dyadic factors alone did not bring Canada to its political paralysis. Other systemic catalytic factors included the replacement of England by North America as the major world power in competition against the USSR, Canada's geo-military and political defense strategy etc., as well as Britain's post second World War II decision to subordinate its Canadian interest to its special relation agreement with the U.S., in the context of the developing U.S. theory of manifest destiny and the Monroe Doctrine. As Charles de Gaulle implied in his visit to Quebec, the Canadian role in this theory was to become absorbed not only in the American dream but also subsumed into the North American socio-economic, political and cultural umbrella. As this was all to be accomplished gradually though the continual intensification of trade, investment and socio-cultural interchanges, any barrier to these interchanges (whether cultural, socio-economic, or politico-military) would have to be viewed by politicians on both sides of the border as contrary to the interest of both states.

From this perspective, then, the repatriation of the Canadian constitution may be viewed by the French or First Nations as not so much a triumph for Canadian nationalism, but rather a further step in the fulfilment of the post World War II British- U.S. agreement (or as referred to by some French scholars, " the special Anglo-American accord") for Canada's full absorption (including Quebec) into the dominant North American socio-economic and Anglophone cultural milieu. From this vista, the landmarks of Quebec's nationalist concern with constitutional repatriation as well as the CBC's partially successful demands for Canadian governmental protection of Canadian TV and radio programming (an indicator of Canadian nationalism) merge into common jigsaw pieces which one must include in order to construct a systemic picture of the Canadian (social policy <-> North American restraint <-> nationalist input) dynamic.

[25] See Annex A, Norma-Jean Byrd, "Urban First Nations and Self-Government," The Circle Project, Regina, 1996.

ANNEX A

Urban First Nations and Self-Government

Norma-Jean Byrd[1]

The Circle Project in the City of Regina represents a particularly striking instance of what may be regarded as a nation-wide problem posed by urban First Nations people, in the context of the Canadian government's commitment to institutionalize and facilitate the constitutionally-recognized inherent right of Canadian First Nations to self-government.

Originally launched in 1986 in the City of Regina by a group of community leaders, elders[2] and organizations to respond to the situation of numerous groups (low socio-economic people, Métis, urban First Nations people) in the inner city of Regina, and supported initially by the Archdiocese of Regina, which funded one position and overhead costs for project operations in the St. Luke School, the Circle Project received additional support from Indian and Northern Affairs Canada (INAC) for four researchers to investigate and determine program needs of this community. The results of the Indian Affairs-sponsored research were documented and categorized, the program desires of the community determined, and a basic orientation outlined.

When the Circle Project sought to access further funding from INAC, this was blocked by the Federation of Saskatchewan Indian Nations (FSIN), which indicated its desire that all budget resources be devoted to on-reservation projects and needs, and protested the allocation of monies from the INAC budget to off-reserve projects, even when these were primarily used by urban First Nations people. INAC complied with the wishes of FSIN, presumably without alternative, insofar as its legally-institutionalized relationship is with FSIN. As a result, The Circle Project enjoys no official relationship or funding support of any kind with either FSIN or INAC as a First Nations institution in law, though in fact it functions as a First Nations institution by orientation, personnel, and the primary population it serves, and is understood as a First Nations institution in the community.

While the urban First Nations population may represent as much as half of the total of the Canadian aboriginal population, and in Regina is a significant proportion of the city population,[3] it remains in a kind of "no man's land" between the tribal and the federal legal system, provided for by neither, and belonging to neither. Unable to enjoy federal government funding for the purpose of institutional development and cultural protection *as an ethnic / national minority*, in a manner similar to that enjoyed by the French-speaking population outside of Quebec, and as may be their right within the context of international minority rights, the off-reservation First Nations ethnic national minority population has been compelled to seek provisions for programs addressing its needs in a manner similar to other socially disadvantaged groups, such as low socio-economic groups, the handicapped, etc..

Accordingly, rather than functioning as an institution empowered by public sources through constitutional-legally recognized and empowered national minority structures, the Circle Project was incorporated (January, 1988) as a charitable organization under the non-profit corporation Act, receiving support variously from the Archdiocese of Regina, the Secretary of State, Canada Employment and Immigration, the City of Regina, Regina United Way, and the community at large. The institutional document outlining the Circle Project's philosophy and organizational structure describes it as "a native spiritually based organization that uses traditional Indian culture and teachings as a framework within which to offer programs and services to all who request help... [whose] doors are open to all people in the community."

As an institution operating on the basis of First Nations cultural norms, and providing for primarily urban First Nations people[4] while maintaining openness to non-aboriginal persons, the Circle Project might be seen as functioning nonetheless in accordance with the ideal mix (in an international minority rights sense) of ethnic orientation and nondiscrimination for a minority-controlled institutional structure: practicing nondiscrimination in relation to the admission/servicing of individuals from other groups, while maintaining a sense of institutional ethnic identity, and utilizing institutional conceptualizations which are ethnically related, e.g. the concepts of wholism,[5] of life as a journey towards wisdom, of the importance of understanding gained through personal experience over the passage of time (as opposed to academic knowledge), of egalitarian grassroots participation (as opposed to subservience to the dictates of elites or professionals), non-hierarchical mutual aid (as opposed to professional/client relationships), and the unity of socio-economic and spiritual wellness, etc..

One cannot even begin to talk about the Circle Project and the implementation of First Nations cultural orientation without talking about wholism. Wholism as understood, practiced and institutionalized by the Circle Project is so much an organic part of its existence on every level, that to attempt to remove this culturally-based skeleton might well be impossible, without totally supplanting the organization. The intent of the Circle Project is not simply to surround First Nations participants with the physical trappings and regalia of their pre-contact cultures which have been smashed and batttered by the varying efforts of the Canadian government either to segregate or to assimilate the aboriginal population, but much more importantly, *to operationalize for contemporary therapeutic effect,*[6] the social, philosophic and spiritual attitudes and understandings which might be said not only to have existed, in general, among pre-contact cultures, but also are presently functional in First Nations communities today, irrespective of tribe. Within the context of the Circle Project's wholism, the word "therapy" itself requires adjustment, as the connotations adhering to the word through its use by the dominant culture are overladen with dichotomies of "sickness" as opposed to "wellness," of those who are "all right" as opposed to those who "need help," those who are "criminal" as opposed to those who are "law-abiding," etc. According to the philosophy informing Circle Project not only theoretically but functionally, life itself is a journey from the cradle to the grave whose purpose is the acquisition of wisdom, and through wisdom, peace, harmony and appropriate action. No one was born with full understanding, all of us are en route to acquiring this. Some of us have our pathways blocked by more difficult situations than others, frequently due to our "environment," i.e. the situation of those who have impacted our lives in the most intimate way — our families, our peers, our communities — which in turn has been buffeted and molded by the greater world outside, through all the complex of processes generally summarized as "history." Some are further along this road, due to having walked on it longer, or having had fewer barriers along the way. There is no great divide on this journey between the knowledgeable and the incompetent, the good and the bad. We all make mistakes; we all need to learn; we are all on this journey towards understanding and harmony. Our experience, often most effectively through trial, error and recuperation, provides us with an invaluable tool not only for our own personal growth, but for assisting others whom we see as enmeshed in similar circumstances.

The Circle Project's wholistic approach to problem-solving means that it applies the same healing circle paradigm to those problems which might concern the criinal justice system, such as domestic violence or substance abuse, as to those which are usually seen as falling within a "learning" rather than a "therapeutic" focus, such as parenting, women's development, etc.. The view of lived experience (as opposed to academic training) as providing an effective basis for understanding in problem areas allows the Circle Project to use "non-professional" staff as leaders in the healing circles, their credentials being simply that they have personally experienced the problem concerned, have struggled with it, have passed through it, and have thereby come to understand it with an intimacy that can never be paralleled by those who deal with such a problem third hand. The role of circle leader is not as a professional, who somehow functions above and beyond the problem, and is in a role of superiority to the group, but rather as a kindred sufferer, who is further along (or now on) the road to recovery.

In a healing circle, the leader begins the session by passing a rock around the circle. Whoever is in possession of the rock has the right to speak about whatever they may have on their mind, at whatever length they may desire. When they have finished, the rock is passed to the next person, who in turn may speak on whatever subject he/she may desire, at whatever length, referring to the conversation of previous persons only by indicating in passing, say, "I felt like he/she did, too"... and then pass on into their own situation with no further reference to that of others. Other participants listen, but do not counsel or offer parallel experience. Insofar as no reference other than this is to be made to the comments of previous participants, no criticisms or judgments of others' behaviors can be rendered, and this in turn leaves all more free to express themselves. Once the rock has passed around the circle once, it is then sent around a second time, and this time, perhaps those will speak who didn't speak before, or some will elaborate on what they have said earlier. Again, no reference to the comments of others is permitted. The third time the rock goes around, participants talk about their resentments — of the system, of family members, etc. — and on the fourth time it goes around, group members try to think of positive thoughts to express, so that the group ends on a positive note.

The healing circle's apparently simple combination of philosophy and functional technique has complex manifestations, ramifications and uses which could be — and deserve to be — written on at great length. Suffice it to say, for the purposes of this paper, that it creates situations of problem assistance which are *non-hierarchical and nonjudgmental* — which are among the quintessential elements in the greater appeal of Circle Project assistance to the urban First Nations community in Regina over the assistance provided by mainstream (or more accurately put, the dominant culture's) social service agencies. First Nations people come to the Circle Project because they feel more at home here, and this is not simply because they are going to a Project which is primarily staffed by members of their ethnic group (in which case the solution to effective service delivery would simply be the further training and employment of First Nations professionals within the social services), but because they are dealt with *in a way which differs* from the approach customary to the majority community (as evidenced by the social service institutions it has established, which deal with persons of its own ethnicity as well) — a way which not only reflects the communitarian and egalitarian social and spiritual values of First Nations peoples, but which may also have a great deal to teach the majority culture, as it concerns assistance to what is categorized as social maladjustment.

Under the present constitutional-legal and institutional arrangements, however, the Circle Project cannot exercise primary jurisdiction over those who use its services. Patients may be referred from other agencies, or may come voluntarily. While the recommendations of sentencing circles[7] (which in themselves are a form of healing circle) as to treatment of offenders are offered as a form of consultation to the courts, they remain just that: recommendations, which the courts may bring to bear to whatever degree they choose, which may range from ignoring them completely, to instituting them, to then, subsequently, repealing them.[8]

It remains questionable to what extent the Circle Project is able to fully exercise First Nations cultural predominance while remaining financially dependent upon funding from non-First Nations agencies (and therefore forced to be adjudicated by and respond to non-First Nations assessments of project need and project success). As a charitable organization, it endures the hazards and burdens of intermittent funding, rather than the relative security of ongoing support derived from a right (in the sense of a national minority's international-legal special right) to a share of public monies. Government and non-government agencies fund Circle Project programs on a year to year and project to project basis. There is nothing in theory to prevent the termination of this support, and this in turn serves as among the many levers by which the Circle Project is kept under the thumb of other (non-First Nations) groups. A further difficulty as it concerns sentencing circles is acquiring the funding necessary to conduct them, since the uniting of victims, families and community elders usually necessitates travel expenses. These costs, rather than being seen as essential costs as might be the case within a First Nations-determined system, are seen by the dominant majority's system as frills which are nice if they can be afforded, a consultative part — like a character reference — rather than a central and necessary part of the judicial process, simply a factor to be taken account of in the more important sentencing determinations (deciphering what is required by the law) of the judge.

While as yet there are no legally-institutionalized processes concerning the establishment of relationships between the Federal government and those institutions which might be developed for the purposes of self-government by urban First Nations peoples, plainly the manner in which urban First Nations' institutions are forced to function — as dependent upon, and therefore necessarily responsive to, non-Indian supervision — serves to debilitate the full expression of their cultural orientations. Funding agencies and sponsors often require voluminous documentation (numerous pages of reports) on Circle Project programs. Presumably these form the basis by which they judge the effectiveness of Circle Project programs for they have never come over to the Circle Project facility to take a personal look around, and see how things are going, and to assess program success by measures which the Circle Project itself has seen its success demonstrated (i.e. the successful functioning of a hot lunch program, basic education, evening programs for children and youth, etc.). While it cannot be determined to what extent the capacity to respond to their paperwork requirements is equated by these agencies as *symptomatic of capacity to function effectively for the purposes for which the programs were established*, i.e. to change dysfunctional behavior, to help people, to respond to community needs, to provide more effectively for a sector of the community which has evidenced a higher degree of social suffering, etc., it is certain that this means of assessment enforces the processes, attitudes and expectations of the dominant culture upon this First Nations institution.

Indeed, one might question to what extent this very relationship between "donors" and the Circle Project — which is, but cannot be called a First Nations institution — acts to inhibit rather than promote the effective realization of *the Circle Project's vision* of how it should function in relation to that population which forms the bulk of persons it serves — urban First Nations people — and thereby serves in actuality to decrease the effectiveness of the services provided. While it may occur that Circle Project is given the lattitude to pare existing programs as it desires when funding is decreased, it also occurs that funding agencies are empowered to exercise preferential choice in relation to proposed projects, and to allocate funding, by choosing to fund one project over another, or respond to one need over another. This enables funding agencies to prioritize Circle Project programs according to funding agencies' priorities, which may in turn relate to factors which are not directly concerned with the Circle Project itself or its service population, or to its assessment of greatest need.

Further, the funding or donor agencies remain impervious to what is meant by the wholistic orientation of the Circle Project — insofar as this is not just an ephemeral quasi-poetic notion, but an actual structural organizing principle with concommitant requirements — as indicated by their various responses to Circle Project requests which, say, advise Circle Project staff that the Circle Project "cannot be all things to all persons," or when they cannot see why the inclusion of a recreational facility such as a swimming pool might form an essential part of the full functionality of the Project's "therapeutic" mission (by integrating recreation with problem-solving as a normal part of every human's experience, thereby removing the stress caused by feelings of isolation, alienation and abnormality which often accompany and exacerbate dysfunctional behavior, and re-enforcing the notion of a nonjudgmental, friendly and caring environment).

Which approach to serving community needs, particularly those of the urban First Nations population of the City of Regina, should hold sway? That of an institution which reflects that community's cultural traditions and to which the community itself is inclined to turn, or that of the social service sector of the dominant community which to date, as indicated by the disproportionality in numbers of First Nations' people involved with social services and with criminal justice in particular, has been staggeringly ineffective? How fully or effectively can the former operationalize its own unique healing / service potential, so long as it is under the direction and control of the latter? These questions take on greater significance as the ramifications of the response are realized. It will impact upon the vested interests not only of funding agencies ' exercise of varying degrees of control and jurisdisction, and their function as a primary rather than a secondary source of support (as would be the case within a minority rights framework) as far as the urban First Nations population is concerned, but also of the whole apparatus of social services, including not only service administration and delivery but also service training and formation, etc. There are, in short, significant resources involved here — necessarily so when it concerns a group which represents not only a sizeable portion of the civic population, but also a major component of the population "processed" by the social service sector.[9]

The ongoing failure of the mainstream (dominant culture's) social service apparatus to resolve urban First Nations people's disproportionate involvement with its criminal justice system and with other social service agencies responding to socio-economic need and malaise, clearly speaks to the need for an alternative approach for urban First Nations people.

---

[1] Norma-Jean Byrd, at the time of writing of this article, was Director of the Circle Project. The article was edited by Diana G. Collier.

[2] Elders within the community are determined on the basis of their experience and history of active community concern. The process of determining "who is an elder" occurs naturally, within an ebb and flow of self-proposal through participation, and acceptance by the community as such.

[3] While the 1991 census of Canada figures indicate that Regina's aboriginal population is less than 10%, this figure is contested by urban First Nations, who indicate that these statistics were taken prior to the option of ethnic self-identification in the Canadian census. When a similar self-identification was introduced in the American census, the American Indian population increased by some 37% (see Devon A. Mihesuah, *American Indians: Stereotypes & Realities*, Clarity Press, Inc., Atlanta, 1996).

[4] Around 90% of the people served by the Circle Project are urban First Nations people.

[5] We spell "wholism" with a "w" in order to emphasize the notion of the whole, which serves as more than just an abstract philosophic label for the Circle Project's activities, in effect functioning so as to determine in concrete form every aspect of the program, from the nature of physical facilities required in order to properly institute programs, to therapeutic practices, to hiring of personnel and empowering of volunteers. This will be dealt with later in this paper.

[6] See following.

[7] Circle Project staff are in the process of seeking a different terminology to replace "sentencing," used by the dominant system to describe the process of imposing penalties or prison terms on those found to have transgressed the law. Given its connotations of prison terms, punishment, criminality, etc. and the social opprobrium that surrounds these, the term "sentencing" has been found to be laden with punitive dichotomies (criminal, law-abiding; bad, good; anti-social, social) which are contrary to and prevent thoughtful repentence and rehabilitation into the community, notions which underpin First Nations approaches to justice.

[8] See, for instance, the case of the young man from La Ronge, who was sentenced to banishment in a remote cabin for the offense of rape, a sentence which was later repealed on what might be seen as a pretext — that serving such a sentence in a "well-stocked cabin," to use the words of the presiding justice who likely could not have borne the sentence himself, was too lenient a penalty to be satisfactory to womens' groups protesting rape. It is open to contention, however, whether the real intent of the repeal was to rescind this initiative towards First Nations jurisdiction in the justice system.

[9] Population with aboriginal origins: 12,765. Source: *Aboriginal Data: Age and Sex*, Statistics Canada, Catalogue 94-327, 1993. (from 1991 census figures)

ANNEX B

L'intervention en milieu multiethnique

Sylvie Riopelle

Ces quelques pages seront je l'espère porteuses de germes qui feront grandir toutes les multiples facettes de l'intervention en milieu multiethnique. Ces réflections pourraient servir à amorcer des pistes d'interventions et de les approfondir par la suite. Cependant, je n'ai pas la prétention de faire le tour de la question. Je ferais une réflection qui me laisse dans certain cas perplexe et dans d'autres remplie d'espoir, qui me permet de continuer. Voici donc, sans aucune prétention ces quelques-unes des questions que la pratique en milieu multiethnique m'amène à vouloir partager.

Quels sont les critères pour travailler avec des personnes différentes, avec des cultures qui semblent aux antipodes, sans aucun point en commun les unes des autres? Suite à cette question que les gens me posent je leurs demande, "Selon vous, qu'est-ce que ces personnes de différents milieux de différentes cultures, de différents ethnies, aiment?" La connaissance permet-elle de créer des éléments qui permettent à l'intervention de se distancer du milieu multiethnique? Poser cette questions, c'est mettre de l'avant toute la problématique de l'approche, des pratiques en service sociale. Je m'explique, "Est-il nécessaire d'avoir une perception précise, tout à fait rationnelle de la problématique dans laquelle se fera intervention? Est-ce que le fait de connaître la problématique favorise une attitude particulière dans la perception et dans l'approche qu l'on fait avec les personnel du groupe? D'une part, la connaissance permet la distanciation entre la personne qui pratique l'intervention et le groupe qui la reçoit. D'autre part, elle permet aussi cette connaissance, d'uniformiser la pratique en conformité avec les politiques sociales qu'une nation se donne. Ceci semble cohérent à la pratique sociale. Je ne m'attarderai pas plus sur cette remarque qui pourrait faire partie de débat touchant le pratique en service social. Cependant, il m'a semblé important d'en souligner la préoccupation, puisqu'elle permet de faciliter la compréhension de ma réflexion dont la question de base est: "Qu'est-ce qui favorise l'intervention psychosociale en milieu multiethnique?" La prémisse à cette question repose sur le fait que le travail se fait avec des éléments qui sont des humains. C'est pourquoi l'aptitude en intervention humaine repose sur des qualités humaines, sur des types de personnalités qui permettent la création de relation de confiance et sont ouvertes à différentes éventualités pour répondre aux besoins des personnes du groupe et ce tant en milieu homogène qu'hétérogène. Ceci étant dit, il me semble implicite que la connaissance devient un accessoire pouvant faciliter la pratique de l'intervention quoique je ne crois pas qu'elle en soit le facteur déterminant.

J'ai eu à travailler avec des personnes très connaissantes qui' n'étaient pas nécessairement très compétentes lors de l'application de leur connaissances sur le terrain même.

Il faut avoir des traits de caractères spécifiques pour faire de l'intervention en milieu multiethnique. D'une part, le fait d'avoir de l'éxpérience dans plusieurs milieux ayant différentes problématiques et d'autre part d'avoir travaillé avec différents experts, m'a amené à croire que la qualité fondamentale de l'intervenant est celle d'être capable de ne pas porter de jugement ... ne pas juger. La personne qui intervient, devrait comprendre le besoin du groupe selon ce groupe et non en fonction de ce qu'il devrait avoir comme besoin. Cette reconnaissance de leur propre besoin a une incidence positive pour l'établissement d'une relation de confiance. Cette reconnaissance du besoin de part sa l'établissement d'une relation de confiance. Cette reconnaissance de besoin de part sa propre reconnaissance devient le toile sur laquelle se dessinera les bases de la relation de confiance qui est nécessaire dans l'intervention en milieu multiethnique. Ce processus est nécessaire pour donner à l'intervention sa synergie et ainsi de permettre aux personnes du groupe d'entreprendre des démarches et/ou une action qui permettra de répondre au besoin. Une fois enclenché, le processus offrira différentes situations permettant au groupe ou â l'individu de pouvoir se repositionner, d'identifier d'autres besoins et d'entreprendre de nouvelles actions pouvant permettre de répondre au besoin. Ce processus devrait être reconnu implicitement part l'intervenant. Cette reconnaissance renforce le sentiment positif que le groupe à de l'action que lui-même a entrepris. Ce renforcement positif sert à régénérer le "désir" de continuer sa propre prise en charge ou du moins à permettre de prendre conscience que l'action a une incidence sur son propre milieu qu'il soit multiethnique ou autre. Il semble que ce processus devrait être enclenché par les personnes du groupe. Le fait de ne pas porter de judgement de valeur processus de prise en charge. L'une des effets secondaires est de rendre le groupe autonome face à la personnel qui pratique l'intervention sociale. En ce sens, l'intervenant devrait pouvoir offrir différentes possibilités et être en mesure de respecter le choix du groupe et ce même si le choix ne porte pas sur ses solutions proposées. Le simple fait de laisser le groupe choisir a une incidence positive sur la perception de groupe face à sa capacité de pouvoir faire ses propres choix. En quelque sorte, l'un des rôles de l'intervenant est de confirmer l'individu ou le groupe. Il va de soi que le simple fait de reconnaître le besoin et le choix de l'action porte en elle-même le germe de la reconnaissance des capacités du groupe de pouvoir répondre à ses besoins. Cette reconnaissance contribue principalement à redonner la dignité au groupe d'ou l'importance de ne pas porter de jugement. Il m'apparaît que le jugement est porteur de ce double message: "Tu me demandes mon aide alors j'identifie tes besoins, je te trouve tes solutions et je te dis comment et quoi faire au moment où je jugerai opportun que tu le fasses et les personnes du groupe aidé n'ont qu'à exécuter ce que moi j'aurai choisi pour elles. Comment en groupe ou un individu peut-il désirer sa propre prise en charge si on le fait à sa place. Le message indirecte que l'on lui livre en jugeant ses choix est de semer un doute face à ses propres choix et part conséquent de le confirmer dans sa perception d'incompétence. L'effet pervers est aussi très grand puisqu'il crée des liens de dépendance entre le groupe et l'intervenant.

Lorsque l'intervention se fait en milieu multiethnique, le risque d'être confronté avec ses propres valeurs est omniprésent. En ce sens la personne qui intervient se devrait d'avoir un esprit ouvert et une grande curiosité pouvant lui permettre lorsque ses valeurs sont confrontées, de dépasser les frustrations. Cette curiosité permet de dépasser les limites que la frustration peut engendrer.

Parler d'intervention en milieu multiethnique renferme une dimension rarement discuté quoique très présente dans ce milieu pluriculturel. C'est à mon avis une dimension qui contient tellement de facettes et d'impacts sur la pratiqe que je prendrai quelques lignes pour du moins soulever sa dimension. Le contexte du multiethnisme porte en lui-même le double germe soit celui de l'ethnie en soi et soit celui du pluriethnique. Il ya a le groupe ethnique qui porte son propre regard. Il y a les autres qui tout comme elle, porte leurs regards. Cette dimension est généralement dévoilée et acceptée de part et d'autre. Un deuxième élément contextuel est aussi omniprésent. Ce'est celui de l'individu ou du groupe de la "société d'accueille" qui a un perception, une compréhension ou / et une prédisposition même face au milieu multiethnique, à un groupe ethnique en particulier dans lequel une personnel pratique son intervention. C'est en ce sense qu'il lui est rendu permis de faire sa pratique en d'en établir ses paramètres. Quoique rarement discuté, ce questionnement face au contexte, à son intervention, semble implicitement faire partie de l'ensemble contextuel. Cependant, l'information ou / et le questionnement ne se pose pas ou rarement ouvertement face à la perception, aux attentes qu'a le groupe d'une ethnie spécifique face à celle dont provient la pratique de l'intervetion et face aux autre culture qui font parties de l'ensemble du contexte multiethnique. La question étant d'identifier le "comment" est perçu la société d'acceuille par le groupe ethnique dans lequel se pratiquera l'intervention? Cette question est d´licate puisqu'elle signifie pour l'intervenant d'arriver à dépasser cette tapisserie de brume dans laquelle il exerce sa pratique.

Certes ce qui vient d'être dit ci-haut ne sous-tend pas que le connaissance des caractéristiques ethniques soit inutile. Il est important de pouvoir avoir un cadre de références. L'une des façons de l'obtenir se fait par de connaissance de l'ethnie avec laquelle l'intervention se pratiquera. Il me semble que se soit tout aussi important de connaître les similitudes et les différences fondamentales. Ces connaissances permettent d'établir les paramètres du cadre de la pratique de l'intervention. C'est par ces connaissances qu'on dessine et transmet le cadre de la pratique. Ceci engendre l'uniformisation de l'intervention en milieu multhethnique et l'établissement de règles pour son application. C'est part la transmission de connaissances et par l'application de l'intervention, que les bases du contrôle de la pratique de l'intervention en milieu pluriethnique se façonnent et se transmettent. L'apprentissage des connaissances ethniques sert de canevas à sa pratique et de façon implicite, à son controle. Cependeant, ce processus ne parvient pas à faire de la pratique en milieu multiethnique une réussite. Une des posite de la réponse pourrait se trouver dans cet "éspace-temps" qui permet aux personnes du groupes de se faire une idée, une représentation de la société d'accueille, de se créer des attentes pour répondre à leurs besoins. Je pose cette questions naît de la première: "Quels sont les facteurs qui permettront aux critères ayant servis à établir la grille de besoins, de s'adapter à ceux pour qui se pratique l'intervention?" Cette dimension n'est pas encore discuté lorsque l'on examine la pratique de l'intervention en milieu multiethnique pour moi, l'exception de cette situation se retrouve dans l'approche de contrôle et de représentant de Pouvoir de l'intervention sociale. C'est comme si la pratique de l'intervention sociale devenait le reflet, le micro-système qui régit les lois, les politiques, la nation.

Cette explication n'est pas stérile en soi puisqu'elle renferme des pistes concernant l'étude des besoins des différentes enthnies en fonction du pays d'origine versus la société d'accueille. Que connaissent ces personnes de leur société à leur arrivé? Ces mêmes personne sont-elles prêtent à modifier quoique se soit de leurs coutumes, de leurs habitudes? Si oui, ces modifications impliquent quoi? Sinon, quels en sont les principales conséquences pour la pratique de l'intervention en milieu multiethnique? Il est tabou de poser ces questions. Peut-être que ces questions veulent rester sans réponse, puisqu'elles questionnent tant la pratique que les lois que les politiques. Ce questionnement peut avoir un impact positif dans le cadre d'une pratique dans un système démocratique. Il me semble intrinsèque à ces questions dêtre porteuses de principes démocratiques. Cette réflexion renforce ma prémisse de départ qui émet que l'intervention repose sur des qualités humaines. Cette prémisse sous-tend par conséquent que ces mêmes qualités peuvent être acceptées ou refusées selon le système dans laquelle se pratique l'intervention. C'est comme si le type de personnalité qui pratique l'intervention en milieu multiethnique devait être porteur des idées du système dans lequel se pratique l'intervention, ou du moins en devient un des transmetteurs. Il est facile de vérifier ce que vient d'être mentionné. Elles se fait par l'étude de l'évolution de pratiques en intervention sociale. Elles se modifaient au fur et à mesure qu'il y avait transformations tant de l'Appareil d'Etat que de l'Appareil Clérical. Des modifications voient le jour selon la pace et le rôle que l'on donnait à la pauvreté.

Cependant il y a des transormations qui viennent modifier tant la forme que le rôle de la pauvreté, et qui affectent aussi son image. Un des nombreaux impacts est de rendre encore plus difficile la pratique de l'intervention et ce tant en milieu multiethnique que dans une culture homogène. D'une part il est de plus en plus difficile d'identifier la pauvreté et d'autre part, elle se manifest différemment selon la culture d'origine et le degré de développement de la société. Le phénomène est de plus en plus complexe et nécessite aussi, de plus en plus de polyvalance de la part de la personne qui pratique l'intervention. Cependant, de part son ouverture d'esprit et sa curiosité, la personnel devrait être en mesure de parfaire ses connaissances et de pouvoir adapter sa pratique aux réalités du milieu. C'est important de ce questionner et de trouver des réponses à des questions comme: "Comment est évalué, perçue la culture d'origine du groupe avec lequel je fais l'intervention? Si les personnes de ce groupe avaient à évaluer sa société d'origine et sa société d'accueille, sur une échelle de 1 à 10 quel ciffre accorderaient-ils pour chacune d'entre elles? Que pensent ces gens de ce groupe des autres groupes ethnique qui les entourent? Ces questions quoique fort intéressantes et fort utiles dans la pratique, ne font pas encore partie des notions théoriques lors de l'apprentissage de l'intervention en milieu multiethnique.

Un autre aspect me semble fondamentale. Elle concerne notre fin de siècle et les transformations qui en découlent. En ce sense devrions-nous maintenir les mêmes formes d'interventions? Cette fin de siècle serait-elle un des moments propices à la remise en question, à l'approfondissament des pratiques en intervention psychosociale?

Il va s'en dire que l'intervention en milieu multiethnique se pratique depuis plusieurs décennies. Cependant depuis au moins les dix dernières années, un "flottement" semble s'intaller. J'attribue ce flottement à de nombreuses causes.

Je ne les explorerai pas toutes puisque ce n'est pas le but de ce texte. J'en retiens deux qui me sont apparues prédominantes. La première repose sur le fait que les personnes, les groupes n'immigrent plus pour les mêmes raisons qu'il y a dix ans. La seconde concerne la circulation de l'information. Elle est plus rapide et plus accessible. Conséquemment, elle influence la perception des cultures, des nations. Ces phénomènes interfèrent dans la pratique de l'intervention psychosociale qu'on le reconnaise ou pas.

Ces éléments ci-haut mentionnés augmentent les facteurs inconnus que l'on rencontre dans la pratique en milieu multiethnique. Ce qui revient à accroître l'impondérabilité et part ricochet l'imprévisibilité des résultats. La pratique en milieu multiethnique est de plus en plus complexe. Les variables inconnues pour établir un grille d'intervention, sont de plus en plus présentes et en affectent la pratique. C'est en ce sens, que le risque de manifestation d'effet pervers a augmenté.

Maintenant il me faut terminer cette réflexion. L'intervention en milieu multiethnique dépasse de beaucoup le context du lieu de son intevention, de sa pratique. Les raisons qui ont amené à immigrer, le degré de développement de la société d'origine, l'information qu'a reçu la personne de sa société d'accueille. Les connaissances de la personne qui pratique l'intervention, ses information qu'elle a du milieu dans lequel elle pratique et tout le jeu d'attentes rendent la pratique en milieu multiethnique très complexe et demande des qualités humaines comme l'ouverture d'esprit, la tolérance, de ne pas porter de jugement de valeurs et cette curiosité qui permet d'aller plus oin que le confort des acquis. Ces acquis qui sont illusoires bien qu'ils permettent de se sécuriser dans la pratique. Il y a des interférences entre la pratique de l'intervention et ce que se passe à cette fin de siècle. Il devrait pouvoir y avoir un lieu, un temps qui permettraient de connaître les attentes des personnes du groupe d'une ethnie face à sa terre d'acceuille. Il devrait aussi avoir un "espace temps" qui permettrait d'échanger et de connaître les aspirations une fois intégré dans cette nouvelle société. La pratique devrait prendre en considération les acquis d'un groups dans le but de les adaptés ou de les appliqués. La pratique en milieu multiethnique comme dans d'autre milieux, touchent certain problèmatiques qui sont perçues différemment selon la culture d'origine. C'est une des raisons qui expliquent la complexité de l'intervention. Ceci signifie que si l'on perçoit différemment la problématique un des effet est que nous pouvons tantôt créer le problème et tantôt applique une pratique qui n'a aucun impact réel ou que des effets pervers.

Est-ce faire une erreur d'aborder un contexte par le problème? Ce processus est-il l'intervention de la problématique sans pour autant avoir pratiqué une intervention dans un milieu selon sa spécificité qui est vécue et perçue par les personnes du groupe. Cette façon d'intervenir me semble rigide puisqu'elle apparait être que l'application de connaissances et de diverse techniques sans pour autant les avoir adaptées aux réalités du milieu. Des recettes toutes faites existent mais ne mènent pas nécessairment là où elles le devraient. Il y a des facteurs impondérables certes, mail il y a aussi le manque de flexibilité et de souplesse dans la pratique qui nous font devenir des "Don Quichot".

Cette conclusion ou moins je l'espère permettra de poursuivre le questionnement de ce texte et de l'approfondir pour en arriver à donner des éléments de réponse puvant tant faciliter que rendre plus efficace la pratique de l'intervention psychosociale en milieu multiethnique.

APPENDIX I

International Instruments for Minority Protection*

A. UN normative instruments dealing directly with the rights of persons belonging to national minorities

1. The International Covenant on Civil and Political Rights

Though the protection of minorities was not recognized in United Nations normative instruments, the rights of persons belonging to minorities are mentioned by several of them. The International Covenant on Civil and Political Rights accepted by the United Nations General Assembly in 1966 is of particular importance in this context as its Article 27 states:

> In those States in which ethnic, religious or linguistic minorities exist, persons belonging to such minorities should not be denied the right, in community with the other members of their group, to enjoy their own culture, to profess and practise their own religion, or to use their own language.

This provision gives, if the conditions foreseen by the Optional Protocol of the *International Covenant on Civil and Political Rights* are fulfilled, the possibility of individuals to present communications to the Human Rights Committee concerning the violation of their rights. The implementation of Article 27 is also verified through the reporting system.

2. The Convention on the Rights of the Child

Article 27, with small alterations, was incorporated in the *Convention on the Rights of the Child*[4] which, in its Article 30, stipulates: "In those States in which ethnic, religious or linguistic minorities or persons of indigenous origins exist, a child belonging to such a minority or who is indigenous shall not be denied the right, in community with other members of his or her group, to enjoy his or her own culture, to profess and practise his or her own religion, or to use his or her own language".

The implementation of this provision is subject to the verification procedure based on reports presented to the Committee on the Rights of the Child.

---

*Excerpt from John Packer and Kristian Mytti, eds., *Ethnic and Linguistic Minorities in Europe*, Abo Akademi University, Finland, 1993

3. *The Declaration on the Rights of Persons Belonging to National or Ethnic, Religious and Linguistic Minorities*

On 18 December 1992, the General Assembly by its resolution 47/135 adopted the *Declaration on the Rights of Persons Belonging to National or Ethnic, Religious and Linguistic Minorities.* Thus the work which had been started by the Commission on Human Rights in 1978 by the establishment of a working group came to a successful conclusion. The Declaration formulates the obligation of States to protect the existence and identity of minorities within their respective territories.

Among rights of persons belonging to minorities it lists: the right to enjoy their own culture; to profess and practise their own religion; to use their own language; to participate effectively in cultural, religious, social, economic and public life, as well as in the decision-making process concerning the minority to which they belong; to establish and monitor their own associations; to establish and maintain without any discrimination, free and peaceful contacts with other members of their group or other citizens of other States to whom they are related by national or ethnic, religious or linguistic ties. To eliminate any misinterpretation, it *expressis verbis* provides that nothing in its text may be construed as permitting any activity contrary to the purposes and principles of the United Nations, including sovereign equality, territorial integrity and political independence of states.

The Declaration foresees a number of measures to be taken by States to ensure that persons belonging to national minorities may exercise fully and effectively all their human rights; to enable them to express their characteristics and to develop their culture, language, religion, traditions and customs, *except where specific practices are in violation of national law and contrary to international standards;* to create for them adequate opportunities to learn their mother tongue. States should, where appropriate, take measures to encourage knowledge of the history, traditions, language and culture of the minorities existing within their territory and enable persons belonging to national minorities to participate fully in economic progress and development in their country. Critics of the Declaration point out that it has no control procedure; lacks a definition of minorities; that States obligations from a legal point of view are circumspect, as linguistic and educational measures should be taken only "wherever possible", that States should only "consider appropriate measures" to enable persons belonging to national minorities to participate fully in economic progress and development. It is also noted that there is no reference to the case of minority languages before public authorities.

Despite this justified criticism, the importance of the *Declaration on the Rights of Persons Belonging to National or Ethic, Religious and Linguistic Minorities* can hardly be overestimated. No doubt, it is the first comprehensive, universal standard-setting instrument dealing with the rights of persons belonging to minorities and will influence the State practice and national legislation.

4. *The Vienna Declaration and Programme of Action of the World Conference on Human Rights (Vienna, June 1993)*

The Vienna Declaration and Programme of Action adopted on 25 June 1993 by the World Conference on Human Rights[5] called on the Commission on Human Rights to examine ways and means to promote and protect effectively the rights of persons belonging to minorities as set out in the *Declaration on* the

Rights of Persons Belonging to National or Ethnic, Religious and Linguistic Minorities. It urges states and the international community to promote and protect the rights of persons belonging to minorities. Measures to be taken should include facilitation of their full participation in all aspects of the political, economic, social, religious and cultural life of society and in the economic progress and development in their country.

In paragraph 19 of the Vienna Declaration and Programme of Action, the World Conference on Human Rights underlined that the promotion and protection of the rights of persons belonging to minorities contributes: "... to the political and social stability of the States in which such persons live". It confirms once again that persons belonging to minorities "... have the right to enjoy their own culture, to profess and practise their own religion and to use their own language in private and in public, freely and without interference or any form of discrimination.

5. Other UN normative instruments

Several United Nations instruments, though they do not speak expressly about the rights of persons belonging to minorities, have a direct bearing on the guarantee of non-discrimination and equality of treatment.

The *Universal Declaration of Human Rights* (1948) did not mention the "protection of minorities", though, during the debate, proposals in this respect were presented. They were rejected because of a fear that they might create incentives for separatist tendencies and movements. In consequence, the Universal Declaration contains only general clauses prohibiting discrimination. Article 2 declares: "Everyone is entitled to all rights and freedoms set forth in this Declaration, without distinction of any kind, such as race, colour, sex, language, religion, political or other opinion, national or social origin, property, birth or other status".

Other United Nations instructions which can be mentioned in this context are:

- *Convention on the Prevention and Punishment of the Crime of Genocide*[6];
- *International Convention on the Elimination of All Forms of Racial Discrimination*[7];
- *Convention on the Elimination of All Forms of Discrimination against Women*[8];
- *Declaration on the Elimination of All Forms of Intolerance and of Discrimination based on Religion or Belief*[9].

B. The UNESCO normative instruments concerning the rights of persons belonging to minorities

1. The UNESCO Convention Against Discrimination in Education (1960)

The first international convention adopted after 1945 which contains provisions *expressis verbis* relating to the rights of persons belonging to minorities is the *UNESCO Convention against Discrimination in Education*[10]. The States Parties to the Convention agreed in Article 5, point 1c:

> It is essential to recognize the right of members of national minorities to carry on their own educational activities, including the maintenance of schools and, depending on the educational policy of each state, the use of the teaching of their own language, provided however:
>
> (i) that this right is not exercised in a manner which prevents the members of these minorities from understanding the culture and language of the

community as a whole and from participating in its activities, or which prejudices national sovereignty;

(ii) that the standard of education is not lower than the general standard laid down or approved by the competent authorities; and

(iii) that attendance at such schools is optional.

The Convention imposed in Article 7 on States Parties an obligation to give, in periodic reports submitted to the General Conference, information on the legislative and administrative provisions which they have adopted and any other action which they have taken for its application.

2. The Resolution of the World Conference on Cultural Policies (1982)

The World Conference on Cultural Policies convened by UNESCO in 1982 in Mexico City[11] adopted resolution 146: Cultural cooperation and protection of the rights of persons belonging to minorities, which:

> 1. Recommends that Member States take active and appropriate measures to give effect to the rights set forth in Article 27 of the International Covenant on Civil and Political Rights;
>
> 2. Recommends that UNESCO base international cultural cooperation on, amongst other things, the fundamental principles of the protection of the rights of persons belonging to minorities and on genuine respect for the cultures, religions and languages of ethnic, religious and linguistic minorities.

3. UNESCO Declarations

It is worth noting that, among UNESCO Declarations, two are of a special importance for the recognition of rights of persons belong to minorities: the *Declaration on Race and Racial Prejudice*[12] which provides that: "All individuals and groups have the right to be different, to consider themselves as different and to be regarded as such", and the *Declaration of the Principles of International Cultural Co-operation*[13] stipulating that:

> 1. Each culture has a dignity and value which must be respected and preserved.
>
> 2. Every people has the right and duty to develop its culture.

II.

STANDARDS CONCERNING THE PROTECTION OF RIGHTS OF PERSONS BELONGING TO NATIONAL MINORITIES AND RIGHTS OF MINORITIES IN EUROPEAN INSTRUMENTS

A. Standard-setting instruments adopted by the CSCE

1. The Helsinki Final Act (1975)

The Final Act of the CSCE adopted in Helsinki[14] mentioned the rights of persons belonging to minorities. Principle VII: Respect for human rights and fundamental freedoms, including the freedom of thought, conscience, religion or belief proclaimed: "The participating States on whose territory national minorities exist will respect the right of persons belonging to such minorities to equality before the law, will afford the full opportunity for the actual enjoyment of human rights and fundamental freedoms and will, in this manner, protect their legitimate interests in this sphere".

This formulation was in line with the concept still prevailing in the 1970s that the elimination of any discrimination, guarantees of equality before the law, and the full enjoyment of human rights and fundamental freedoms satisfies all claims that persons belonging to minorities may present. The stipulation of the *Final Act* was limited in its scope as only the existence of national minorities was taken into account. Indirectly, Principle VII confirmed also the rights of persons belonging to religious minorities, providing that the participating States "... will recognize and respect the freedom for the individual to profess and practise, along or *in community with others*, religion or belief" . No doubt, the very fact that at the outset of the CSCE process, minority rights were put on the European agenda by all thirty-five participating Sates, without any objection, should be seen as an important, though from the substantive point of view, rather a modest step forward.

2. The Vienna Concluding Document

During the Vienna follow-up meeting,[15] the questions linked with the protection of minority rights were discussed within the framework of the first and third baskets. In a new, much improved, international atmosphere, the meeting made substantive, qualitative progress in the protection of human rights and fundamental freedoms. This new approach was also reflected in stipulations concerning minorities.

The participants agreed to refrain from any discrimination and to take all necessary legislative, administrative, judicial and other measures and apply all binding international instruments to ensure the protection of human rights and fundamental freedoms of persons belonging to national minorities. The *Vienna Concluding Document* did not limit itself to the obligation to guarantee them full equality with others but went further, imposing on participating States in Paragraph 19 the duty to "(...) create conditions for the promotion of the ethnic, cultural, linguistic and religious identity of national minorities on their territory". Thus, for the first time in the CSCE process, the positive commitment to preserve the rights of minorities — their ethnic, cultural, linguistic and religious identity — was recognized. Though Paragraph 19 does not contain any specific indications how these "conditions" should be understood and interpreted, nevertheless in part "Co-operation in humanitarian and other fields", the *Vienna Concluding Document* stipulates that persons belonging to national minorities can establish and maintain contacts through travel and other means of communication "including contacts with citizens of other States with whom they share a common national origin or cultural heritage".

3. The Copenhagen Document of the CSCE Meeting on the Human Dimension (1990)

The second meeting of the Conference on the Human Dimension, lasting from 5 to 29 June 1990, was preceded by a discussion and exchange of ideas, with proposals and documents coming from States and international non-governmental organizations.

The Copenhagen meeting was for some Central and Eastern European countries, a convenient forum to demonstrate and articulate their new positive approach to minority rights. This, as well as dangers linked with the revival of nationalist and, in some cases, even chauvinist resentments in parts of Central and Eastern Europe gave a special importance to the negotiations conducted in Copenhagen by the Working Group on Minorities. The result of these negotiations, paragraphs 30-39 of the Concluding Document[16], have to be qualified, despite their shortcomings, as the opening of a new phase in the protection of minorities within the framework of the CSCE process.

This new approach to the protection of minorities finds its expression not only in a detailed enumeration of rights but also in a general assumption formulated in paragraph 30 of the document that as questions concerning national minorities are essential factors for peace, justice, stability and democracy, they can only be solved within the frameworks of democratic policies based on the existence of a state of law, effective judicial control of government, pluralism and tolerance. The participating States recognized that non-governmental organizations (parties, trade unions, organizations of human rights and religious groupings) play an important role in the promotion of tolerance, cultural diversity and solution of procedures concerning national minorities.

The Concluding Document, in confirming the principle of nondiscrimination and equality, listed specific rights of persons belonging to national minorities:

> ... to use freely their mother tongue in private as well as in public:
>
> - to establish and maintain their own educational, cultural and religious institutions, organizations or associations, which can seek voluntary financial and other contributions as well as public assistance, in conformity with national legislation;
>
> - to profess and practise their religion, including the acquisition, possession and use of religious materials, and to conduct religious educational activities in their mother tongue;
>
> - to establish and maintain unimpeded contacts among themselves within their country as well as contacts across frontiers with citizens of other States with whom they share a common ethnic or national origin, cultural heritage or religious beliefs;
>
> - to disseminate, have access to and exchange information in their mother tongue;
>
> - to establish and maintain organizations or associations within their country and to participate in international non-governmental organizations.

Participating States agreed not only to protect the ethnic, cultural, linguistic and religious identity of national minorities but also to create conditions for this protection. For this purpose, necessary measures will be undertaken after appropriate consultations, in particular with minority organizations or associations.

Among means to promote identity, the Copenhagen meeting mentioned the organization of local administration or autonomy corresponding to the historical and territorial specificity of minorities, as well as the possibility to learn or to be educated in their mother tongue, and to use it, when possible and necessary, in relations with public authorities. The participants underlined the need to improve constructive cooperation among the nations involved in the CSCE process to encourage mutual understanding, confidence, friendly relations, peace, security and international justice. They agreed to favour the creation of a propitious climate for cooperation and solidarity among their citizens and to search for solutions to existing problems by dialogue.

The Concluding Document stressed that none of its provisions concerning the protection of minorities can be interpreted as justifying any action in contradiction with the aims and principles of the UN Charter and other obligations prescribed by international law and the *Helsinki Final Act*, including the principle of territorial integrity.

4. The 1990 Charter of Paris

The *Charter of Paris* adopted by the heads of states or governments at the CSCE Summit meeting on 21 November 1990[17], declares that friendly relations among peoples, as well as peace, justice, stability and democracy in Europe require that the ethnic, cultural, linguistic and religious identity of national minorities be protected, and conditions for the promotion of that identity be created. The Summit also stressed that questions related to national minorities can only be satisfactorily resolved in a democratic political framework.

The Summit Meeting decided that the meeting of experts on national minorities would take place in Geneva in July 1991 with the objective of increasing international cooperation as well as creating conditions for the better protection of national minorities.

5. The Final Report of the CSCE Meeting of Experts on National Minorities

The meeting which took place in Geneva from 1 to 19 July 1991 adopted a Final Report[18] which, in eight parts, presents the results of the thorough discussion on the issues of national minorities and of the rights of persons belonging to them.

It declares that the observance and full exercise of human rights and fundamental freedoms, *including those of persons belonging to national minorities*, are the foundation of the New Europe.

The representatives of the participating States reaffirmed that friendly relations among their peoples, as well as peace, justice, stability and democracy, require that the ethnic, cultural, linguistic and religious identity of national minorities be protected, and that conditions to the promotion of that identity be created. They recognized that the questions relating to national minorities can only be satisfactorily resolved in a democratic political framework based on the rule of law, with a functioning independent judiciary.

Aware of the diversity of situations and constitutional systems in their countries, participating States recognized that various approaches to the implementation of CSCE commitments regarding national minorities are appropriate.

In this context, underlining that the diverse and varying constitutional systems among them make no single approach generally applicable, they noted the positive results obtained by some of them in an appropriate democratic manner by, *inter alia*, advisory and decision-making bodies in which minorities are represented; elected bodies and assemblies on national minority affairs; local and autonomous administration; self-determination by a national minority; decentralized or local forms of government; bilateral and multilateral agreements; erection of special educational institutions; funding the teaching of minority languages to the general public; creation of governmental research agencies to review legislation and disseminate information; provision of financial and technical assistance to persons belonging to national minorities who wish to exercise their right to establish and maintain their own educational, cultural and religious institutions, organizations and associations; the establishment of permanent mixed commissions either inter-state or regional to facilitate dialogue between the neighbouring countries concerned.

Recognizing the fundamental importance of the principles of equality and nondiscrimination, the Report lists among the rights of persons belonging to national minorities: the right to effective participation in public affairs; economic activities and building of their societies; the right to freely express, preserve and develop their ethnic, cultural, linguistic or religious identity and to maintain and develop their culture in all its aspects, free from any attempts at assimilation against their will; the right to the preservation of the cultural heritage; the right to establish and maintain organizations and associations; the right to establish and maintain their own educational, cultural and religious institutions; the right to information and exchange of ideas without interference by public authorities and regardless of frontiers.

The Geneva meeting also reconfirmed the importance of adopting, when necessary, *specific measures* for the purpose of ensuring equality with other citizens in the exercise and enjoyment of human rights and fundamental freedoms to persons belonging to national minorities.

6. The character of the commitments foreseen by the CSCE documents

The CSCE standard-setting instruments cannot be qualified technically as international treaties, for they are in fact political decisions adopted by consensus. Nevertheless, they are recognized by all participants as binding and as having legal consequences.

In the discussions concerning this question, a number of views were tabled:

- the CSCE instruments incorporate decisions of a differentiated legal character, among them principles which are binding in international law;
- they may *mutatis mutandis* be treated as decisions of an international organization;
- they systematize and spell out political norms of differing but essential legal importancewhich reinforce existing international legal rules or contribute to their development.

Putting aside the scholastic debate concerning the political or legal character of CSCE documents, one has to acknowledge that in determining State practice concerning human rights, these instruments can lead to the creation of regional customary norms and, therefore, they may be seen as means of the progressive development of regional international law.

In the discussion concerning the character or rather the legal consequences of the commitments adopted by the participating States, two additional elements should be taken into account: the terms in which these commitments are formulated and the existence of procedures which can be used in the case of their violation.

The analysis of texts allows us to observe that, in some cases, the formulations impose strict obligations, whereas in others the margin for interpretation is rather broad and there is in fact an absence of an intention to create an obligation. Thus, for example, the provision: "the participating States note the efforts undertaken to protect and create conditions for the promotion of the ethnic, cultural, linguistic and religious identity of certain national minorities by establishing as one of the possible means to achieve these aims, appropriate local or autonomous administrations corresponding to the specific historical and territorial circumstances of such minorities and in accordance with the policy of the State concerned"[19], cannot be interpreted as creating an obligation.

It is worth noting that the Vienna follow-up meeting introduced an obligatory supervisory mechanism for the human dimension of the CSCE. This mechanism comprises four stages. First, participating States have the right to exchange and request information on questions relating to the Human Dimension of the CSCE. Second, they may hold bilateral meetings with other States in order to examine questions in this area, including situations and specific cases, with a view to resolving them. Third, they may bring situations and cases to the attention of their States through diplomatic channels and, fourth, they may provide information on the responses to their requests, on the results of bilateral meetings, as well as present information on situations and specific cases at the meetings on the Conference on the Human Dimension of the CSCE and of the main follow-up meetings.

The participating States have decided that the Conference on the Human Dimension of the CSCE will review the implementation of the relevant CSCE commitments, evaluate the functioning of the procedures of the supervisory mechanism and consider practical proposals for new measures aimed at improving the implementation of the commitments relating to the Human Dimension of the CSCE.

The Moscow Conference on the Human Dimension (September 1991) further developed the CSCE human dimension mechanism providing that CSCE missions and CSCE rapporteurs can be sent to participating States in cases of conflicts related to the human dimension. In the case of a particularly serious threat to the fulfilment of the provisions of the CSCE human dimension, a commission or a rapporteur can also be sent to a country against its will, if at least ten participating States support such a measure. The Vienna and Moscow mechanisms can be also applied in cases involving national minority issues as they belong to the human dimension of the CSCE. To eliminate any doubt on this question, the Moscow Document[20] confirms the provisions and commitments of the Copenhagen and Geneva Documents and calls for "... their full and early implementation". The participating States also expressed their belief that "... the use of the new and expanded CSCE mechanisms and procedures will contribute to further protection and promotion of the rights of persons belonging to national minorities".

In 1992, during the CSCE follow-up meeting in Helsinki, a decision was taken to nominate a High Commissioner on National Minorities[21]. The High Commissioner has no competence to adjudicate but only to provide "early warning" and as appropriate "early actions" at the earliest possible stage in regard to tensions involving national minority issues which have, in his opinion, the potential to develop into a conflict within the CSCE area, affecting peace, stability or relations between participating States. The post of High Commissioner on National Minorities (Mr Max van der Stöel was appointed as High Commissioner) has therefore to be seen as an important institution for the monitoring of developments and situations of minorities in Europe.

7. Bilateral treaties concluded by the CSCE participating States

Bilateral treaties on friendship and cooperation or on good neighbourliness, friendly relations and cooperation concluded by Central and Eastern European countries in the recent years contain as a rule provisions concerning the protection of the rights of national minorities and persons belonging to national minorities.

Thus Poland alone in 1991-1993 concluded treaties with: Federal Republic of Germany (17 June 1991); Czechoslovakia (6 October 1991); Hungary (6 October 1991); Ukraine (18 May 1992); Russian Federation (22 May 1992); Belarus (23 June 1992); Latvia (2 July 1992); Estonia (2 July 1992); Romania (25 January 1993) and Lithuania (26 April 1992).

In these agreements, signatories declare their intention to respect rights and fulfil obligations concerning minorities in accordance with international standards, as formulated by international conventions and other documents concerning minorities. Special importance is attached to standards formulated by the CSCE instruments, in particular the *Copenhagen Document* as well as the *Helsinki Final Act* and the *Paris Charter.*

All treaties recognize as members of minorities only citizens of their respective countries which means that their provisions do not apply to immigrants. The signatories confirm their obligation to protect and promote the ethnic, cultural, linguistic and religious identity of minorities. Among positive rights of persons belonging to national minorities, treaties list the use of their mother language in private and public life as well as in contacts with administrative authorities (in accordance with national laws: the right to access to information and education in their mother tongue; the right to set up institutions, associations and economic, educational, cultural and religious organizations. Some agreements also add the right to use names in the mother language , the right to have free and unimpeded contacts within the country and across borders.

In some cases, treaties underline the necessity to learn the official language of the country by persons belonging to national minorities. The treaty with Lithuania prohibits expressly the forced assimilation and deliberate demographic changes of the regions in which national minorities are settled.

Treaties formulate the obligation of loyalty of persons belonging to national minorities towards the country of their citizenship. The possibility of the interpretation of these provisions contrary to the purposes and principles of the United Nations as well as to obligations formulated by the *Helsinki Final Act,* including the principle of territorial integrity, is expressly excluded.

B. The standard-setting instruments of the Council of Europe

The importance of the minority problem was unanimously recognized by the Commission on Legal and Administrative Affairs of the Consultative Assembly already in 1949. The *European Convention on Human Rights* (1950) contains in its Article 14 a general nondiscriminatory clause which provides that the enjoyment of the rights and freedoms recognized by the Convention must be secured without any distinction based, *inter alia,* on association with a national minority. This situation led to a discussion concerning the way in which positive rights of minorities might be formulated. In 1961 the Assembly adopted Recommendation 285 inviting the Committee of Ministers to include in the second additional protocol to the *European Convention on Human Rights* an article designed to guarantee certain rights to national minorities.

Due to an unfavourable opinion from the Committee of Experts appointed for this purpose, the Committee of Ministers in 1973 refused to take any further action on this proposal. The Parliamentary Assembly in its Recommendation 1134 (1990) on the rights of minorities recommended that the Committee of Ministers draw up a protocol to the European Convention or a Special Convention to protect the rights of minorities.

1. The Draft of a European Convention for the Protection of Minorities

In May 1990, the European Commission for Democracy through Law started to examine the problem of the protection of minorities in Europe. It agreed on a number of principles which apply to national minorities. The Commission expressed the view that the drawing up of a binding European legal instrument would offer, in the long run, the best solution to these problems.

The draft,[22] apart from general principles, lists rights of minorities and persons belonging to a minority, obligations of States and obligations of minorities. It recognizes the collective rights of minorities "... to the respect, safeguard and development of their ethnic, religious, cultural and linguistic identity" and "... to be protected against any activity capable of threatening their existence". Furthermore, it stresses that, whenever the minority reaches a high percentage of the population of a region or of the total population, its members should have the right to communicate orally and in writing in their own languages to the authorities of the region or the State. In State schools, obligatory schooling should be given in the mother tongue of the pupils belonging to a minority. The States are obliged to refrain from pursuing or encouraging policies aimed at the assimilation of minorities or aimed at modifying intentionally the proportions of populations in regions inhabited by minorities. On the other hand, persons belonging to a minority should fulfil loyally their obligations resulting from their status as nationals of a State.

The draft underlines that the international protection of minorities does not permit any activity which is contrary to the fundamental principles of international law and, in particular, to the sovereignty, territorial integrity and political independence of States. It also gives a definition of minority[23] and foresees the possibility of establishing a European mechanism for the protection of the rights of minorities.

The Parliamentary Assembly did not take up the proposal of the European Commission for Democracy through Law because of the assumption that, instead of the creation of a new mechanism for the protection of the rights of minorities, it is better to enable persons belonging to national minorities to benefit from the well-functioning system of protection foreseen by the European Convention - the right of individual and collective petitions to the European Commission and subsequently the European court of Human Rights which can be achieved only through the additional protocol.[24]

2. The Recommendation of the Parliamentary Assembly of the Council of Europe on an Additional Protocol on the Rights of National Minorities to the European Convention on Human Rights

In Recommendation 1177 (1992) on the rights of minorities, the Parliamentary Assembly advocated that the Committee of Ministers:

- conclude as soon as possible the work underway for the elaboration of a charter for regional and minorities languages;

- draw up an additional protocol to the European Convention on Human Rights on the rights of minorities;

- provide the Council of Europe with a suitable mediation instrument.

The Parliamentary Assembly by its Recommendation 1201 (1993) adopted the text of the proposal for an additional protocol to the Convention for the Protection of Human Rights and Fundamental Freedoms concerning persons belonging to national minorities.

The proposal offers a definition of "national minorities" and formulates general principles; membership of a national minority is a matter of personal choice; each person belonging to a national minority has the right to express, preserve and develop in complete freedom his/ her religious, ethnic, linguistic and/ or cultural identity; all persons belonging to national minorities shall be equal; any discrimination based on membership of a national minority as well as deliberate changes of demographic composition of the region in which a national minority is settled shall be prohibited.

The list of substantive rights of persons belonging to national minorities formulated in six articles foresees that they shall have:

a) the right to set up their own organization, *including political parties;*

b) the right to use freely their mother tongue in private and public;

c) the right to use names in the mother tongue;

d) in the regions in which a substantial number of members of a national minority are settled, the right to use their mother tongue on contacts with administrative authorities and in proceedings before the courts and legal authorities; and the right to display in their language local names, signs, inscriptions;

e) the right to learn their mother tongue in an appropriate number of schools as well as the right to set up and manage their own schools and educational establishments (within the framework of the legal system of the State);

f) the right to have free and unimpeded contacts with the citizens of another country with whom this minority shares ethnic, religious or linguistic features or a cultural identity;

g) in the regions where they are in the majority, the persons belonging to national minorities shall have the right to have at their disposal appropriate local or autonomous authorities or to have a special status.

The list of rights, though very long, still does not take into consideration all standards formulated by the CSCE documents; for example, the right to participate in political, economic and cultural life, as well as in the decision-making process concerning minorities or the right to receive financial subsidies. On the other hand, one can observe that duties of persons, as formulated in the proposal, speak exclusively about the respect of territorial integrity which seems to be unsatisfactory and frustrating the necessary balance between rights and duties.

3. The European Charter for Regional or Minority Languages

In 1992 the Council of Europe adopted the *Charter for Regional or Minority Languages*.[25] The Charter is based on the assumption that the protection and promotion of regional or minority languages in the different countries and regions of Europe represent an important contribution to the building of a

Europe based on the principles of democracy and cultural diversity within the framework of national sovereignty and territory integrity. Stressing the value of interculturalism and multilinguism and considering that the protection and encouragement of regional or minority languages should not be to the detriment of the official languages and the need to learn them.

The Charter recognizes that the right to use of regional or minority language in private or public life is an inalienable right.

The Charter imposes an obligation on parties to present periodically to the Secretary-General of the Council of Europe a report on their policies and the measures taken to promote the use of regional or minority languages in public life. The reports shall be examined by a committee of experts.

---

1 UN Doc. E/CN.4/Sub.2/1991/43.

2 UN Doc.E/CN.4/Sub.2/1992/87.

3 UN Doc.E/CN.4/Sub.2/1993/30.

4 A/Res. 44/25, 20.11.1989.

5 UN Doc.A/CONF. 157/23, paras 25-27.

6 UNTS, vol. 754, p. 73, 26.22.1948.

7 UNTS, vol. 660, p. 195, 21.12.1965.

8 UNTS, vol. 1249, p.13, 18.12.1979.

9 A/Res. 36/55, 25.11.1981.

10 UNTS, vol. 429, p. 93, 14.12.1960.

11 UNESCO, Final Report, 1982, Mondiacult CLT/DM/1.

12 Adopted by the General Conference, 20th session, 21.11.1978.

13 Adopted by the General Conference, 14 Session, 4.11.1966.

14 The first stage of the Conference on Security and Co-operation in Europe opened on 3.7.1973 in Helsinki. The negotiations of the CSCE second stage took place in Geneva from 18.9.1973 to 21.7.1975. During the third stage of the CSCE in Helsinki, the formal signing ceremony, the Final Act was signed by the leaders of 35 States of Europe and North America on 1.8.1975.

15 The meeting was opened on 4.11.1986 and ended on 19.1.1989. (See the Vienna Concluding Document in 10 HRLJ (1989), p. 270). In the discussions, the participating States took into account, *inter alia*, the results of the Ottawa meeting, as well as the meeting of experts on human contacts held in Berne in April-May 1986.

16 Text in 11 HRLJ (1990), p. 232. In order to find a common denominator, the Working Group on Minorities was forced to eliminate too far-reaching suggestions and based its agreed text on a (compromise) proposal submitted on the first day of the meeting, 5.6.1990, by the delegations of Austria, Czechoslovakia, Hungary, Italy and Yugoslavia. Doc. CSCE/CHDC.5. This draft proposed twenty principles which should be observed by States in the formulation of policies concerning national minorities.

17 Text in 11HRLJ (1990), p. 379.

18 Text in 12 JRLJ (1991), p. 332.

19 The Copenhagen Document, *loc. cit.*, Principle 34.

20 Text in 12 HRLJ (1991), p. 471.

21 Text in 13 HRLJ (1992), pp. 2890290.

[22] Text in 12 JRLJ (1991), p. 269.

[23] For the purpose of this text, "minority" means a group which is smaller in number than the rest of the population of a State whose members, although nationals of that State, have ethnic, religious or linguistic features different from those of the rest of the population, and are guided by the will to safeguard their culture, traditions, religion or language.

[24] Report on an additional protocol on the rights of minorities to the *European Convention on Human Rights*. Rapporteur Mr. Worms, Council of Europe, Parliamentary Assembly, 29.1.1993, Doc. 6742, p. 10.

[25] ETS, No. 148, 5.11.1992.

APPENDIX II

Implementation of OSCE Standards on National Minorities*

The following are excerpts from the 1995 correspondence of Mr. Max van der Stöel, High Commissioner on National Minorities, Organization for Security and Cooperation in Europe (OSCE) and Ministers of OSCE member governments from eastern European states concerning appropriate constitutional and politico-legal measures to ensure protection of states' national minorities in accordance with OSCE and international standards for minority protection.[1] OSCE standards for minority protection must be fulfilled by all states requesting admission to the OSCE, and are applicable to all its member states.

His Excellency, Mr. Hennady Udovenko
Minister for Foreign Affairs of Ukraine
Mykhaylivska Sor. 1
252018 KYIV
Republic of Ukraine
The Hague
15 May 1995
Reference : No 635/ 95/ L

Dear Mr. Minister,

...

1. Our first comment is that everything ought to be avoided which could lead to an escalation of existing tensions. In this connection, we urge the Parliament of the Autonomous Republic of Crimea not to proceed with its plan to submit to a referendum the Crimean Constitution which was abolished by the Ukrainian parliament. We also feel that it would not bring the solution of the existing problems any nearer if the Crimean Parliament were dissolved.

2. Regarding the constitutional differerences OSCE has consistently taken the view that any solution would have to be based on the respect for the sovereignty and territorial integrity of Ukraine and for the fundamental

*These excerpts concerning the High Commissioner's activities have been taken from internet gopher: URL:</ / gopher nato.int:70/ 1>.

principles of the Ukrainian Constitution. Looking for solutions on this basis, we were especially struck by the fact that a considerable number of participants in the Round Table, who often differed in the past, expressed the view that the law of Ukraine on the demarcation of powers between the organs of state power of Ukraine and the Republic of Crimea of June 1992 (which did not enter into force) contained important elements for an eventual solution of the problem. We share this view for the following reasons:

a) Article 1 of this law lays down some basic principles which usually govern the relationship between an autonomous republic and the central state organs. In our view, the acceptance by the Crimean Parliament of these principles would constitute a major step towards a solution of the constitutional problems;

b) Article 3 and Article 11 of the law on the demarcation of powers summarize the competencies reserved for the Autonomous Republic of Crimea and those of the state organs of Ukraine in a way which makes it clear that the Autonomous Republic of Crimea would have substantial autonomy... 13 gives the Parliament of the Autonomous Republic of Crimea the right to appeal to the future Constitutional Court of Ukraine if it considers that Ukrainian legislation infringes the plenary powers of the Autonomous Republic of Crimea...

d) Article 15 lays down the important principle that autonomous power, once granted can not be altered unilaterally. We would recommend that a determined effort be made as soon as possible to reach agreement on the future status the Autonomous Republic of Crimea on the basis of these principles. One could even envisage that the essential parts of the law on the demarcation of powers, with some modifications and additions, could constitute the future constitution of the Autonomous Republic of Crimea, and that the Ukrainian Parliament would adopt parallel constitutional law with the same content. ..

3) On a number of specific subjects we should like to make the following recommendations:

a) If the division of competences as laid down in Articles 3 and 11 of the law on the demarcation of powers is followed, which we hope will be the case, it will be necessary to start negotiations as soon as possible between the central authorities of Ukraine and those of the Autonomous Republic of Crimea on the implementation of Article ... point 8, which on the one hand gives to the Autonomous Republic of Crimea the right to own the land, mineral wealth, water and other natural resources on its territory, but which, on the other hand opens the possibility of curtailment of this right by Ukraine;

b) Quite often, the need of dual citizenship of Ukraine and the Russian Federation has been brought up by the Parliament of the Autonomous Republic of Crimea. The motivation for this is especially the problems which the many pensioners living in Crimea have with the transfer of their pensions from the Russian Federation, and the opportunities which this could open for Crimeans wanting to study in the Russian Federation. However, these problems could be solved by a special agreement between the Russian Federation and Ukraine regarding these issues.

c) We have noted that there is still a considerable number of Tatars who after having returned to Crimea, have not yet been able to acquire the citizenship of Ukraine. They would, therefore, not be able to participate in the local elections on 25 June. For this reason, the Tatar leadership is reluctant to take part in these elections. We hope that ways can be found to solve this problem in the coming weeks in order to ensure appropriate representation of the Tatars in local government.

d) Pending the setting up of the Constitutional Court, it is, in our view, desirable that the Parliaments of Ukraine and of the Autonomous Republic of Crimea create an organ of conciliation with the task of suggesting solutions to differences arising in the course of dialogue about relevant legislation...

Yours sincerely,

(Max van der Stöel)

On the demarcation of plenary powers between the organs of state power of Ukraine and of the Republic of Crimea [articles 1, 3, 11, 13, and 15]

Article 1. The Republic of Crimea is an autonomous, constituent part of Ukraine. The Republic of Crimea independently decides questions assigned to its competence by the Constitution of Ukraine, the Constitution of the Republic of Crimea, and the present Law. The Constitution of the Republic of Crimea may not contradict the Constitution of Ukraine, the basic principles of its democratic, legal and political structure, or its guarantee of individual rights and freedoms.

Every citizen of the Republic of Crimea is a citizen of Ukraine.

[...]

Article 3. The competence of the Republic of Crimea in the person of its highest organs of power, embraces:

(1) adopting, amending and interpreting the Constitution (Fundamental Law) of the Republic of Crimea and its laws, and monitoring their observance;

(2) participating in the formation and execution of Ukraine's domestic and foreign policy on questions touching the interests of the Republic of Crimea;

(3) resolving questions concerning the territorial structure of the Republic of Crimea, the establishment and alteration of the boundaries of districts and populated areas, the upgrading of populated areas to the status of towns, and the naming and renaming of towns, districts, districts within towns, settlements and villages;

(4) determining the form of organization and activity of republic (Republic of Crimea) and local organs of power, local self-government and citizens' organizations;

(5) calling elections of people's deputies of the Republic of Crimea and determining the composition of the Central Electoral Commission for elections of people's deputies, calling elections of deputies to local Soviets of people's deputies of the Republic of Crimea;

(6) holding referendums of the Republic of Crimea on matters within its competence;

(7) creating and establishing organs of judicial power in accordance with the judicial system of Ukraine;

(8) exercising the inalienable right to own the land, mineral wealth, water and other natural resources located on the territory of the Republic of Crimea. This right may be curtailed by Ukraine in the course of its realization of the exclusive plenary powers specified in Article 11 of the present Law and by agreement with the Republic of Crimea;

(9) within the bounds of its competence, exercising the legislative regulation of property relations and ensuring the equality of different forms of property;

(10) determining the structures and priorities of the economic development of the Republic of Crimea, assuring scientific and technical progress; setting up and overseeing the functioning of free economic zones in accordance with Ukrainian legislation; licensing and assigning quotas for the export of goods;

(11) elaborating, approving and implementing programs relating to the economic, social, and national-cultural development, and the protection of the environment, of the Republic of Crimea;

(12) determining the budgetary revenues of the Republic of Crimea;

(13) independently drawing up and approving the budget of the Republic of Crimea on the basis of the single taxation policy of Ukraine; forming mutual budgetary relations between the governments of Ukraine...

(14) designating localities as spas, setting zones of sanitary protection of health-resorts, and ensuring that they function according to the law;

(15) deciding matters of ecological security; the rational use, protection and replenishment of natural resources; declaring quarantines and zones of natural disasters and carrying out policy in the spheres of education, culture, healthcare, physical culture and sports, social welfare, and protection and use of historical and cultural monuments;

(17) guaranteeing the rights and freedoms of citizens, civic and national accord, maintenance of law and order and public security

(18) initiating the introduction of a state of emergency on the territory of theRepublic of Crimea, in agreement with the President of Ukraine;

(19) regulating internal migration in the Republic of Crimea, elaborating and executing scientifically-based demographic, urbanisation and housing policies;

(20) guaranteeing the functioning and development of national languages and cultures in the territory of the Republic of Crimea;

(21) participating in the elaboration and execution of state programs for the resettlement of peoples deported from Crimea;

(22) establishing honorary titles of the Republic of Crimea and instituting other awards.

[...]

Article 11. The supreme organs of state power of the Republic of Crimea may not decide questions relating to the exclusive competence of the state organs of Ukraine, namely: defense, the armed forces; foreign policy; the organization and protection of state borders, customs and security; the single, pan-state electoral system; all-Ukrainian referendums; the single currency and monetary emission; the pan-state taxation and system of weights and measures, standardization; citizenship; states of emergency; civil law, criminal law, civil and criminal procedures, penal policy, labor law, and social welfare legislation; the preparation and realization of pan-state programs regarding the economy or scientific, technical, social, and national-cultural development; the protection of the health of people and environmental protection; the organization and direction of a single system of communications and information, the transport system, the fuel and energy system, space exploration.

[...]

Article 13. Pending the adoption of a definitive decision by the Constitutional Court of Ukraine, the Supreme Soviet of the Republic of Crimea may halt the execution of normative acts of the organs of executive power of Ukraine on the territory of the Republic of Crimea if these infringe the plenary powers of the Republic of Crimea.

The Supreme Soviet of the Republic of Crimea may appeal to the Constitutional Court of Ukraine to declare inoperative normative acts of the Verkhovna Rada of Ukraine that infringe the plenary powers of the Republic of Crimea. In the event that the Constitutional Court of Ukraine declares inoperative, on the territory of the Republic of Crimea, normative acts of Ukraine, the Verkhovna Rada of Ukraine or, when applicable, the President of Ukraine, regulates the legal relations arising as a result of the operation of these acts.

[...]

Article 15. The plenary powers of the Republic of Crimea established by the present Law may not be changed without the agreement of the supreme legislative organs of Ukraine and the Republic of Crimea.

*

Letter from Mr. Sev Crvenkovski
Minister, Republic of Macedonia Ministry of Foreign Affairs
3June 1995
To: Mr. Max van der Stöel
OSCE High Commissioner on National Minorities

Dear Mr. High Commissioner,

....

The Government holds that your suggestion for the establishment of a private higher education establishment is not only in harmony with the Constitution, but is a follow-up to the intensive activity of the Government aimed at the privatization of all spheres of life including education. In this regard, the Government accepts your idea and considers that in our further discussion it could be elaborated and adapted to the existing legislation in force and to the laws to be passed. As you may know, there is still no new law regulating these issues. The Law on Higher Education which is currently being prepared, covers this problem, and what remains to be done is that essential aspects of private education such as financing, harmonization of programmes and alike are regulated by a special law. Your initiative will undoubtedly represent an encouragement for speedy legal regulation of this sphere.

The Government agrees with your observation that Article 45 of the Constitutionof the Republic of Macedonia is almost identical to Para 32.2 of the CSCE Copenhagen document of 1990. You rightly point out that "both.... open the option of private educational institutions; both equally stress the need of conformity with the relevant national law.

However, there are certain substantial differences between the two provisions. Namely, whereas according to the mentioned Copenhagen Document the only option for persons belonging to national minorities is private education, the laws and practice of the Republic of Macedonia are at a rather higher level in regard to the education of national minorities in elementary and secondary education, rendering it a duty of the state. As you may know, the fundamental issues pertaining to the rights of national minorities are regulated by Article 48 of the Constitution; hence we would like to suggest that Article 45 be read together with the said Article of the Constitution. On the basis of Article 48, there is a legal provision having existed in the law we have had thus far and incorporated in the new Law on Higher Education, prescribing that tuition in higher education is conducted in the Macedonian language exclusively, naturally with the exception of subjects most closely linked with fostering ethnic identity and culture of persons belonging to national minorities, what is foreseen by the new Law on Higher Education.

Any solution regarding a private university in the Republic of Macedonia has to take into account that such an establishment can be founded in the constitutional and legal framework, meaning in the Macedonian language or under specific conditions in one of world languages. Your initiatives for assisting the Republic of Macedonia in this sphere should have this fact in view...

Stevo Crvenkovski
Minister

*

Her Excellency Mrs Roza Otunbaeva
Minister for Foreign Affairs of the Republic of Kyrgyzstan
BISHKEK Republic of Kyrgyzstan
7 August 1995
Reference : No 897/95/L

Dear Mrs. Minister,

...

1. Within the Assembly, an Executive Council should be created composed of representatives of the various National Cultural Centers and representatives of various Ministries which have competences which affect the interests of the various minorities in Kyrgyzstan.

2. The Council should meet at least once a month; under its aegis commissions can be formed to deal with specific subjects.

3. The competences of the Council should include :

a. to give advice to the Government regarding draft legislation concerning matters which affect national minorities;

b. to suggest to the Government legislation for submission to Parliament which in the Council's view could help to solve minority problems;

c. to study questions relating to educational questions confronting minorities;

d. to study the question of the access of minorities to the mass media;

e. to maintain contacts with local or regional public authorities regarding specific minority issues and to suggest possible solutions.

f. to investigate complaints by National Cultural Centers, non-governmental organizations and individuals related to the respect of rights of persons belonging to national minorities and to make recommendations regarding these complaints to the relevant governmental agencies;

g. to take the initiative in investigating specific situations which might cause inter-ethnic tensions; report at regular intervals to the Government and to the Assembly of the People of Kyrgyzstan about its activities.

I would also recommend that one of the departments of the office of the President should be assigned to concentrate exclusively on questions relating to minorities. In order to achieve maximum coordination, the head of the department, supported by a well qualified staff, could also be charged with the secretariat of the Executive Council.

Finally, it is in my view essential to create an institute (or use an existing institute) for research relating to possible sources of inter-ethnic tension. Such an institute could also be of help to the Executive Council when it decided to start an investigation concerning a specific minority question.

The intensification of the work of the Assembly is in my view justified because it can greatly contribute to inter-ethnic harmony, and, heretofore to the lasting stability of Kyrgyzstan. Special attention to minority problems also seems desirable because the number of persons belonging to national minorities in Parliament (15 out of 105) is smaller than one might expect considering the fact that the national minorities taken together constitute more than 40% of the total population of Kyrgyzstan.

I do realise that the measures proposed have financial consequences, which, while small considering the vitally important purpose they will be used for, might presently be too much of a burden for your Government. But I am not without hope that international financial assistance could be mobilised.

...

(Signature)
Max van der Stöel
OSCE High Commissioner on National Minorities

*

His Excellency Mr. Juraj Schenk
Minister for Foreign Affairs of the Slovak Republic
20 Stromov=A0 1
833 36 Bratislava
Slovak Republic
The Hague
24 August 1995
Reference: No 899/ 95

Dear Mr. Minister,

... I have also taken into account the text of the treaty on good neighbourliness and friendly cooperation which was concluded last March between the Slovak Republic and the Republic of Hungary, because it contains a number of important principles regarding the treatment of persons belonging to national minorities. I feel entitled to do so, because, even though the treaty still has to be approved by the National Council of Slovakia, its contents can be considered as reflecting the views of the Slovak Government.

The concept of alternative education

One of the subjects most discussed recently in your country is the introduction of a system of alternative education in linguistically mixed regions. This question is especially relevant for the Hungarian minority in Slovakia. According to the data regarding the school year 1993/1994 published in a publication of your Ministry, 77% of the total number of children, 13% belonging to the Hungarian minority attending kindergarten go to kindergarten with Hungarian as the language of instruction. Approximately 80% of the total number of pupils of Hungarian nationality at the elementary school level attend elementary schools with Hungarian as the language of instruction (the Slovak language being taught as a compulsory subject during the school period of attendance to elementary school). The others go to mixed elementary schools, i.e. those with Slovak classes besides Hungarian ones.

On the basis of the conversations the Team of Experts and I had with the Minister of Education Mrs. Slavkovska, and various publications on the subject, I understand that the concept of alternative education has the following elements :

1. In kindergarten with Hungarian as language of instruction, teachers in charge of teaching in Slovak would teach in two classes according to the following pattern : one week, in one class, on Monday, Wednesday and Friday; in the other class, on Tuesday and Thursday; the other week vice versa. Thus it is estimated that every week a total of 28 hours would be available for education inthe Slovak language;

2. For elementary schools, two options are being envisaged for introducing bilingual classes in addition to the existing classes in the Hungarian language. The more restricted option foresees bilingual classes starting only in the fifth year of primary schools. In secondary schools, the choice of two options is also foreseen.

In the conversation the Team of Experts and I had with the Minister of Education, she stressed that participation in the alternative education system would be on a strictly voluntary basis. Parents would not be obliged to send their children to the alternative classes. Such classes would only be started if there were sufficient interest for them. In this connection a number of 20 pupils was mentioned, with exceptions to be made for special circumstances in individual localities. In the near future, the alternative system would start on an experimental basis.

In recent months, parents of the Hungarian minority have been asked to give their views on the plans of the Government. A very strong majority of them have apparently given a negative reaction. The protagonists of the alternative education system stress that this is probably due to a misunderstanding of what is intended, and express the hope that further explanations will lead to a more positive response. The reactions in the Hungarian community in Slovakia against the plan are so strong, however, that I doubt that a major shift in favour of the plan in the coming years is likely. On the other hand, the Government has committed itself - and has continued to commit itself after the reaction of the parents became known - to respect the free choice of the parents. Fears have been expressed that the Government might resort to indirect pressure on the parents, for instance by implying that pupils of Hungarian schools would suffer the consequences of their choice in their future careers, or by taking steps which would be to the financial disadvantage of Hungarian language schools. It is my assumption that the

Government will firmly reject such a cause of action because this would mean a breach of its promise to respect the free choice of the parents.

In the policy statement of 12 January 1995 your Government announced its intention to create the conditions for the thorough learning of the state language in the linguistically mixed areas of the Slovak Republic. In this context it mentioned the concept of alternative education at state schools operating in the linguistically mixed territories of Slovakia.

In my view, your Government acts in full conformity with international standards when it tries to ensure that all citizens of your country have a proper knowledge of the statelanguage. In this context, I refer to paragraph 34 of the 1990 OSCE Copenhagen 5 Document which refers to "the need to learn the official language or languages of the state."

On the other hand, there are other ways than the concept of alternative education to achieve this end. In the light of the opposition of most of the parents of the Hungarian minority to the concept of alternative education on the one hand, and the commitment of the Government to respect the choice of the parents on the other, I would recommend that an investigation will be made about the quality of the teaching of the Slovak language in Hungarian schools and the ways to ensure its improvement where necessary. In order to avoid any complaints about partiality, it might be advisable to use international expertise in such a study.

The draft law on the state language of the Slovak Republic

With great interest I studied e draft law on the state language of the Slovak Republic. Its main aim is clearly that the role of the Slovak language as the state language will be ensured and protected. Other European states have laws with similar objectives. On the other hand, in states with national minorities, the question inevitably arises how to find a balance betweenthe right of a state to ensure that the position of the state language is safeguarded and the need to ensure that the languages of the national minorities are protected in accordance with international standards. In this context I mention Article 1 of the UN Declaration on the Rights of Persons belonging to National, or Ethnic, Religious and Linguistic Minorities (legally binding for Slovakia once the treaty with Hungary comes into force) which requires i.a. that states shall protect the linguistic identity of minorities within their respective territories, and shall encourage conditions for the promotion of their identity. Article 15.2g of the treaty concluded with Hungary also makes several references to the linguistic rights of persons belonging to minorities. So do paragraphs 32.1 and 34 of the Copenhagen Document and Article 10.1 of the Council of Europe Framework Convention. The existing law on the official language contains (Article 1, paragraph 2) a reference to "international obligations in the field of human rights." I would suggest a similar reference to international obligations and commitments in the text of the new law.

In making these remarks, I am of course aware of the repeated assurances of your Government that it intends fully to respect its international commitments. In addition, Article 34 of the Constitution of the Slovak Republic is of major significance in this respect. I also noted that the draft law on the state language of the Slovak Republic contains a number of references to the linguistic rights of persons belonging to minorities. What causes me some concern, however, is that in a number of fields the draft law is formulated in such a way that it leads to uncertainty about the position of the minority languages. I will illustrate this with a few examples. Article 10 of the draft law states that law no 428/1990 on the official language of the Slovak Republic is null and void. This has i.a. as a consequence that section 6, paragraph 2 of that law ("if persons belonging to a national minority constitute at least 20% of the population of a town or village, they have the right to use their language in such towns and villages in official communications") is no longer valid. On the other hand, Article 34.2 sub b of the Constitution of the Slovak Republic refers to "the right to use a minority language in official communications." However, this right is granted "under provisions fixed by law". If the draft law would be adopted, no such law would exist anymore. I would, therefore, recommend that the text of Article 6 paragraph 2 of the law on the official language will be incorporated in the draft law.

The reference in footnotes to various Articles of other laws also lead to doubts about the continued validity of other sections of such laws. For instance, Article 5.1 of the draft law states that broadcasts in the languages of the ethnic minorities are regulated by special provisions. A footnote then refers to Article 5 of law 255/1991 on Slovak Radio, and Article 3 of law 254/1991 on Slovak Television. No reference is being made to a number of other Articles in laws relating to Slovak Radio and TV and their role to promote the identity of the national minorities quoted in the publication of your Ministry on the status of the Hungarian minority in the Slovak Republic (Section 9, paragraph 2, item c, law on the operation of Radio and TV broadcasting no 268/1993; Section 6, item d, law on the Slovak Radio no 270/1993; Section 3, paragraph 3 and Section 6, item j, law on Slovak Television 271/1993.) In my view it would be desirable that the draft law would confirm their identity.

Article 4.3 of the draft law states that text books and teaching aids (video, film, electronic recordings and so on) used in the teaching process are issued in the state language; they can be issued in another language only to the extent determined by special provisions. As the question of text books in minority schools is an important one, it would in my view be preferable to deal with this matter in the text of the law itself. I hope that the question of the import of text books and other educational material from Hungary will be solved in the spirit of Article 12.7 of the treaty concluded between Slovakia and Hungary (each contracting party shall endeavour to expand the opportunities for learning about culture, literature and language of the other contracting party).

A number of provisions in the draft law could be interpreted in a way which might not be intended at all. For instance Article 2,7 paragraph 2, sub c, could be interpreted as excluding the language of a minority as the means of communication within such a minority.

Article 3, paragraph 1, might be interpreted as making it impossible for a state university to employ foreign teachers if they don't know the Slovak language. Article 4, paragraph 3 could be interpreted as obliging teachers in minority language schools to use only the Slovak language in the teaching process. Reformulation of these paragraphs must be considered desirable.

Article 9, paragraph 3 refers to the supervision of the obligations under the draft law by the Ministry of Culture. My assumption is that the way this task will be implemented shall be the subject of a subordinate set of regulations. I would recommend that these regulations shall be published as they will give a clearer insight into the way the law will be implemented.

Minorities and Cultural Policy

In 1995, the overall budget of the Ministry of Culture was increased considerably compared with 1994. On the other hand, the direct contributions from the budget of the Ministry to various cultural activities of natural minorities have been considerably reduced. The most severe cuts have been made in the contributions of the Ministry to periodicals and other publications in the language of national minorities. Considerable reductions were also made in the contributions to the functioning of various national minority organisations, the percentage of the reduction being the highest for CSEMADOK, the social and cultural Alliance of Hungarians in Slovakia. I can only express the hope that in thc coming year this downward trend will be reversed, also taking into account the fact that subsidies are the most effective and sometimes the only way to implement the commitment contained in para. 33 of the CSCE 1990 Copenhagen Document regarding the protection and the creation of conditions for the promotion of the cultural identity of national minorities.

In the statement on government policy of 12 January 1995 it is announced that norms will be drafted for the support of minority cultures. I express the hope that these norms, before being presented to the National Council in the form of a draft law, will be the subject of discussion in the Government Council for Nationalities. I would also recommend that the formulation of these norms should be accompanied by a change of the decision-making process regarding the allocation of funds for various cultural activities of national minorities. At presentthe Ministry of Culture is making these decisions, and as a consequence, it is also the target of criticism if it rejects specific projects or provides less money for a project than has been asked for. In my view it would be preferable to delegate this responsibility to the minorities themselves. Once the National Council has decided on the total budget for cultural activities of all the national minorities, the funds made available, could be divided amongst the various national minorities, the percentage allotted to each to be decided on the basis of their numerical strength with a certain minimum for the smallest national minorities. The decision on how to divide up the funds available of various cultural projects planned within each national minority could be left to a committee of representatives of that minority. The task of the Ministry of Culture would be to ensure that the norms would be respected. If this would not be the case, the relevant decision could be annulled. Such a policy would be very much in line with Article 15 of the Framework Convention which states: "the parties shall create the conditions necessary for the effective participation of persons belonging to national minorities in cultural, social and economic life and in public affairs, in particular those affecting them."

The declaration on government policy of January 12, 1995 also states that special attention will be given to "strengthening the position of the culture of the Slovaks living in the territories imbued with the culture of the ethnic minority." As long as such a policy has as its sole aim to strengthen Slovak culture in areas where a national minority constitutes a majority, and refrains from steps to weaken the culture of the other ethnic group, such a policy is in my view compatible with international norms. I would recommend, however, that such a policy will not be financed by reducing the funds available for supporting the culture of the national minorities living in Slovakia, because it is difficult to see why it would have to be implemented at their expense.

Finally, I noted that a number of periodicals have been given subsidies totalling SK 27.70 mn in order to publish supplements in the languages of national minorities. This new policy has been explained by the need to provide objective and relevant information of an apolitical nature, especially for people who have problems with the Slovak language. As this new policy is specifically designed for, and of immediate relevance to the various national minorities, I would recommend that the Council of the Government for National Minorities, making use of the competence given to it under Article 4 of its Statutes, will establish a special working group to follow and analyze its implementation. On the basis of the report of the working group, the Council could then, when it would fit the need to do so, come forward with suggestions and recommendations regarding this policy as foreseen in Article 12, 1 (d)f its Statutes.

... It is my firm belief that, if both national minorities and the Government choose a constructive approach, they can be solved in a satisfactory way. In this respect, I want to emphasize the importance I attach to what is stated so clearly in the policy statement of your Government : "In dealing with all the questions related to the situation and the rights of persons belonging to national minorities, the Government will abide by the Constitution of the Slovak Republic and the international legal and political commitments of the Slovak Republic."

Yours sincerely,

Max van der Stöel

*

His Excellency Mr L. Kovacs
Minister for Foreign Affairs
of the Republic of Hungary
BUDAPEST, Republic of Hungary
The Hague
24 August 1995
Reference :No 923/95/L

Dear Mr. Minister,

...

I submit to you, as I did on previous occasions, a number of comments and recommendations regarding a number of current questions relating to the Slovak national minority in your country.

In doing so, I have also taken into account the text of the treaty on good neighbourliness and friendly cooperation which was concluded last March between the Slovak Republic and the Republic of Hungary and subsequently ratified by your country, because it contains a number of important principles regarding the treatment of persons belonging to national minorities.

According to the 1990 census 10,459 persons declared that they belonged to the Slovak national minority while 12,745 persons declared that Slovak was their mother tongue. It is likely that the number of persons of Slovak descent is considerably higher; the policies followed by previous regimes have had considerable consequences for the cultural and linguistic identity of the Slovak national minority in Hungary and has also weakened its national self-identification. The maintenance of the national identity of the Slovaks in Hungary was also affected because they are not living in one compact area, but are spread over 103 localities in various parts of the country.

Against this background, I can only welcome the determination of the Hungarian Government, as shown in its declaration before Parliament when assuming office in 1994, to strengthen the identity of the various national minorities. However, the implementation of his policy has led to a number of problems which have caused me to formulate some comments and recommendations.

Slovak minority self-governments

One of the major steps undertaken by your country to strengthen the identity of the various national minorities was the introduction of legislation which provided the option of elections for self-governing bodies in addition to those for municipal councils. In the elections of 11 December 1994 Slovak minority 8 candidates received over 149,000 votes, and this in turn led to the creation of Slovak minority self-governing bodies in 39 of the 103 localities where persons belonging to the Slovak national minority constitute an important part of the population. In 18 communities without a Slovak minority self-governing body, Slovaks have elected a spokesperson. New elections are planned in November next in towns and villages where no minority self-governing bodies have been created so far. In addition a national self-governing body consisting of 53 members was elected by a group of 206 persons composed of minority representatives elected as such in municipal councils and of Slovaks belonging to the self-governing bodies.

The existence of such a body strengthens the system for the protection of the interest of the Slovak national minority in Hungary and can also contribute to its cohesion. The importance of the local minority self-governing bodies is demonstrated by the fact that in questions relating to local public education and culture and the use of the minority language the municipal council can only adopt bylaws if these have the consent of the local minority self-governing body. (In other fields, such as the protection of the environment and local public transport the local self-governing body has to be consulted.)

Undoubtedly, the system of local minority self-government reflects an original and innovative approach to the problem of ensuring the various minorities the optimal chances for protectingtheir interests and developing their identity. However, there is in my view need to take two further steps to ensure that the system works effectively. Frst is that the minority self-governing bodies must be given a more solid financial basis. The original subsidy of HUF 114,000 for each minority self-governing body is apparently now being doubled; but even then the funds available cannot be considered sufficient for a proper functioning of these bodies. In a number of cases municipalities have helped by providing facilities or by giving subsidies. But the municipalities are themselves often confronted with financial difficulties and it seems preferable to avoid situations in which such subsidies can only be provided at the expense of projected municipal activities. I hope therefore that ways can be found to increase the direct income of the minority self-governing bodies.

In accordance to the text of Chapter VIII of the Act on National and Ethnic Minorities as recently modified a public foundation will be established soon in order to subsidise activities that help preserve the identity of minorities, maintain their traditions and transmit them to new generations, promote and develop their mother tongue, preserve their spiritual and material heritage and attenuate cultural and political disadvantages resulting from the minority status. It is the intention that subsidies allocated by the public foundation are part of the system of financing by the state of minority related activities. In the Board of Trustees, representatives of the minorities (either persons delegated by each of the national self-governments of the minorities elected by their general assemblies or persons elected by minority organizations in case minorities might not have a national self-government) will occupy 13 of the 25 seats.

According to my information, HUF 400 million have been reserved for the new foundation. I express the hope that it will start its work soon and that most of the funds will be allotted to the national self-governments or to national minority organizations, thus giving them more opportunities to decide for themselves which projects for the strengthening of the identity of the minority in various fields would have to be given priority.

My second comment relates to the interaction of state administration, municipal authorities and minority self-governing bodies, a fairly complicated subject. It is in my view useful that various one-day training programmes concerning this subject have been planned for the current year. I suggest, however, that, in addition, an analysis will be made to introduce further constitutional and administrative legislation with the aim of reducing the risk of conflict of competences between the various organs.

Educational questions facing the Slovak minority

In the 1994 Declaration on Government policy I noted the following passage: "It is the chief condition of the strengthening of the identity of minorities that there should be real progress in minority education. In observation of the autonomy of the minorities, the Government will assure adequate conditions for the operation of minority nursery schools, teaching in minority languages in elementary and secondary schools, tuition in institutes of higher education, furthermore, the running of libraries and other cultural facilities and the upgrading of mass media in minority languages. It is a governmental function to assure the training of minority teachers, the training of bilingual lecturers, and the supply of textbooks and teaching aids needed for minority education."

In my view, the consistent implementation of the policies as quoted above is especially important in the case of the Slovak minority because under past regimes there were great deficiencies in the system of teaching the Slovak language. At present, at the level of primary education, there are 71 schools where the Slovak language is taught as an optional subject and as a foreign language. Only 6 schools can be considered as being bilingual. Furthermore, there are two grammar schools with Slovak as the language of instruction, and a hotel school where students are taught in both the Hungarian and Slovak languages. Teachers for schools where Slovak is a subject are trained in the Teachers Institute in Esztergom, the department of Slavonic at ELTE university in Budapest and the Pedagogical college in Szeged. Slovak minority self-governing bodies could try to improve the present instruction either by trying to create a unilingual Slovak school with Hungarian as a compulsory subject, by increasing the number of bilingual schools or by stimulating the interest of parents and pupils for optimal classes in the Slovak language. The programme of your Government makes it clear that it would be willing to support such efforts, even though the creation of new schools might meet financial difficulties. Considering the need to strengthen the linguistic identity of the Slovak minority in Hungary, it would in myview be of considerable importance to create unilingual Slovak schools, or, in case this would be the preference of the parents, to make a major effort to increase the number of bilingual schools and to secure greater interest for optional courses in the Slovak language.

Finally, I should like to recall Article 12, paragraphs 6 and 7 of the treaty between the Slovak Republic and Hungary. I hope that the close cooperation foreseen both in the linguistic and cultural fields will soon become a reality.

Parliamentary representation of ethnic minorities

In your letter of 8 November 1994 you recalled that although members of various minority groups gained seats in Parliament on party lists in the 1994 elections, no persons were elected who could be considered as representing the various national minorities as such. This has created a complicated situation because on the one hand paragraph 20 of the Minorities Act mentions the right of parliamentary representation of minorities, while on the other hand the Constitution of the Republic of Hungary requires that the members of Parliament have to be elected directly, and not by delegation. As changes in the Constitution are required to resolve this question, it has to be assumed that parliamentary representation of the minorities can be expected to begin only after the next general elections, due in 1998.

As you also mentioned in your letter of 8 November 1994, however, the Government envisioned an interim solution : the establishment of a Minority Interest Mediation Council, consisting of representatives of 92 political parties, representatives of government organizations involved in minority questions, and independent experts. Also under consideration was the convening of a committee alongside the Parliamentary Committee on Human Rights and Minority and Religious Affairs, consisting of members delegated by the national self-governing bodies of the minorities who would be enabled to take part in the work of Parliament without the right of vote. During my visit in June, however, this idea had still not been implemented. I express the hope that ways will be found to introduce such an interim system or a formula on similar lines without further delay.

Parliamentary Commissioner for Minority Affairs

In the 1994 Declaration on Government policy it was stated that there should be no delay in electing a parliamentary commissioner for minority affairs. I do realise, however, that the amending of the Constitution in order to enable Parliament to change from a collegiate form of commissionership to a single commissioner inevitably takes time. Still I hope that it will be possible to elect a parliamentary commissioner for minority affairs. The importance of the role of such a commissioner in the system of protection of the rights of minorities is obvious.

....

Yours sincerely,

Max van der Stöel
OSCE High Commissioner on National Minorities

APPENDIX III

UN Methods of Recruitment*

A. General observations

Despite all the deficiencies of the United Nations recruitment system, it needs to be recognized that a number of positive changes have been introduced over the last several years. These include:

i) recruitment of occupational groups;

ii) recruitment at P-1 and P-2 levels exclusively through competitive examinations;

iii) setting up of a Senior Review Group to consider candidates for D-2 posts.

In addition to the above improvements, htere had been some progress in complying with the request of Member States, formulated in a number of General Assembly resolutions, including 35/210, to the effect that no posts, offices, or divisions should be considered as the domain of particular Member States or groups of Member States. However, in its resolution 47/226, the General Assembly reaffirmed that no post should be considered the exclusive preserve of any State or group of States. The Inspectors observed that these resolutions have not yet been fully implemented. They found that, despite the above resolutions, the practice of replacing senior level positions with nationals of the same country remains in effect in many cases.

Finally, a new system of "secondment" has been established. The Assembly, at its forty-seventh session amended the Staff Regulations to make provision for the appointment of staff on secondment from government service. It decided that secondment should be based on a tripartite agreement involving the Organization, the government and the staff member concerned, and that extension of secondment would require the agreement of all three parties.

There are effectively two formal recruitment procedures for United Nations professional staff. One - competitive examinations - which is widely used for junior staff, and the other, for employees entering at the P-3 level and above is ordinary or regular recruitment.

* The following document was provided by the Library of the UN Center for Human Rights in Geneva upon request for UN guidelines for recruitment of personnel. It illustrates UN efforts to respond to the multicultural nature of the global state system, in furtherance of its function as a global social service agency.

B. Competitive examinations

The system in place for junior staff (P-1 and P-2 grades) utilizes internal and external competitive examinations for all language posts or posts subject to geographical distribution, which are the majority of career-path positions.

General Assembly resolution 33/143 of 20 December 1978 provided that up to 30 per cent of the total posts available at the P-1 and P-2 levels should be made available for movement of staff from the General Service to the Professional category and that such recruitment should be conducted exclusively through competitive methods of selection from General Service staff with at least five years' experience. The resolution also recommended, in consultation with the governments concerned, the use of competitive examinations for the remaining P-1/P-2 vacancies. Subsequently, the General Assembly, in its resoltuion 38/210 of 17 December 1980, decided that recruitment to grades P-1 and P-2 would, as a general rule, be based on competitive examinations. It should be added that recruitment to P-2 posts account4d for a little over a third of total annual recruitment in all professional grades.

a) Internal (G-to-P) examinations

Internal examinations have been held each year since 1980 in one or more of the 11 occupational groups of the United Nations. These standardized written tests which contain analytical and essay sections as well as sections specific to the occupational group's skill, are the only avenue through which individuals in the General Service category of the United Nations can advance to the professional service...

Actually, as required by resolution 33/143, 30 per cent of the P-2 posts vacant annually are allocated for the G to P examination while the 70 per cent balance of P-2 vacancies is allocated for the successful candidates in the national competitive recruitment examinations. On average, about 20 vacancies were made available annually for transition from category G to category P. Over the period under review these targets have been closed adhered to...

Since they wre instituted in 1979, the internal examinations for G to P promotion have generally raised the quality of employees entering professional grades through internal promotion. In view of some Member States, G to P examinations can be seen not only as a means of promotion but also as part of recruitment. Therefore, they hold that the principles and policies of the Organization in the area of recuitment — such as certain educational requirements, due regard to equitable geographical distribution and gender balance — should be adhered to as well.

In this connection, OHRM observes that any limitation on the participation of staff in the General Service and related categories in the G to P examination process on the basis of nationality or gender would constitute discrimiantion and run contrary to the Staff Regulations and Rules. The G to P examinations proved to be a major contributor in the effort to achieve gender balance in the Secretariat, since 63 per cent of the candidates promoted through the G to P examination since 1979 have been women.

b) External examinations

As for the external examinations, they had become the rule by 1985, which means that non-competititve recruitment to P-1/P-2 posts subject to geographical distribution was practically ended. External examinations, also conducted annually and by occupational group, are held in countries whose nations are under-represented in the Secretariat. Like the interal G to P tests, the national competitive examinations have generally improved the calibre of professionals entering the United Nations since their institution in 1981. Moreover, they brought some talented youth to the Organization. They have also been an effective means of increasing the percentage of new employees from countries with traditionally low levels of representation on the staff.

The success of the external examinations in identifying candidates for recruitment indicated that they might be equally useful in the recruitment of candidates at higher levels. Following the recommendations of the International Civil Service Commission and the Joint Inspection Unit, the General Assembly, at its forty-third session, requested the Secretary-General to introduce competitive examinations for candidates to P-3 posts...

The first national competitive examinations at the P-3 level were held in 1991 in four Member States: Czechoslovakia, Hungary, Italy and Japan. Two occupational groups were selected on the basis of prospective vacancies in these groups, administration and economics. In 1992 P-3 examinations were held in five Member States: Finland, Germany, Japan, Russia and United States of America in the occupational groups of economics, social affairs statistics. Within the group of social affairs an examination was also held in demography. In 1994, P-3 examinations were held in Germany, Gabon and Japan in the occupational groups of economics, social affairs and statistics. In 1995, P-3 examinations are planned to be held in Japan, Republic of Korea, Norway, Poland, Romania and Ukraine in the occupational groups of administration, economics, political affairs and statistics. The Inspectors hope that more examinations will be held in developing countries and in the new Member States. The Inspectors also believe that the regional competitive examinations may, in some cases, prove to be more cost-effective than national examinations.

c) Recruitment through language examinations

In addition to the above, recruitment of staff requiring special linguistic qualifications is carried out through national languages examinations. These, differnet in nature, organization and cost from examinations held for other categories of profesisonals, are announced in those Member States where the language of examination is the principal language....

During a normal year, the number of language staff recruited is estimated to be between 80 and 90. The freeze on recruitment which was initiated on 1 March 1992 was extended to all posts requiring special language competence. These included intepreters, editors, proofreaders, translators and verbatim reporters in all six official languages, plus German. As a result, the number of competitive examinations for language posts was reduced and long term recruitment nearly stopped. Only examinations for candidates who were staff members were requested during this period. Examinations initiated before the freeze were completed on a low priority basis. Because of the freeze and as a saving measure, the Secretariat has been using more free-lancers as intepreters, translators and other language staff. This has affected the quality of the conference services in respective areas.

By way of concluding this section, it may be noted that there seems to be a consensus for maintaining the competitive examination system....

The examinations, indeed, may well yield more candidates than there are vacancies and the list of recommended candidates is thus a reserve list which goes beyond the number of posts committed to each examination. However,

OHRM recognizes that the past reserve lists have been too liberal. OHRM intends, therefore, to limit their validity to one year....

Without prejudice to the statement that as a result of the competitive examinations over the years some talented young staff members had been recruited, the general level of candidates is rather low... the vast majority of candiates do not pass the competitive examinations.

Moreover, there are complaints from programme managers that the performance of many staff recruited through competitive examinations is inadequate. The Inspectors were informed that the contracts of about 11 per cent of those are not renewed. It appears, however, that the number of some of those whose contracts they would wish not to extend is much higher.

In the Inspectors' view there is a certain laxity in applying staff rule 104.12(a), concerning the probationary form of appointment, despite the fact that it provides for separation. The reason is that this rule creates greater expentancy for this category of staff members since it mentions that they "are recruited for career service". Therefore, some programme managers act as if conversion from probationary into permanent appointment were automatic.

Other critical remarks are related to the quality and procedures of the competitive examinations themselves. Firstly, there seem to be no ojbective criteria for selection of candidates which would allow to select the best talents available in the countries where examinations are held. In the course of their analysis of some of the files, the Inspectors could not understand why some of the successful candidates with relevant academic background were only "recommended", and some others with inadequate academic background to the post were "highly" recommended. Secondly, interviews held within the framework of competitive examinations focus much more on personal attributes than on job-related issues. This hampers determining the degree of competence of the candidate.

An interview may be described as a conversation with a purpose. It is a conversation because the candidate should be drawn out to talk frankly with the interviewer about him - or herself and career. But the conversation has to be planned, directed, and controlled to achieve the main purpose of the interview, which is to make an accurate prediction of the candidate's future performance in the job for which he or she is being considered, as well as to identify how their professional perspective is related to the functions they are expected to carry out. Therefore, assessment criteria commonly used in interviews held outside the United Nations, include not only "personality characteristics" and "overall impression", but above all "qualifications and training", "experience", and "knowledge and skills".

Concurrently with criticism, some Member States suggest that, whilst not abandoning the use of national competitive examinations, the number of such examinations should be limited. In their view a less costly means of identigying qualified candidates for entry-level and mid-level positions would be the use of recruitment missions where structured inteviews would be held and representatives from OHRM as well as the substantive office would be present.

C. Recruitment missions

Another modality of recruitment is recruitment missions to unrepresented and under-represented Member States. During the period under rview, 8 such missions were undertaken: 2 in 1989 (Japan, Mongolia); 2 in 1990 (Albania,

Soviet Union), and 3 in 1991 (Papua-New Guinea, Solomon Islands, Vanuatu). Owing to the retrenchment exercise and the restructuring of various departments followed by the freeze on recruitment (1992-1994), no other missions were undertaken. As recruitment missions are sometimes referred to as an alternative to competitive examinations, the question of their cost-effectiveness inevitably arises. The Inspectors requested OHRM to provide information on the cost of recruitment missions organized in 1989 and 1991 as well as on the number of reviewed, recommended and recruited candidates. Unfortunately, this request has not been met.

D. Regular recruitment procedures for P-3 level and above

At the middle and senior levels -- P-3, P-4, P-5 and D-1 -- a lengthy, formal set of procedures for recruitment is in place: a job is prepared by the department where the opening occurs; a vacancy announcement is produced and circulated by OHRM, which also selects candidates from its internal and external rosters who fit the job description, screens the names, and forwards them to the department. The department then interviews, evaluates, and selects a candidate from among these names as well as those submitted by the United Nations agencies and the governments of member countries. If the candidate is from the outside, the department's selection is reviewed by one of the selection bodies, whose recommendation is submitted for final decision by the Secretary-General. The Appointment and Promotion Board is the viewing body for candidates at the P-5 and D-1 level; the Appointment and Promotion Committees conduct the view of candiates at the P-3 and P-4 level. Despite the existence of these procedures, in many cases, especially in attractive duty stations, vacancy advertising becomes a formality since the names of future incumbents are known well in advance.

E. Recruitment for D-2 level

In 1991, following consultations on the manner in which vacancies at the Director (D-2) level should be filled, the Secretary-General established a Senior Review Group to advise him on the filling of these posts. This measure was intended to serve a threefold purpose: (a) to provide the Secretary-General with more structured advice in the consideration of candidates; (b) to ensure consistent implementation of personnel policies and recruitment guidelines; and (c) to satisfy members aspiring to such posts that their candidacies are given adequate consideration.

The Senior Review Group which is appointed by the Secretary-General consists of four officials at the Under-or Assistant Secretary-General level. One is the Chairperson of the Appointment and Promotion Board, another represents the Executive Office of the Secretary-General, a third is appointed in consultation with the staff, and the fourth is the Assistant Secretary-General for Human Resources Management (ex-officio).

a) Procedures

The Secretary-General's administrative instruction on prcoedures of the Senior Review Group provides that, in principle, prior to the submission of any recommendation for an appointment or promotion to the D-2 level, the head of the department or office concerned will request the Office of Human Resources Management to circulate a vacancy announcement for the post. Depending on the circumstances of the case, the head of the department or office concerned, in consultation with the Assistant Secretary-General for Human Resources Management, may decide to advertise the vacancy internally only, or internally and externally. In exceptional circumstances, however, the Senior Review Group may decide not to advertise a post. After initial screening by the Office of Human Resources management to establish basic eligibility, applications received by that Office will be forwarded to the head of the department or office concerned for evaluation.

After reviewing the applications, the head of the department or office will forward a recommendation to the Director of Personnel, who will present it to the Senior Review Group. It is the responsibility of the Group to ensure that all qualified candidates are given due consideration.

If a vacancy announcement has initially been circulated internally only and the Group concludes that there is no internal candiate fully qualified for the post, it may recommend that the post be advertised externally.

After deliberation, the Senior Review Group prepares a short list of all fully qualified candidates in ranking order and submits it to the Secretary-General for a final decision. Should the names put forward by the Review Group not include the candidate recommended by the department or office concerned, the recommendations of the Group, together with the views of the head of the department or office, are forwarded to the Secretary-General for a decision.

It should be noted that this procedure in no way detracts from the discretion of the Secretary-General as regards appointment to posts at the D-2 level. At his discretion, the Secretary-General may request the Group to review candidatures for senior management positions at levels higher than D-2.

b) Activities

The information provided by OHRM on the activities of the Senior Review Group from March 1992 to the end of May 1994 suggests that the Group considered 157 candidates, including 30 external, for 36 D-2 posts and 1 ASG post. Sixteen of the candidates were already at D-2 level and one candidate for the post of Assistant Secretary-General was already at that level.

As a result, 30 appointments were made. As to the other 6 posts, either consideration of candiates was deferred or vacancy announcements were re-circulated. It also needs to be mentioned that for 8 posts only one candidature each was submitted. Seven of these posts have been filled.

APPENDIX IV

UN Primary Service Areas

The following is a selective listing of the primary subject areas in which the United Nations Secretariat, indicating its various programs and its specialized agencies.

Africa. See also UN New Agenda for the Deveopment of Africa. DPA; DOPCSD, ECA
ageing DESIPA; DPCSD; INSTRAW; WHO
Agenda 21. See also environment. DPCSD; FAO; INSTRAW; UNNGLS; UNCH; UNDP; UNEP; UNESCO; UNFPA; UNU; WMO
agriculture FAO; IAEA; IFAD; UNDP; WFP; World Bank Group, WTO
AIDS/HIV CHR; UNDP, UNESCO; UNFPA, UNICEF; UNICRI; WHO
air law conventions ICAO
air navigation plans ICAO
air worthiness ICAO
animal health FAO; IAEA
apartheid CHR; DPA; DPI
aquaculture FAO, UNDP
arms embargo DPA; UNOG
arms sales DPA; UNIDIR; UNOG
Asia and the Pacific DPA; ESCAP
aviation security ICAO
balance of payments. See also Debt. DESPIRA; IMF
biological diversity FAO; UNDP; UNEP, UNESCO
biotechnologyFAO; UNU; WHO
capital punishment CHR
Caribbean region DPA; ECLAC
chemical weapons DPA; UNIDIR
child health. See also maternal and child health. UNICEF; UNRWA; WHO
child labour CHR; ILO; UNICEF
children. See also juvenile delinquency. CHR; ILO; UNICEF; UNICRI; WHO
children's rights CHR; UNICEF; UNICRI
civil and political rights CHR; UNCHS
civil aviation ICAO
climate change DPCSD; FAO; UNDP; UNEP; UNESCOP WMO; World Bank Group
coastal zone management IAEA; UNEP, UNESCO
commodities. DESIPA; FAO; ITC; UNCTAD; World Bank Group
communcation media DPI; INSTRAW, UNESCO
communcation satellites ITU; WMO
community participation IFAD; UNCHS; UNDP; UNFPA, UNICEF; UNRISD, WHO
conflict resolution
cooperatives ILO; UNDP
coordination within UN system

'*Source*: *A Guide to the UN*, published by the Department of Public Information, UN, 1995. DPI/1444 - Feb., 1995

APPENDIX V

Instances of Major Armed Conflict within Multinational States*

Country or area	Year formed / Year joined	Parties to Conflict	Casualties (including 1990)
Africa			
Angola			
	1975/1975	National Union for the Total Independence of Angola (UNITA)	1975-1989:
	1975/1975	Liberation front for Cabinda (FLEC)	25,000
	1975/1975	National Front for the Liberation of Angola (FNLA)	
Chad			
	1982/1987	Islamic Legion	
	1989/1989	Mouvement patriotique du salut	
	1973/1979	Libyan Government (Aozou Strip)	
Ethiopia			
	1970/1971	Eritrean People's Liberation Front (EPLF)	1962-1900:
	1976/1976	Tigray People's Liberation Front (TPLF)	500,000
	1975/1980	Ethiopian People's Democratic Movement	
	1977/1977	Oromo Liberation Front (OLF)	
	1974/1975	Ethiopian People's Revolutionary Party (EPRP)	
	1975/1975	Afar Liberation Front (ALF)	
Liberia			
	1989/1989	National Patriotic Forces (NPLF)	1989-1990:
	1990/1990	Independent National Patriotic Forces (INPLF)	10,000-13,000
	1990/1990	Economic Community of West African States (ECOWAS) Monitoring Group (ECOMOG)	
	1990/1990	Government of Burkina Fasco	

Source: Selected excerpts from *World Armaments and Disarmament Yearbook 1991*, Stockholm International Peace Research Institute (SIPRI).

Country or area	Year formed Year joined	Parties to Conflict	Casualties (including 1990)
Morocco			
	1975/1976	Polisario	1975-1989: 10,000-13,000
Mozambique			
	1975/1976	National Resistance Movement	100,000 (civilian)
Somalia			
	1981/1981	Samoli National Movement (SNM)	1981-1990:
	1989/1989	Samoli Patriotic Movement (SPM)	50,000-60,000
	../1990	United Somali Congress (USC)	
South Africa			
	1950/1984	African National Congress (ANC)	1984-1990:
	1979/1983	Inkatha versus ANC	over 7,750
	1990/1990	White rightist groups	
Sudan			
	1980/1983	Sudanese People's Liberation Army	1983-1990:
	1990/199	Military factions	over 33,000
Uganda			(military)
	1986/1986	Uganda People's Democratic Movement (UPD)	1986-1990:
	1987/1987	Uganda People's Army (UPA)	over 11,000
	1987/1987	United Democratic Christian Movement UDCM)	(military)
South Asia			
Afghanistan			
	1978/1978	Mujahideen based in Afghanistan, Republic of Iran, Pakistan	1978-1990: 1,000,000
Bangladesh			
	1971/1982	Parbattya Chattagram Jana Sanghati Samiti (JSS) Shanti Bahini (SB)	1975-1990: 1,200-3,000
India			
	1947/1981	Khalistan Commando Force	1983-1990:
	1947/1982	Jammu and Kashmir Liberation Front	over 19,800
	1990/1990	Hizbul Mujahideen	
	1988/1988	Bodo Student Union/Bdo Voulontiers Force	
	1967/1967	Naxalites, People's War Group	
Myanmar			
	1948/1949	Karen National Union	1948-51: 8,000 1950: 5,000
	1948/1948	Kachin Independence Army	1981-1984: 400-600 yearly
	1949/1949	Mon State Party	1985-1987: over 1,000 yearly
	1965/1965	Shan State Army	1988: 500-3,000

Country or area	Year formed / Year joined	Parties to Conflict	Casualties (including 1990)
	1989/1989	Burma National United Party	
	1989/1989	Noom Suk Harn	
	1989/1989	National Democratic Army	
Sri Lanka			
	1976/1983	Liberation Tigers of Tamil Eelam	
	1969/1987	People's Liberation Front (JVP)	
Pacific Asia			
Cambodia			
	1975/1979	Democratic Kampuchea (Khmer Rouge)	1979-1989:
	1979/1979	Khmer People's National Liberation Front (KPLNF)	35,300
	1979/1979	Front Uni pour un Cambodge Indepéndant Neutre, Pacifique et Coopératif/ Armée Nationale Sihanoukiste (FUNCINPEC/ ANS)	
Indonesia			
	1975/1975	Revolutionary Front for an Independent East Timor (Fretilin)	1975-1990: 15,000-16,000 (military)
	../1989	Aceh Merdeka	
	../1989	National Liberation Front of Aceh	
		Lao People's Democratic Republic	
	1975/1975	United Lao National Liberation front (ULN□F) (1980) and other	1975-1990: over 1,000
Philippines			
	1968/1986	New People's Army	1972-1990:
	1982/1986	Reform Army Movement	over 37,5000
	1972/1986	Mindanao National Liberation Front	
	1990/1990	Military faction	
Central and South America			
Colombia			
	1949/1978	Fuerzas Armadas Revolucionarias de Colombia	1980-1990:
	1965/1978	Ejército de Liberación Nacional (ELN)	over 8,500
	1968/1977	Ejército Popular de Liberación (EPL)	
El Salvador			
	1976/1979	Farabundo Marti Front for National Liberation (FMLN)	1979-1990: 76,000
Guatemala			
	1967/1968	Guatemalan National Revolutionary Unity	1962-1990: 20,000-60,000
Nicaragua			
	1981/1981	Contras	1981-1990: over 30,000 (military)

Country or area	Year formed Year joined	Parties to Conflict	Casualties (including 1990)
Peru			
	1980/1981	Sendero Luminoso	1981-1990:
	1984/1986	Movimiento Revolucionaario Tupac Amaru (MRTA)	11,500-20,000
Middle East			
Iran			
	1961/1980	Kurdish Democratic Party	1980-1989: 5,000-6,000
	1975/1980	Patriotic Union of Kurdistan	
Israel/Palestine			
	1964/1964	Palestine Liberation Organization (PLO	1948-1990: over 11,000
Lebanon			
	1975/1975	Lebanon Army (Aoun)	1975-1990:
	1985/1985	Lebanese Forces (Gaegea)	150,000
	1979/1979	Amal	
	1975/1975	Islamic Resistance/Hezbollah	
	1964/1964	Palestine Liberation Organization (PLO)	
	1959/1965	Al Fatah	
	1969/1969	Democratic Front for the Liberation of Palestine (Hawatmah)	
	1967/1968	Popular Front for the Liberation of Palestine (Habash)	
	1968/1968	Popular Front for the Liberation of Palestine -- General Command	
	1968/1975	Palestine Popular Struggle Front Lebanese Forces	
	1974/1976	Fatah Revolutionary Council (Nidal)	
	1977/1977	Palestine Liberation Front (Yaqoub)	
	1961/1975	Syrian Socialist Nationalist Party	
	1975/1975	Lebanese National Resistance Front	
	1975/1975	Popular Nasserite Organization	
	1975/1975	Lebanese Baath Party	
	1978/1978	South Lebanese Army	
	1976/1976	Government of Syrian Arab Republic	
	1978/1982	Government of Israel	
Turkey			
	1974/1984	Kurdish Worker's Party	1984-1990: 2,000-2,500
Europe			
United Kingdom of Great Britain and Northern Ireland			
	1969/1969	Provisional Irish Republican Army (IRA)	1969-1990: 2,000